Tolworth, Surrey, 3rd November, 2023

Referendum Authorization Procedures in Europe

ELGAR STUDIES IN EUROPEAN LAW AND POLICY

Series Editor: Herwig C.H. Hofmann, *Professor of European and Transnational Public Law, Faculty of Law, Economics and Finance and Robert Schuman Institute for European Affairs, University of Luxembourg*

Elgar Studies in European Law and Policy is a forum for books that demonstrate cutting-edge legal and politico-legal analysis of the pertinent policies in a multi-jurisdictional Europe. The series is as relevant for academic reflection as for practical development of the matters addressed therein, such as policy relevance, its origins and the possibilities of future development. Books in the series take a multidisciplinary or multi-jurisdictional approach to the topics at their centers, with an aim to facilitating understanding of European law and policy matters and demonstrating their connectedness throughout jurisdictional levels. The series will provide coverage and analysis of various regulatory areas at the forefront of EU law and policy, including: the development of new European policy fields, issues of market regulation, economic and monetary matters and social dimensions of EU law.

Referendum Authorization Procedures in Europe

A Comparative Analysis

Anna Forgács

PhD candidate, University of Zurich, Switzerland

ELGAR STUDIES IN EUROPEAN LAW AND POLICY

Cheltenham, UK • Northampton, MA, USA

The prepress of this publication was supported by the Swiss National Science Foundation.

Published by
Edward Elgar Publishing Limited
The Lypiatts
15 Lansdown Road
Cheltenham
Glos GL50 2JA
UK

Edward Elgar Publishing, Inc.
William Pratt House
9 Dewey Court
Northampton
Massachusetts 01060
USA

A catalogue record for this book
is available from the British Library

Library of Congress Control Number: 2023941875

This book is available electronically in the **Elgar**online
Law subject collection
http://dx.doi.org/10.4337/9781035311217

ISBN 978 1 0353 1120 0 (cased)
ISBN 978 1 0353 1121 7 (eBook)

Printed and bound in Great Britain by
TJ Books Limited, Padstow, Cornwall

To my father

Contents

Acknowledgements

This book grew out of the research project 'Popular Sovereignty vs. the Rule of Law? Defining the Limits of Direct Democracy' (LIDD) at the University of Zurich. I am thankful for the support of all my colleagues at the university and I am immensely grateful to Professor Daniel Moeckli for his guidance and insightful comments throughout my work.

I would like to thank the European Research Council for funding the research project (grant agreement 7721160) and the Swiss National Science Foundation for supporting the publishing of the book.

Finally, I would like to thank my family for their unwavering support.

Abbreviations

AEI	American Enterprise Institute
Art	Article
App	Application
AS	Amtliche Sammlung (Official Collection of the Swiss Confederation)
BBl	Bundesblatt der Schweizerischen Eidgenossenschaft (Official Gazette of the Swiss Confederation)
BGE	Entscheidungen des Schweizerischen Bundesgerichts (Decisions of the Swiss Federal Supreme Court)
BuA	Bericht-und-Antrag-Nummer (Report number of Government decisions in Liechtenstein)
C2D	Centre for Research on Direct Democracy
CC	Constitutional Court
CEC	Central Election Commission
Ch	Chapter
DCU	Dublin City University
DR	Decisions and Reports of the European Commission on Human Rights
ECHR	European Convention for the Protection of Human Rights and Fundamental Freedoms
ECHR (in case citation)	Reports of Judgments and Decisions of the European Court of Human Rights
ECtHR	European Court of Human Rights
ECPR	European Consortium for Political Research
edn	edition
ed/eds	Editor/editors
e.g.	exempli gratia (for example)
ETS	European Treaty Series
EU	European Union

ff	and following
Gov	Government
Ibid	from the same place
ICCPR	International Covenant on Civil and Political Rights
IDEA	Institute for Democracy and Electoral Assistance
i.e.	id est (that is)
LGBTQ	Lesbian, Gay, Bisexual, Trans, and Queer/Questioning Community
LIDD	'Popular Sovereignty vs. the Rule of Law? Defining the Limits of Direct Democracy' research project
LSE	London School of Economics
n	Footnote number
No/Nos	Number/numbers
ODIHR	Office for Democratic Institutions and Human Rights of the Organization for Security and Co-operation in Europe
OJ	Official Journal of the European Communities
OSCE	Organization for Security and Co-operation in Europe
para	paragraph
Parl.	Parliament
Pres.	President
TFEU	Treaty on the Functioning of the European Union
TISCO	Tilburg Institute for Interdisciplinary Studies of Civil Law and Conflict Resolution Systems
UN	United Nations
UNTS	United Nations Treaty Series
U.S.	United States Supreme Court Reports
Vol	Volume
VS	Verlag für Sozialwissenschaften (Publisher for Social Sciences)

Table of cases

Italy

Latvia

Switzerland

United States

European Court of Human Rights

UN Human Rights Committee

Table of legislation/table of legal sources

1. Introduction to *Referendum Authorization Procedures in Europe*

The instruments of direct democracy are often seen as antithetical to representative democracy.[1] In a representative democracy, decisions are reached through a careful deliberation process with the involvement of multiple state institutions, whereas voters decide free of constraints in referendums.[2] Jean-Jacques Rousseau powerfully depicts this antithetical relationship when he writes

> When we see among the happiest people in the world bands of peasants regulating the affairs of state under an oak tree, and always acting wisely, can we help feeling a certain contempt for the refinements of other nations, which employ so much skill and effort to make themselves at once illustrious and wretched?[3]

However, direct democracy does not mean that citizens decide questions completely free, under an oak tree, without any intervention from state institutions. In modern democracies, direct-democratic instruments co-exist with representative democracy.[4] The organization of a referendum requires the assistance

---

[1]   David Butler, Austin Ranney (eds), *Referendums: A Comparative Study of Practice and Theory* (American Enterprise Institute 1978) 36; Markku Suksi, *Bringing in the People: A Comparison of Constitutional Forms and Practices of the Referendum* (Kluwer Academic Publishers 1993) 2; Georg Brunner, 'Direct vs. Representative Democracy' in Andreas Auer, Micheal Bützer (eds), *Direct Democracy: The Eastern and Central European Experience* (Ashgate 2001) 215; David Altman, *Direct Democracy Worldwide* (Cambridge University Press 2010) 48; Wilfried Marxer, 'Foreword' in Wilfried Marxer (ed), *Direct Democracy and Minorities* (Springer 2012) 8; Theo Schiller, Maija Setälä, 'Introduction' in Theo Schiller, Maija Setälä (eds), *Citizens' Initiatives in Europe: Procedures and Consequences of Agenda-Setting by Citizens* (Palgrave Macmillan 2012) 3–4.

[2]   Anna Christmann, Deniz Danaci, 'Direct Democracy and Minority Rights: Direct and Indirect Effects on Religious Minorities in Switzerland' (2012) 5(1) *Politics and Religion* 133–160, 136.

[3]   Jean-Jacques Rousseau, *Of the Social Contract* (Yale University Press 2002) Book IV, Chapter 1, paras 1–2.

[4]   Francis Cheneval, Mónica Ferrín, 'Direct Democracy in the European Union: An Option for Democratic Empowerment?' in David Levi-Faur, Frans van Waarden, *Democratic Empowerment in the European Union* (Cheltenham: Edward Elgar 2018)

of state institutions. The referendum process from the initiation until the vote entails several decisions by the state. State institutions validate the results of the signature collection, set the date for the vote, decide about the legality of campaign actions, and declare the official results.

Arguably, the most important decision state institutions make in the referendum process is the selection of issues for the vote. In the procedure authorizing the referendum issue, the state institutions review the content of the referendum proposal and are able to block the whole referendum process from going forward. In reaching this decision, the state institutions always have some level of discretion: when reviewing whether the referendum proposal violates any legal limits, the state institutions have some leeway to reach legally acceptable decisions. By authorizing certain issues and refusing others, state institutions exercise considerable control over the whole referendum process.

Thus, the design of the referendum authorization procedure, including the choice of the state institution and the procedural guarantees provided for the initiators and voters, can be decisive for the fate of the referendum. Nevertheless, the intricacies of the institutional and procedural settings of referendum authorization have not been in the focus of comparative research. The present book aims to fill this gap in the comparative constitutional law literature by providing an overview and an analysis of the most common institutional and procedural configurations for authorizing referendums in Europe. The book was completed as part of the 'Popular Sovereignty vs. the Rule of Law? Defining the Limits of Direct Democracy' (LIDD) research project, which is funded by the European Research Council and is hosted at the University of Zurich.[5]

1.   THE IMPORTANCE OF REFERENDUM AUTHORIZATION PROCEDURES

The instruments of direct democracy and particularly referendums have been in the spotlight for some of the most important economic and political events of the last decades in Europe.[6] Central and Eastern European countries organized multiple referendums in the democratic transition of 1989–90 to declare

---

109; Céline Colombo, Hanspeter Kriesi, 'Referendums and Direct Democracy' in Robert Rohrschneider, Jacques Thomassen, *The Oxford Handbook of Political Representation in Liberal Democracies* (Oxford University Press 2020) 437.

[5]   See http://lidd-project.org/about/, accessed 2 October 2022.

[6]   Stephen Tierney, *Constitutional Referendums: The Theory and Practice of Republican Deliberation* (Oxford: Oxford University Press 2012) 2; Matt Qvortrup, 'Introduction: Theory, Practice and History' in Matt Qvortrup (ed), *Referendums Around the World* (Palgrave Macmillan 2018) 11.

their independence and to adopt democratic constitutions.[7] Greece organized
a referendum on the financial bailout plan in 2015, while the UK decided to
leave the European Union (EU) in a referendum in 2016.[8] The ratification of
the Treaty establishing a Constitution for Europe was blocked by referendums
in France and the Netherlands.[9] Since 2010, Croatia, Slovenia, Slovakia, and
Romania have all held referendums to prohibit same-sex marriage, while in
Ireland and Switzerland the right of same-sex couples to marry has been granted
in referendums.[10] Referendums have been held on controversial moral issues
such as abortion, reproduction rights, or divorce in Ireland, Liechtenstein,
Malta, Portugal, Slovenia, and Italy.[11] Even countries with extensive tradition
in direct-democratic decision-making have caused political turmoil with referendums: Swiss voters banned the building of minarets in a popular vote and
adopted constitutional amendments that introduced automatic expulsion for
convicted foreign criminals and lifelong custody for non-treatable, extremely
dangerous, sexual and violent offenders.[12] The perception of referendums has
been controversial both in everyday life and in the legal literature. Some of
the mentioned referendum events, such as the referendums during democratic
transition in Central and Eastern Europe, have been celebrated for their role

---

[7]   Independence referendums have been held in Slovenia, Lithuania, Estonia,
Latvia, Ukraine, Georgia, Croatia, North Macedonia, and Armenia, and referendums on
the new constitutional regimes in Hungary, Romania, Estonia, Lithuania, and Russia.
See LIDD Referendum events dashboard > 'Select topic' > 'State formation' on http://
lidd-project.org/data2/, statistics correct as at 15 March 2022.

[8]   Kevin Featherstone, 'What Those Calling for Brexit Could Learn from the
Greek Bailout Referendum' (LSE Comments, 6 June 2016) <https://blogs.lse.ac.uk/
europpblog/2016/06/06/brexit-and-greek-bailout-referendum/>, accessed 15 March
2022; Andrew Reid, 'Buses and Breaking Point: Freedom of Expression and the
"Brexit" Campaign' (2019) 22 *Ethical Theory and Moral Practice* 623–637.

[9]   Cheneval, Ferrín (n 4) 125.

[10]   Elżbieta Kużelewska, 'Same-Sex Marriage – A Happy End Story? The
Effectiveness of Referendum on Same-Sex Marriage in Europe' (2019) 1(24)
Białostockie Studia Prawnicze 13–27; Jonas Glatthard, 'Schweiz sagt "Ja, ich will" zur
Ehe für alle' (Swissinfo, 26 September 2021) https://www.swissinfo.ch/ger/ehe-fuer
-alle-wird-voraussichtlich-realitaet/46979242, accessed 15 March 2022.

[11]   See LIDD Referendum events dashboard > Select a topic > Moral & Ethics on
http://lidd-project.org/data2/, statistics correct as at 15 March 2022.

[12]   Helen Keller, Markus Lanter, Andreas Fischer, 'Volksinitiativen und Völkerrecht:
die Zeit ist reif für eine Verfassungsänderung' (2008) 109(3) *Schweizerisches
Zentralblatt für Staats- und Verwaltungsrecht* 121,121–154; Giovanni Biaggini, 'Die
schweizerische direkte Demokratie und das Völkerrecht – Gedanken aus Anlass der
Volksabstimmung über die Volksinitiative "Gegen den Bau von Minaretten"' (2010)
65 *Zeitschrift für öffentliches Recht* 325, 325–343; Daniel Moeckli, 'Of Minarets and
Foreign Criminals: Swiss Direct Democracy and Human Rights' (2011) 11 *Human
Rights Law Review* 774.

in democratic empowerment.[13] Others, such as the vote on Brexit, have been criticized for their lack of clarity.[14] Again others, such as the Swiss vote on the ban on building minarets, have been denounced for violating fundamental rights and freedoms as well as international law.[15]

The rise of populist political parties and governments in Europe has also brought direct democracy to the fore – and mostly in a negative light. Populism and direct democracy seem to go hand in hand. Even the definitions of populism suggest that in prioritizing the 'common people' over the 'corrupt elites', populism has a strong preference for popular sovereignty and majority rule over liberalism or rule of law.[16] Populism is a thin-centered ideology,[17] meaning that beyond some core elements such as anti-elitism, anti-pluralism, and the focus on majority will, a variety of other ideas (nationalism, socialism, etc.) can attach to its core.[18] This makes it possible that we see parties from the left to the right claiming to give power back to the people and restore popular sovereignty through initiating referendums. However, the populist claim to represent the people is not an empirical but a moral one, based on identity politics.[19] Referendums only serve the purpose of reassuring the populist standpoint on a certain issue. As Jan-Werner Müller summarizes:

> the referendum isn't meant to start an open-ended process of deliberation among actual citizens to generate a range of well-considered popular judgments; rather, the referendum serves to ratify what the populist leader has already discerned to be

---

[13] Ronald J. Hill, Stephen White, 'Russia, the Former Soviet Union and Eastern Europe' in Matt Qvortrup (ed), *Referendums Around the World* (Palgrave Macmillan 2018) 19.

[14] Reid (n 8) 623–637.

[15] Regina Kiener, Melanie Krüsi, 'Bedeutungswandel des Rechtsstaats und Folgen für die (direkte) Demokratie am Beispiel völkerrechtswidriger Volksinitiativen' (2009) 110 *Schweizerisches Zentralblatt für Staats- und Verwaltungsrecht* 237, 239; Moeckli, 'Of Minarets and Foreign Criminals: Swiss Direct Democracy and Human Rights' (n 12) 775.

[16] Koen Abts, Stefan Rummens, 'Populism versus Democracy' (2007) 55 *Political Studies* 405–424, 407–408; Jan-Werner Müller, *What is Populism?* (University of Pennsylvania Press 2016) 2–3; Bojan Bugaric, Alenka Kuhelj, 'Varieties of Populism in Europe: Is the Rule of Law in Danger?' (2018) 10 *Hague J Rule Law* 21–33, 21–22; Cas Mudde, Cristóbal Rovira Kaltwasser, 'Studying Populism in Comparative Perspective: Reflections on the Contemporary and Future Research Agenda' (2018) 51(13) *Comparative Political Studies* 1667–1693, 1670; Matthijs Rooduijn, 'State of the Field: How to Study Populism and Adjacent Topics? A Plea for Both More and Less Focus' (2019) 58 *European Journal of Political Research* 362–372, 364.

[17] Abts, Rummens (n 16) 407–408; Mudde, Kaltwasser (n 16) 1670.

[18] Bugaric, Kuhelj (n 16) 21–22; Mudde, Kaltwasser (n 16) 1669–1670.

[19] Müller (n 16) 2–3. and 27.

the genuine popular interest as a matter of identity, not as a matter of aggregating empirically verifiable interests.[20]

Thus, populist politicians are less interested in the genuine will of the people and more in showing off popular support for their own agendas. The Hungarian migrant quota referendum in 2016 served the purpose of turning up the volume on the anti-migrant propaganda, which is shown by the fact that the government celebrated its victory in the media, even though the referendum was invalid due to the low turn-out.[21] Similarly, the Russian constitutional referendum, or 'All-Russian vote', in 2020 was more of a theatrical gesture than an actual openness to popular opinion, as the referendum did not follow the rules of any of the legally recognized direct-democratic instruments. Moreover, it did not even facilitate the expression of voters' opinion as all constitutional amendments had to be affirmed or rejected in their entirety instead of separate questions.[22]

The frequent use of referendums by populist politicians can increase the distrust in the instruments of direct democracy. The populist use of referendums can cause tension between the exercise of popular sovereignty and the protection of the rule of law. It may distort the genuine democratic character of the instruments and give emphasis to those features of direct democracy that are most commonly criticized. Arguments about the competency of voters to decide complex legal and policy questions can surface in relation to votes that determine the future of the country, such as the Brexit vote or the vote on the Greek financial bailout.[23] Concerns can be voiced about the freedom of vote when the referendum proposal is unclear and when the populist referendum campaign – such as the Brexit campaign – only amplifies the misinformation about the legal consequences of the vote.[24] Populist referendums on the rights

---

[20] Müller (n 16) 101.

[21] Gábor Halmai, 'The Invalid Anti-Migrant Referendum in Hungary' (*Verfassungsblog*, 4 October 2016) <https://verfassungsblog.de/hungarys-anti-european-immigration-laws/>, accessed 15 March 2022.

[22] Julian Ivan Beriger, 'Russia' in Daniel Moeckli, Anna Forgács, Henri Ibi (eds), *The Legal Limits of Direct Democracy* (Edward Elgar Publishing 2021) 260.

[23] Laurence Morel, 'The Democratic Criticism of Referendums. The Majority and the True Will of the People' in Laurence Morel, Matt Qvortrup (eds), *The Routledge Handbook to Referendums and Direct Democracy* (Routledge 2018) 149; Matt Qvortrup, 'Judicial Review of Direct Democracy' in Matt Qvortrup, *Direct Democracy: A Comparative Study of the Theory and Practice of Government by the People* (Manchester University Press 2014) 136; Ece Özlem Atikcan, 'The Expression of Popular Will: Do Campaigns Matter and How Do Voters Decide?' in Laurence Morel, Matt Qvortrup (eds), *The Routledge Handbook to Referendums and Direct Democracy* (Routledge 2018) 249.

[24] Reid (n 8) 623–637.

of asylum seekers, foreigners, or other minorities are capable of strengthening the populist notion of 'us against them' and harmfully affect the societal groups that populists deem not to belong to 'the people'.[25] Thus, the populist use of referendums can increase concerns about the 'tyranny of the majority' and that the rights and interests of minorities cannot be effectively protected in a popular vote.[26]

Even if in the recent years some referendum events have been controversial, it must be emphasized that direct-democratic instruments can genuinely ease the disconnect between the people and governments.[27] Direct democracy provides a control over the representative organs[28] and can restore the trust in the government and democracy.[29] Direct democracy opens a new channel between the representatives and the people: it creates an 'institutionalized discussion process'[30] for important policy questions, in which minority and majority opinions are articulated in the public sphere. Studies suggest that direct democracy improves the responsiveness of the government toward the citizens' demands, especially when citizens have the power to influence the political

---

[25]   Abts, Rummens (n 16) 407–408; Ronald F. Inglehart, Pippa Norris, 'Trump, Brexit, and the Rise of Populism: Economic Have-Nots and Cultural Backlash' (Harvard Kennedy School Faculty Research Working Paper Series No. RWP16–026, August 2016) <https://www.hks.harvard.edu/publications/trump-brexit-and-rise-popu lism-economic-have-nots-and-cultural-backlash>, accessed 15 March 2022.

[26]   Marxer, 'Foreword' (n 1) 7; Marthe Fatin-Rouge Stefanini, 'Referendums, Minorities and Individual Freedoms' in Laurence Morel and Matt Qvortrup (eds), *The Routledge Handbook to Referendums and Direct Democracy* (Routledge 2018) 371.

[27]   Saskia P. Ruth, Yanina Welp, Laurence Whitehead, 'Direct Democracy in the Twenty-First Century' in Saskia P. Ruth, Yanina Welp, Laurence Whitehead (eds), *Let the People Rule? Direct Democracy in the Twenty-First Century* (ECPR Press 2017) 1–2; John G. Matsusaka, *Let the People Rule: How Direct Democracy Can Meet the Populist Challenge* (Princeton: Princeton University Press 2020) 7.

[28]   Arthur Lupia, John G. Matsusaka, 'Direct Democracy: New Approaches to Old Questions' (2004) 7 *Annual Review of Political Science* 463–482; Hanspeter Kriesi, *Direct Democratic Choice: The Swiss Experience* (Lexington Books 2005) 5; Simon Lanz, Alessandro Nai, 'How Elections Shape Campaigning Effects in Direct Democracy' in Laurence Morel, Matt Qvortrup (eds), *The Routledge Handbook to Referendums and Direct Democracy* (Routledge 2018) 348.

[29]   Matsusaka, *Let the People Rule: How Direct Democracy Can Meet the Populist Challenge* (n 27) 165–166. For empirical findings: Kriesi (n 28) 5; Isabelle Stadelmann-Steffen, Adrian Vatter, 'Does Satisfaction with Democracy Really Increase Happiness? Direct Democracy and Individual Satisfaction in Switzerland' (2012) 34 *Polit Behav* 535, 538; Julien Talpin, 'Do Referendums Make Better Citizens? The Effects of Direct Democracy on Political Interest, Civic Competence and Participation' in Laurence Morel and Matt Qvortrup (eds), *The Routledge Handbook to Referendums and Direct Democracy* (Routledge 2018).

[30]   Elisabeth Alber, 'Ethnic Governance and Direct Democracy: Perils and Potential' in Wilfried Marxer (ed), *Direct Democracy and Minorities* (Springer VS 2012) 76.

agenda through initiatives or when they have the power to react to government decisions.[31] Direct-democratic instruments can ensure that the policy decisions are more in line with the citizens' preferences than in a purely representative system.[32] The direct-democratic instruments introduce a new veto-player in the political system,[33] an additional check on the representatives beyond the periodical elections, thus reducing chances that the government does not act according to the interests of the majority.[34] The threat of referendums encourages governments to seek consensual decisions and consider minority positions.[35] The right to participate in the decision-making also incentivizes citizens to inform themselves about political issues.[36] An encouraged participation in politics and legislation increases civic engagement and political knowledge and provides a democratic outlet for the dissatisfaction.[37]

However, direct democracy can only fulfill the promise of enhanced civic engagement and genuine democratic will-formation, if the direct-democratic instruments are well constructed. The legal construction of the direct-democratic instruments must ensure that the majorities are able express their genuine will, and at the same time that the rights of the minorities and the rule of law are protected.[38] The careful construction of direct-democratic instruments can reduce

---

[31] Maija Setälä, Theo Schiller, 'Comparative Findings' in Theo Schiller and Maija Setälä (eds), *Citizens' Initiatives in Europe: Procedures and Consequences of Agenda-Setting by Citizens* (Palgrave Macmillan 2012) 258.

[32] Bruno S. Frey, Alois Stutzer, Susanne Neckermann, 'Direct Democracy and the Constitution' in A. Marciano (ed), *Constitutional Mythologies: New Perspectives on Controlling the State* (New York: Springer 2011) 110.

[33] Simon Hug, George Tsebelis, 'Veto Players and Referendums Around the World' 2002 14(4) *Journal of Theoretical Politics* 466.

[34] Gebhard Kirchgässner, 'Direkte Demokratie und Menschenrechte' in Lars P. Feld, Peter M. Huber, Otmar Jung, Christian Welzel, Fabian Wittreck (eds), *Jahrbuch für direkte Demokratie 2009* (Nomos 2010) 66–89; Stadelmann-Steffen, Vatter (n 29) 538.

[35] Matt Qvortrup, 'Direct Democracy and Referendums' in Erik S. Herron, Robert J. Pekkanen, Matthew S. Shugart (eds), *The Oxford Handbook of Electoral Systems* (Oxford University Press 2018) 22.

[36] Frey, Stutzer, Neckermann (n 32) 114; Stadelmann-Steffen, Vatter (n 29) 536.

[37] Qvortrup, 'Introduction: Theory, Practice and History' (n 6) 11; Palle Svensson, 'Views on Referendums: Is There a Pattern?' in Laurence Morel, Matt Qvortrup (eds), *The Routledge Handbook to Referendums and Direct Democracy* (Routledge 2018) 103; M. Dane Waters, 'The Strength of Popular Will: Legal Impact, Implementation and Duration' in Laurence Morel, Matt Qvortrup (eds), *The Routledge Handbook to Referendums and Direct Democracy* (Routledge 2018) 261.

[38] Kiener, Krüsi (n 15) 244; Setälä, Schiller, 'Comparative Findings' (n 31) 258–259; Francis Cheneval, Alice El-Wakil, 'The Institutional Design of Referendums: Bottom-Up and Binding' (2018) 24(3) *Swiss Political Science Review* 294, 295; Stephen Tierney, 'Democratic Credentials and Deficits of Referendums A Case

the chance of controversial referendums taking place and may also counter the populist threat of misusing referendums.

The need for a careful design of direct-democratic instruments also follows from international law. The International Covenant on Civil and Political Rights (ICCPR) states that every citizen shall have the right and opportunity to take part in the conduct of public affairs directly, without discrimination and unreasonable restrictions.[39] The Human Rights Committee emphasizes that the Covenant does not impose any particular form of democracy on its member states, but if the state introduces a direct-democratic instrument, such as referendums, then any restriction on the direct participation must be reasonable and should not constitute a barrier to the use of the instrument.[40]

Meanwhile the Revised Guidelines on the Holding of Referendums ('Revised Code', 'Code') adopted by the European Commission for Democracy through Law ('Venice Commission') highlight that 'a number of guarantees are necessary to ensure that they [referendums] genuinely express the wishes of the electorate and do not go against international standards in the field of human rights, democracy, and the rule of law'.[41] The Venice Commission has determined these necessary guarantees in detail through the adoption of the original Code of Good Practice on Referendums ('Original Code')[42] and its recent revision. These documents are highly important for the European referendum practice, as they are the only international standards adopted specifically for referendums. The Venice Commission drafted the Original Code in 2006–07, which contained the Guidelines on the holding of referendums, and an Explanatory Memorandum. The Guidelines were revised in 2020, in order to better reflect the recent challenges of referendum practice.[43] Although no explicit reference is made to any of the controversial referendums of the

---

Study of the Scottish Independence Vote.' in Laurence Morel, Matt Qvortrup (eds) *The Routledge Handbook to Referendums and Direct Democracy* (Routledge 2018) 193–194; Matsusaka, *Let the People Rule: How Direct Democracy Can Meet the Populist Challenge* (n 27) 84.

[39] Art. 25(a) International Covenant on Civil and Political Rights (adopted 16 December 1966, entered into force 23 March 1976) 999 UNTS 171 (ICCPR).

[40] *Mario Staderini and Michele De Lucia v Italy*, UN Human Rights Committee, No. 2656/2015, para 9.3–9.4.

[41] European Commission for Democracy Through Law (Venice Commission) Revised Guidelines on the Holding of Referendums, CD50-AD(2020)031, Introduction para 8.

[42] European Commission for Democracy Through Law (Venice Commission) Code of Good Practice on Referendums, Study No. 371/2006, CD50-AD(2007)008rev-cor.

[43] Nicos C. Alivizatos, 'Revision of the Code of Good Practice on Referendums' in Daniel Moeckli, Anna Forgács, Henri Ibi (eds), *The Legal Limits of Direct Democracy* (Edward Elgar Publishing 2021).

last years, the introduction of the Revised Code states that the revision of the previous Code was influenced by the recurring concerns about the protection of rule of law in the recent practice.[44] The Revised Code is not binding on the member states but it serves as an important point of reference.[45] The Code is not only cited by the Venice Commission in its legal opinions,[46] but also guides national practice.[47]

There are several elements of the referendum design that can affect the balance between popular sovereignty and the rule of law. The conditions of initiating the referendum; the rules of the signature collection; the legal limits imposed on the formulation and the substance of the referendum question; the authorization procedure enforcing the legal limits; the rules governing the referendum campaign, and the voting event all influence this balance. The Revised Code makes recommendations in all these areas.

First and foremost, it is crucial who has the power to initiate a referendum and determine the issue to be put to a popular vote. Some direct-democratic instruments have inherently more potential for democratic empowerment than others, while some are more prone to populist capture.[48] When citizens have the power to initiate referendums, then direct democracy can be used to correct the failures of representation and to empower the citizens to take action into their own hands.[49] Meanwhile referendums triggered by governments or parliamentary majorities are discretionary tools of the majorities that can be used

---

[44]   Revised Code, Introduction para 5.

[45]   Regina Kiener, 'Einführung/Europäische Mindeststandards zum Parlaments-wahlrecht im Soft Law der Venedig-Kommission' in Andreas Glaser, Lorenz Langer (eds), *Das Parlamentswahlrecht als rechtsstaatliche Grundlage der Demokratie* (Dike Verlag, 2020) 22.

[46]   European Commission for Democracy Through Law (Venice Commission) Azerbaijan – Opinion on the draft modifications to the Constitution submitted to the Referendum of 26 September 2016, CD50-AD (2016)029 para 8; Opinion on 'whether the decision taken by the Supreme Council of the Autonomous Republic of Crimea in Ukraine to organise a referendum on becoming a constituent territory of the Russian Federation or restoring Crimea's 1992 Constitution is compatible with constitutional principles' CD50-AD (2014) para 21; see also Pierre Garrone, 'The Code of Good Practice on Referendums' in Daniel Moeckli, Anna Forgács, Henri Ibi (eds), *The Legal Limits of Direct Democracy* (Edward Elgar Publishing 2021).

[47]   Croatia: Warning of the Constitutional Court of the Republic of Croatia No. U-VIIR-5292/2013 of 28 October 2013, Official Gazette 131/2013, 2869, para 4; Decision of the Constitutional Court of the Republic of Croatia No. U-VIIR-1159/2015 of 8 April 2015, Official Gazette 43/2015, 887, para 24; Lithuania: Decision No. Sp-101 of 7 April 2014 of the Central Election Commission.

[48]   Cheneval, El-Wakil (n 38) 295.

[49]   Ibid, 299.

to enhance their powers and avoid electoral accountability on certain issues.[50] Most populist referendums mentioned throughout the book (e.g. Brexit or the Hungarian migrant quota referendum) fall into the latter category.[51]

It is a crucial element of the referendum design that the conditions of initiating the referendum are clearly regulated. The rules of initiation should not create such technical hurdles for the citizens that would hollow out democratic participation. Among other suggestions, the Revised Code highlights that the necessary number of signatures for initiating a referendums should ensure that citizens are interested in the referendum issue but should not be so high as to make the initiation of referendums impossible.[52] For instance, the introduction of impossible technical hurdles in Russia, where 4500 voters are required to form an initiative group to collect two million signatures, has made citizen-initiated referendums practically unattainable for voters.[53]

The formulation of the referendum question is also important so that the voters are able to understand the legal consequences of the vote and decide according to their actual preferences. The vote on Brexit has been criticized for the lack of clarity in the legal consequences of voting for leaving the EU.[54] The Revised Code emphasizes the importance of clarity as part of free suffrage.[55] The freedom of voters to form an opinion about the referendum question requires the question to be clear and comprehensible. States also have to devise rules for countering misleading and biased referendums where the voters are prevented from expressing their genuine preferences due to the formulation of the question.

Limitations on the permissible scope of direct-democratic decision-making can effectively protect the values of constitutional democracy and the rule of law against the potential misuse of referendums.[56] In this regard, the Revised Code emphasizes that the text submitted to a referendum must comply with all superior laws and international law as well as the principles of democracy, human rights, and the rule of law.[57] Based on empirical studies, there are few

---

[50]   Ibid, 299, Daniel Moeckli, 'Referendums: Tyranny of the Majority?' 2018 24(3) *Swiss Political Science Review* 335, 337.

[51]   See more on this in section 3.2 of this chapter.

[52]   Revised Code III.3.c.

[53]   Beriger (n 22) 260.

[54]   Jacob Eisler, 'Dissonant Referendum Design and Turmoil in Representation' [2019] *Public Law* 622–632; Sandra Kröger, 'Assessing the Democratic Legitimacy of the 2016 Brexit Referendum' (DCU Brexit Institute – Working Paper No. 12 2018).

[55]   Revised Code I.3.1.

[56]   Jürgen Habermas, 'Constitutional Democracy. A Paradoxical Union of Contradictory Principles?' (2001) 29(6) *Political Theory* 766–781, 766.

[57]   Revised Code III.1.

instances when referendums aim to restrict the existing rights of minorities,[58] although they are not without precedent, as the 2009 Swiss minaret ban referendum shows. More often the minorities are harmed by the majority blocking or repealing government efforts to provide more rights for minority groups and eliminate discrimination.[59] For example, the defense of marriage referendums in Slovakia, Slovenia, Croatia, and Romania all aimed at obstructing the legal recognition of same-sex marriage. It has been shown that the 'outgroups' of society, the groups that the given society considers not integrated, such as foreigners or certain racial or religious minorities, can be negatively affected by referendums.[60]

The legal rules governing the initiation of referendums, the formal limits on the wording of the referendum proposal, and the substantive limits excluding certain issues can all contribute to a well-functioning direct-democratic instrument. However, the regulatory framework should not be regarded as static. The different institutional and procedural configurations for enforcing the legal limits and authorizing certain referendums while rejecting others are just as crucial. The institutional choices and the procedural guarantees governing the authorization can hinder both the arbitrary restriction of democratic rights as well as the exercise of uncontrolled majoritarian power.

The Revised Code emphasizes that an impartial body – preferably an independent central commission – must be entrusted with the organization and the supervision of the referendum.[61] The Code also requires an effective system of appeals for referendum matters with an impartial and independent appeal body.[62] Regarding the individual procedural rights, the Code states that all voters must be entitled to an appeal and that the 'applicant's right to a hearing involving both parties must be protected'.[63]

---

[58] Barbara S. Gamble, 'Putting Civil Rights to a Popular Vote' (1997) 41(1) *American Journal of Political Science* 245–269; Todd Donovan, Shaun Bowler, 'Direct Democracy and Minority Rights: An Extension' (1998) 42 *American Journal of Political Science* 1020–1024; Donald P. Haider-Markel, Alana Querze, Kara Lindaman, 'Lose, Win, or Draw? A Reexamination of Direct Democracy and Minority Rights' (2007) 60 *Political Research Quarterly* 304–314; Fatin-Rouge Stefanini (n 26) 373.

[59] Marxer, 'Foreword' (n 1) 9.

[60] Adrian Vatter, Deniz Danaci, 'Mehrheitstyrannei durch Volksentscheide? Zum Spannungsverhältnis zwischen direkter Demokratie und Minderheitenschutz' (2010) 51(2) *Politische Vierteljahresschrift* 205–222; Deniz Danaci, 'The Minaret Ban in Switzerland: An Exception to the Rule?' in Wilfried Marxer (ed), *Direct Democracy and Minorities* (Springer 2012) 157; Christmann, Danaci (n 2) 134, 155.

[61] Revised Code II.4.1.

[62] Revised Code II.4.3.a.

[63] Revised Code II.4.3.f. and II.4.3.h.

The procedural design of referendums is vital to enforce the rules protecting the freedom of vote and other fundamental rights and freedoms. The referendum authorization procedure holds the key to blocking referendums that might go against the fundamental values of constitutional democracy and the rule of law. The institutional choice for the procedure as well as the procedural guarantees provided for the parties can determine how effectively the state can prevent such referendums and protect its citizens.

The procedural design of referendums is also crucial to ensure that the state cannot arbitrarily restrict the exercise of popular sovereignty when exercising discretionary powers. The procedural guarantees such as the independence and impartiality of the decision-maker, the availability of effective remedies, or hearing rights can all ensure that the initiators of the referendum and the voters are protected against the arbitrariness of state action.

Lastly, the procedural guarantees can themselves have an empowering effect. As Jeremy Waldron, a theorist of the procedural understanding of the rule of law, highlights, the essential idea of procedure 'embodies a crucial dignitarian idea – respecting the dignity of those to whom the norms are applied as being capable of explaining themselves'.[64] Social psychology research has shown that the perception of procedural justice can itself represent a value.[65] If the participants perceive that the authorities conducted a fair procedure respecting their dignity, then this perception increases the legitimacy of the authority as well as the acceptance of the decision.[66]

2.   THE UNIQUENESS OF REFERENDUM AUTHORIZATION PROCEDURES

Almost all European states regulate the permissible scope of citizen-initiated referendums, and voters cannot initiate a referendum completely free of legal constraints. Most European states have introduced substantive limits on referendums, most commonly excluding financial matters, questions of amnesty and pardon, and fundamental rights from the scope of referendums.[67] The sub-

---

[64]   Jeremy Waldron, 'The Rule of Law and the Importance of Procedure' in James E. Fleming (ed), *Getting to the Rule of Law* (New York: New York University Press 2011) 347.

[65]   E. Allen Lind, Tom Tyler, *The Social Psychology of Procedural Justice* (New York: Plenum Press 1988) 2; Tom R. Tyler, 'Social Justice: Outcome and Procedure' (2000) 35 *International Journal of Psychology* 117, 118–120.

[66]   For a general overview of this field of research, see Laura Klaming, Ivo Giesen, 'Access to Justice: The Quality of the Procedure' (TISCO Working Paper Series on Civil Law and Conflict Resolution Systems No. 002/2008).

[67]   See LIDD data dashboard > Summaries > By Instrument/Countries on <http://lidd-project.org/data/>, statistics correct as at 15 March 2022.

stantive limits are often supplemented with some form of clarity requirement for the formulation of the question.[68] The legitimacy of limiting the exercise of popular sovereignty is not questioned here but is accepted as a given.

The focus of the book is on the question of how the enforcement of the legal limits can strike a balance between competing interests. In the referendum authorization procedure, the decision-maker must find an equilibrium between protecting the individual and public interests and allowing the exercise of the democratic rights of citizens. Legal limits can serve multiple individual and public interests. Substantive limits can be imposed in order to protect the current constitutional order or more generally the rule of law. Excluding certain issues can also aim to protect fundamental rights and freedoms, the functionality of the state, or the stability of the state organization.[69] Meanwhile formal limits generally aim to protect the right to vote. In the referendum authorization procedure, the state institutions have to assess whether the referendum proposal violates these protected interests in a way that would make the exercise of democratic rights impermissible. At the same time the state has to devise a practice that does not make the instruments of direct democracy dead letter and completely unattainable for citizens.

From a procedural standpoint this means that the competent state institution shall not decide in an arbitrary way. The procedural rules should enable the state institution to consider all relevant arguments on both sides. The final decision should reflect that the exercise of discretion is the result of careful deliberation. Consequently, the main question is how to minimize the risk of arbitrary decision-making and maximize the chance of a balanced decision.

The referendum authorization procedure is an atypical public law dispute where the traditional fair trial guarantees may not seem evidently applicable. Indeed, most European states do not ensure the same procedural guarantees for referendum authorization procedures as for civil or administrative law disputes.[70] The referendum authorization is a future-oriented and mostly abstract review of the referendum proposal. It is not a classic contradictory procedure between individual parties. In most states only the initiators of the referendum are a party to the authorization procedure, although arguably the interests of all voters are affected by the decision since the subject of the procedure is the exercise of their political rights. This last element – the exercise of political rights – warrants the observance of some procedural guarantees. However,

---

[68]   See LIDD data dashboard > Summaries > By Instrument/Countries on <http://lidd-project.org/data/>, statistics correct as at 15 March 2022.

[69]   More on legal limits in Chapter 4, section 3.

[70]   See LIDD data dashboard > Explore data > By Instrument/Item > Theme: Formal procedure or Substantive procedure on <http://lidd-project.org/data/>, statistics correct as at 15 March 2022.

it must be acknowledged that a full-fledged list of fair trial rights may not be applicable to referendum authorization due to its special nature.

When trying to understand the nature of the referendum authorization procedure among public law disputes, multiple questions arise. Is the referendum authorization procedure legal or political in its nature? Is the review of legal limits abstract or concrete? Can this procedure be regarded as legal adjudication where procedural guarantees should be available for the affected parties? And, if so, then what procedural guarantees should be applicable?

The present book aims to answer these questions. I explore in detail the applicability of four procedural guarantees: the independence and impartiality of the decision-maker; the right to a reasoned decision; the right to be heard; the right to an effective remedy. The four procedural guarantees are selected based on the fair trial rights guaranteed by international treaties, on the procedural understanding of the rule of law and on the procedural recommendations of the Venice Commission's Revised Code.[71] I investigate the applicability of these procedural guarantees based on the special nature of referendum authorization procedures. I explore the referendum practice of selected European states in order to flesh out the advantages of certain institutional or procedural solutions in reducing the chance of arbitrary decision-making.

3.   THE SCOPE OF THE BOOK

3.1   Terminology

Instruments of direct democracy can be classified in numerous ways and the terminology used in the literature is also quite diverse.[72] The most commonly mentioned direct-democratic instruments are referendums, popular or citizens' initiatives, plebiscites, agenda initiatives, and recalls.[73] *Agenda initiatives* describe citizen-initiated proposals to representative bodies that aim to put issues on the agenda of the state institution but do not result in a vote. *Recalls* are popular votes specifically about terminating the mandate of certain state officials or representatives: these are votes on persons and not policy issues.[74]

---

[71]   See Chapter 5.
[72]   For some of the most commonly cited catalogues, see Butler, Ranney (n 1) 23; Suksi (n 1) 6–8; Altman (n 1) 8; Laurence Morel, 'Referendums' in: Michel Rosenfeld, András Sajó (eds), *Oxford Handbook of Comparative Constitutional Law* (Oxford University Press 2012) 508; Laurence Morel, 'Types of Referendums, Provisions and Practice at National Level Worldwide' in Laurence Morel, Matt Qvortrup (eds), *The Routledge Handbook to Referendums and Direct Democracy* (Routledge 2018) 28–33.
[73]   Altman (n 1) 7.
[74]   Morel, 'Referendums' (n 72) 456.

The literature either uses the term *referendum* for all events of popular vote on policy issues or it differentiates between referendums and popular initiatives.[75] If used separately, then referendums refer to reactive popular voting events, when citizens confirm, reject, or abrogate legislation and *popular or citizens' initiatives* refer to votes on initiatives formulated by citizens. Meanwhile *plebiscites* carry a negative connotation and traditionally refer to referendums initiated by the government.[76] I will use the term 'referendum' to cover both reactive and proactive popular voting events regardless of the initiator of the vote. Since the referendum authorization procedures take place before the voting event, the terms 'referendum proposal', 'initiative', or 'referendum request' will be used to describe the issue submitted to a referendum.

Referendums can be classified in multiple ways.[77] One dimension of the classification is the *mandatory or facultative* (optional) nature of the referendums: whether the referendum is a compulsory element of the decision-making process on pre-determined issues or the referendum can be freely initiated by state actors or citizens.[78] Another dimension is based on the *legal effect* of the vote: whether the referendum results bind the representative organs or are merely consultative.[79] Yet another categorization can be made according to the *types of questions* that can be submitted to a referendum: is it possible to initiate a popular vote on constitutional revisions, or is it limited to legislative changes?[80] Is it permissible to call referendums on individual administrative acts or only on normative provisions?[81] Referendums can also be differentiated based on their direction: referendums can be *reactive* or *proactive*. A reactive referendum is non-propositive and decision-controlling,[82] as the initiators aim

---

[75] Zoltán Tibor Pállinger, Bruno Kaufmann, Wilfried Marxer, Theo Schiller (eds), *Direct Democracy in Europe: Developments and Prospects* (Springer VS 2007) 19; Schiller, Setälä, 'Introduction' (n 1) 1.

[76] Altman (n 1) 7.

[77] Suksi (n 1) 28; Michael Bützer, 'Introduction' in Andreas Auer, Micheal Bützer (eds), *Direct Democracy: The Eastern and Central European Experience* (Ashgate 2001) 5–6; Altman (n 1) 7–8; Morel, 'Types of Referendums, Provisions and Practice at National Level Worldwide' (n 72) 29–34.

[78] Altman (n 1) 8; Morel, 'Types of Referendums, Provisions and Practice at National Level Worldwide' (n 72) 29.

[79] Altman (n 1) 8; Morel, 'Types of Referendums, Provisions and Practice at National Level Worldwide' (n 72) 33.

[80] Morel, 'Types of Referendums, Provisions and Practice at National Level Worldwide' (n 72) 31.

[81] Andreas Glaser, 'Das Verwaltungsreferendum' (2012) 113 *Schweizerisches Zentralblatt für Staats- und Verwaltungsrecht* 511.

[82] Pier Vincenzo Uleri, 'Institutions of Citizens' Political Participation in Italy: Crooked Forms, Hindered Institutionalization' in Theo Schiller, Maija Setälä (eds), *Citizens' Initiatives in Europe: Procedures and Consequences of Agenda-Setting*

to confirm, veto, or abrogate a state decision. In contrast, a proactive referendum is propositive and decision-promoting,[83] as the initiators formulate the issue put to a popular vote. Finally, referendums can be classified based on the *initiator* of the popular vote. A referendum can be top-down if it is initiated by the political establishment, or bottom-up if by citizens.[84]

I rely on the classification used in the LIDD research project.[85] This classification is based on the initiator of the direct-democratic instrument, thus the entity that has the power to define the subject of the referendum or agenda initiative. Referendums may be initiated by citizens or by state institutions or may be legally mandated. *Citizen-initiated referendums* come in two versions: proactive citizen-initiated referendums allow a certain number of citizens to initiate a referendum and formulate the topic of the referendum, while rejective citizen-initiated referendums allow a certain number of citizens to initiate a ref-

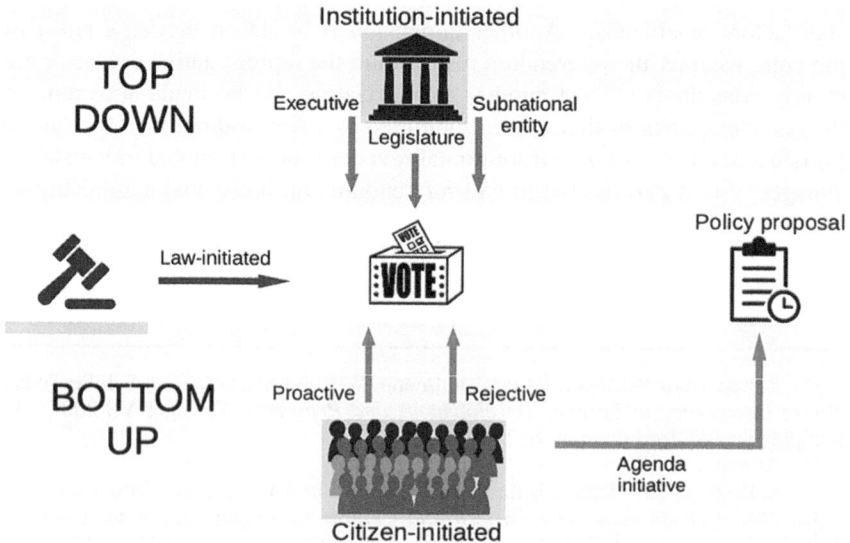

Source: LIDD Project website at http://lidd-project.or/research/.

Figure 1.1   Instruments of direct democracy

---

by Citizens (Palgrave Macmillan 2012) 71–88, 83; Morel, 'Types of Referendums, Provisions and Practice at National Level Worldwide' (n 72) 30.

   [83]   Ibid.

   [84]   Altman (n 1) 8.

   [85]   LIDD Project website <http://lidd-project.org/research/>, accessed 15 March 2022.

erendum that is aimed to prevent new laws from being passed or to repeal existing laws. *Institution-initiated referendums* are optionally initiated by the executive, by the legislature, or by a number of subnational entities, and these institutions define the issue for the popular vote. Meanwhile *law-initiated referendums* are triggered if certain conditions specified by law (i.e. the constitution or a legislative act) are met. The law may determine the topic (e.g. transfer of sovereignty) or the type of legal act (e.g. constitutional amendment) that triggers the referendum process.

3.2 Topical Scope

The instruments of direct democracy have extensive comparative political science literature, where the focus lies mostly on the use of direct-democratic instruments, the campaign, and the voting process.[86] Referendums and other direct-democratic instruments also appear prominently in comparative consti-tutional law scholarship. Some of the comparative constitutional law volumes thoroughly describe the conditions of initiating referendums and the practice of referendums in selected states.[87] In these edited books, the state institutions authorizing referendums are usually mentioned, but procedural details are not provided. Other comparative works highlight the challenges of direct democracy.[88] Some of these works focus on the protection of individual rights or on the imposition of legal limits,[89] but without revealing much about the procedures for enforcing these limits. Similarly, the national literature on direct-democratic instruments offers valuable sources for understanding how

---

[86] Butler, Ranney (n 1); Altman (n 1); Laurence Morel and Matt Qvortrup (eds), *The Routledge Handbook to Referendums and Direct Democracy* (Routledge 2018); Matt Qvortrup (ed), *Referendums Around the World* (Palgrave Macmillan 2018).

[87] Andreas Auer, Micheal Bützer (eds), *Direct Democracy: The Eastern and Central European Experience* (Ashgate 2001); Maija Setälä, Theo Schiller (eds), *Citizens' Initiatives in Europe: Procedures and Consequences of Agenda-Setting by Citizens* (Palgrave Macmillan 2012); Evren Somer (ed), *Direct Democracy in the Baltic States* (Peter Lang 2015); Maria Marczewska-Rytko (ed), *Handbook of Direct Democracy in Central and Eastern Europe after 1989* (Opladen: Barbara Budrich Publishers 2018).

[88] Zoltán Tibor Pállinger, Bruno Kaufmann, Wilfried Marxer, Theo Schiller (eds), *Direct Democracy in Europe: Developments and Prospects* (Springer VS 2007); Wilfried Marxer (ed), *Direct Democracy and Minorities* (Springer VS 2012); John G. Matsusaka, *Let the People Rule: How Direct Democracy Can Meet the Populist Challenge* (n 27).

[89] Marxer (ed), *Direct Democracy and Minorities* (n 88); Robert Podolnjak, 'Constitutional Reforms of Citizen-Initiated Referendum: Causes of Different Outcomes in Slovenia and Croatia' (2015) 26 *Revus Journal for Constitutional Theory and Philosophy of Law* 129; Fatin-Rouge Stefanini (n 26); John G. Matsusaka, *Let the People Rule: How Direct Democracy Can Meet the Populist Challenge* (n 27).

the legal limits imposed on referendums are interpreted in specific countries, but rarely reflects on the procedural aspects of referendum authorization.[90] The only question about referendum authorization that occasionally appears in the national literature is the question of institutional choice.[91] Meanwhile, the constitutional law literature on the state institutions authorizing referendums also provides little guidance, because referendum authorization is never the core constitutional function of the given institution. For instance, most of the comparative works on constitutional courts focus on their constitutional review functions and only mention election and referendum disputes as possible ancillary tasks.[92]

I analyze primarily the various institutional and procedural guarantees applied in authorizing *citizen-initiated referendums*. Citizen-initiated referendums are selected due to their high potential for democratic empowerment.[93] Both types of citizen-initiated referendums allow people to start the referendum process and ultimately decide about the issue. Citizen-initiated referendums are specifically designed to allow citizens to interact with the representative government: rejective referendums are called for the confirmation or rejection of the decisions of the representative organs, while proactive citizen-initiated referendums are able to bring up issues that are disregarded by the representative government.[94] Thus, citizens can voice their discontent with decisions or the lack of decisions through initiating referendums and can keep the elected representatives accountable.[95]

---

[90] Switzerland: Keller, Lanter, Fischer (n 12) 121. Slovenia: Ciril Ribičič, Igor Kaučič, 'Constitutional Limits of Legislative Referendum: The Case of Slovenia' (2014) 12(4) *Lexlocalis – Journal of Local Self-Government* 899. Croatia: Dario Čepo, Dario Nikić Čakar, 'Direct Democracy and the Rise of Political Entrepreneurs: An Analysis of Citizens' Initiatives in Post-2010 Croatia' (2019) 16(1) *Anali* 27.

[91] Kiener, Krüsi (n 15) 237; Giovanni Biaggini, 'Die schweizerische direkte Demokratie und das Völkerrecht – Gedanken aus Anlass der Volksabstimmung über die Volksinitiative "Gegen den Bau von Minaretten"' (n 12) 325; Andreas Auer, Nicolas Aubert, Evren Somer, 'So besser nicht: Kritische Anmerkungen zum materiellen Vorprüfungsverfahren für Volksinitiativen im Bund' [2013] *Aktuelle Juristische Praxis* 659.

[92] Andrew Harding, *Constitutional Courts: A Comparative Study* (Wildy, Simmonds & Hill 2009); Maartje de Visser, *Constitutional Review in Europe: A Comparative Analysis* (Oxford: Hart 2014); John Bell, Marie-Luce Paris (eds), *Rights-based Constitutional Review: Constitutional Courts in a Changing Landscape* (Edward Elgar Publishing 2016); Martin Belov (ed), *The Role of Courts in Contemporary Legal Orders* (Eleven International Publishing 2019).

[93] Cheneval, Ferrín (n 4) 116.

[94] Frey, Stutzer, Neckermann (n 32) 108.

[95] Matsusaka, *Let the People Rule: How Direct Democracy Can Meet the Populist Challenge* (n 27) 155.

Examples of referendums initiated by state institutions are highlighted briefly to provide contrast to citizen-initiated referendums. These instruments have the least democratic potential.[96] Being completely at the service of state actors, these referendums rarely serve civic empowerment, regardless of their procedural design. Instead, these direct-democratic instruments are often used by (populist) governments to further their agenda and to claim that their ideas are in fact supported by the electorate.

Citizen-initiated referendums and state institution-initiated referendums accentuate different aspects of the tension between popular sovereignty and rule of law. Citizen-initiated referendums represent the fullest exercise of popular sovereignty among the direct-democratic instruments, these confer the most power to citizens. However, this also means that these instruments can be potentially in conflict with the rule of law and the fundamental values of a liberal democracy. For these reasons, citizen-initiated referendums are usually extensively regulated, including the referendum authorization procedures. In contrast, referendums initiated by state institutions are controlled forms of the exercise of popular sovereignty, because the state institutions have discretion to select the issues put to a vote. Traditionally, these instruments are deemed purely political and the legal constraints – including the authorization procedures – imposed on these instruments are not comparable to referendums initiated by citizens. However, the increasing populist use of these instruments has shown that referendums initiated by state actors can also be in conflict with the rule of law. Still, the fact that these instruments are underregulated and authorization procedures are rarely devised for them makes it difficult to analyze these direct-democratic instruments from a legal (procedural) perspective. Consequently, only a few examples of government-initiated referendums are highlighted in the comparative analysis of referendum authorization decisions.[97]

I use the term *referendum authorization procedure* to describe the procedure of the competent state institution that reviews whether the citizen-initiated referendum complies with the legal limits imposed on the instrument. According to the type of legal limits, the referendum authorization procedures can be categorized into three groups.

All citizen-initiated referendums have to comply with certain *technical limits*: the legal rules determine the number of signatures that is needed to initiate a referendum and, in some states, prescribe the formation of an initiative group, the use of certain submission forms, or time-limits for submitting

---

[96]   Daniel Moeckli, 'Referendums: Tyranny of the Majority?' (n 50) 337; Cheneval, El-Wakil (n 38) 299.
[97]   See Chapter 5.

questions. In the corresponding *technical authorization procedure*, the state institution counts and verifies the signatures and officially registers the initiative or referendum request. The technical limits and procedures can be decisive for the accessibility of a referendum.[98] Especially the number of required signatures is crucial for the practical use of the direct-democratic instrument. However, these limits are unrelated to the issue of the referendum: the content of the referendum proposal is not assessed in these procedures. Additionally, the review of technical limits rarely requires the exercise of discretion. The procedures are usually very straightforward, thus they are excluded from the analysis.

The second group of limits encompasses the *formal limits* that determine how the referendum issue or question has to be worded. Such formal limits ensure that the voters can express their genuine preferences at the ballots, thus that they are not misled or confused by the formulation of the referendum question. They can base their answer on a clear understanding of both the question and its potential legal consequences. This way the formal limits protect all voters and the freedom of the vote. The most common formal limits are the clarity, the unity of form, and the unity of substance requirements.[99] The unity of form requirement ensures that the referendum issue is not a mix of a generally worded proposal and a draft legal text. The unity of substance guarantees that the issues put to a vote are connected to each other. Meanwhile, the clarity requirement is a broader category that can cover any requirement that ensures the free will-formation of the voters. The corresponding *formal authorization procedures* are for reviewing the formulation of the initiative or the referendum question. As the content of the referendum proposal is evaluated in these procedures and the state institutions exercise considerable discretionary powers, formal authorization procedures are a fundamental part of the present research.

Lastly, *substantive limits* exclude certain subject matters from being put to a popular vote. Some substantive limits aim to protect fundamental rights and freedoms or the constitutional order of the state. Other substantive limits ensure that decisions about the core functions of the state (e.g. national security, emergency powers, or finances) or decisions about the state organization (e.g. election rules, competences of government branches, civil service laws)

---

[98]   For instance, in Russia, the lack of practical experience with citizen-initiated referendums is due to the extensive technical limits. See: Beriger (n 22) 245.

[99]   These limits may also appear under different names in the literature or in the national legislation. For instance, the Swiss legislation uses the terms 'consistency of subject matter' and 'consistency of form'. See Art. 75 Federal Act on Political Rights. Here I rely on the terms used in the Revised Code III.2.

are reserved for the elected representatives.[100] In the corresponding *substantive authorization procedures* the state institutions review whether the issue proposed for a popular vote falls under one or more of the prohibited topics. These procedures are also part of the analysis, because – similarly to formal authorization procedures – the content of the referendum proposal is evaluated in them, and state institutions exercise discretionary powers.

Most states do not have a clear-cut separation between the different types of authorization procedures in practice.[101] In some states the technical and formal authorization procedures are carried out together, for instance the formulation of the question is checked when the initiative group is registered, and the signatures are counted. In other states the same institution reviews the formal and substantive limits in a single procedure. The reason for still using this distinction is mostly to signal that the pre-vote referendum authorization procedures can fulfill different functions: checking that technical requirements are complied with, ensuring that the referendum request has gathered enough popular support, protecting the free will-formation of all voters, and protecting individual rights or other public interests.

I focus exclusively on pre-vote authorization procedures. In terms of the timing of the referendum authorization procedure, three possible solutions exist: the citizen-initiated referendum may be reviewed before the signature collection starts, after the necessary number of signatures have been collected, or after the vote has taken place. The Council of Europe member states all use pre-vote review procedures, while post-vote review is typical in the United States.[102] Pre-vote review ensures that the subject of the authorization is in fact only a proposed question and not the expressed will of the people. If a referendum request is blocked from reaching the ballot, the pre-vote review protects the people from the frustration of a decision that is impossible to implement. So, in reality, the pre-vote review fosters not only the rule of law, but also the democratic process by not allowing fruitless popular votes to take place.[103] It also mitigates the political pressure on the state institutions, which may be more reluctant to find an initiative unconstitutional after the voters have showed their support for it. In contrast, the post-vote review effectively means the review of the legislative act that was adopted in the referendum process. Most European states have established constitutional courts or authorized

---

[100] See Chapter 4, section 3.1.

[101] See Chapter 1, section 4.

[102] Kenneth P. Miller, *Direct Democracy and the Courts* (Cambridge University Press 2009) 99; Henry S. Noyes, *The Law of Direct Democracy* (Carolina Academic Press 2014) 145.

[103] Douglas C. Michael, 'Preelection Judicial Review: Taking the Initiative in Voter Protection' (1983) 71 *California Law Review* 1216, 1233–1234.

regular high courts to review the constitutionality of legislative acts.[104] The assessment of these post-vote review systems is excluded from the analysis, because they would raise different questions than the pre-vote review. While the pre-vote review focuses on deciding whether popular sovereignty should be exercised, the post-vote review is about the legislative change following the referendum. The post-vote review procedures are not able to fully remedy the potential defects of the referendum proposal. Most evidently, these remedies are *ex post facto*: the vote on a potentially unlawful or unconstitutional referendum has taken place and the results of the successful referendum have become part of the legal system. This means that while certain defects such as violation of fundamental rights and freedoms can be corrected after the vote, other defects such as the misleading formulation of questions are final.

Other state interventions during the referendum process are also excluded from the scope of this book. Once a citizen-initiated referendum has been authorized as fulfilling all the technical, formal, and substantive requirements, the next stages of the referendum process are the campaign, then the vote itself and the verification of the results. These stages also entail a number of decisions by state institutions. Campaign rule violations, irregularities during the vote, or even the final results of the referendum may be challenged. These procedures are excluded because these are not linked to the content of the referendum and are not decisive for the popular vote taking place.

3.3   Temporal Scope

I analyze the referendum authorization procedures currently in force, without going into details about their historical development. Institutional and even procedural choices are often rooted in constitutional traditions or can be traced back to certain constitutional events. Historical references are only used when they can contribute to interpreting the current institutional and procedural settings.

I primarily focus on referendum authorization decisions and referendum events that occurred between 1989–90 and 2022. The one exception from the temporal scope is an Italian referendum case from 1978.[105] This case is included in the analysis because the Italian Constitutional Court introduced new legal limits, which are highly influential in the current practice of the Court.

---

[104] de Visser (n 92) 99; Wojciech Sadurski, *Rights Before Courts: A Study of Constitutional Courts in Postcommunist States of Central and Eastern Europe* (Springer 2005) 5.

[105] Judgment no. 16 of 1978 of the Constitutional Court, Official Gazette, 1st Special Series no. 39 of 8 February 1978.

The main reason for choosing 1989–90 as a starting point is that the new constitutions of the Central and Eastern European countries were adopted in or after 1989. Thus, in this region, direct democracy was introduced or reintroduced then. Drawing on more than 30 years of practice also makes it possible to include countries that are sporadic users of direct democracy.[106]

3.4   Geographical Scope

The geographical scope of the book is limited to Europe and to national referendums. The member states of the Council of Europe are assessed to establish the general trends of referendum authorization, while a smaller set of member states is used for the more detailed analysis. The member states of the Council of Europe have committed themselves to protect the rule of law and ensure the enjoyment of human rights and fundamental freedoms.[107] Focusing on these states offers an opportunity to assess how they can balance these fundamental principles in their referendum practice. The member states of the Council of Europe are also subject to the only international standards guiding referendums: the Revised Guidelines on the Holding of Referendums. Consequently, the fulfillment of the institutional and procedural requirements of the Revised Code is a relevant question regarding the referendum practice of these states.

Limiting the analysis to Europe also provides a manageable set of states that still represent a wide variety of different systems and practices. Some countries are on the world-wide frontline of referendum practice (Switzerland, Liechtenstein), while others are frequent or regular users.[108] Some states impose many limits (Portugal, Hungary), while others none or only few (Switzerland, Croatia). Several different institutional solutions appear in Europe for referendum authorization, from election commissions through presidents and parliaments to regular and constitutional courts. The procedural rights of the parties are also varied.[109]

The smaller set of states is selected based on the following criteria: (1) the selected states need to have some form of citizen-initiated referendum at the national level, (2) the citizen-initiated referendum has been used in practice since 1989–90, (3) the states need to represent prevalent institutional choices for referendum authorization in Europe and (4) the states should represent

---

[106] Morel, 'Types of Referendums, Provisions and Practice at National Level Worldwide' (n 72) 52–53.

[107] Art 3 Statute of the Council of Europe, ETS No. 001, London 5 May 1949.

[108] Morel, 'Types of Referendums, Provisions and Practice at National Level Worldwide' (n 72) 52–53.

[109] See Chapter 2, section 3.

both 'old' and 'new' democracies. Including 'new' democracies contributes to an even geographic distribution of states. More importantly, several 'new' democracies have introduced citizen-initiated referendums after the fall of the Soviet Union and a couple of them have organized multiple referendums since. Meanwhile relatively few 'old' democracies use these instruments.

Of the member states of the Council of Europe only 25 have legal institutions for citizen-initiated referendums at national level.[110] Since 1990 only 15 of these states have had national referendum events initiated by citizens: Bulgaria, Croatia, Georgia, Hungary, Italy, Latvia, Liechtenstein, Lithuania, Malta, North Macedonia, San Marino, Slovakia, Slovenia, Switzerland, and Ukraine.[111] For the selection of the smaller set of states I focus on states that have had multiple citizen-initiated referendums since 1989–90, because the exceptional use of citizen-initiated instruments does not allow for developing a practice in referendum authorization procedures. This selection step excludes Georgia, Malta, North Macedonia, and Ukraine. Croatia has also had only one citizen-initiated referendum. However, the referendum was on the issue of same-sex marriage, which allows for a comparison with Slovakia and Slovenia where citizens also initiated referendums on same-sex marriage.

Out of the 'old' democracies, San Marino is excluded because it has similar institutional settings to Italy (authorization by the Constitutional Court). This leaves Italy, Liechtenstein, and Switzerland. Out of the 'new' democracies in Central and Eastern Europe and the Baltics, Bulgaria and Lithuania are excluded based on similar considerations. They both leave referendum authorization decisions to the parliaments, an institutional setting that is already represented by other states (Croatia, Liechtenstein, Slovenia, and Switzerland). Consequently, the book highlights the referendum practice of the following eight states: Croatia, Italy, Hungary, Latvia, Liechtenstein, Slovakia, Slovenia, and Switzerland.

---

[110] Albania, Armenia, Azerbaijan, Bulgaria, Croatia, Georgia, Hungary, Italy, Latvia, Liechtenstein, Lithuania, Luxembourg, Malta, Moldova, Montenegro, North Macedonia, Poland, Portugal, Russia, San Marino, Serbia, Slovakia, Slovenia, Switzerland, Ukraine. See LIDD data dashboard > Summaries > By Instrument/ Countries on http://lidd-project.org/data/, statistics correct as at 15 March 2022. The data collection was carried out when Russia was still a member of the Council of Europe. The figures and tables illustrating the data collection and analysis incorporate the Russian rules on referendums as well as the practice, and the book contains references to this practice.

[111] See LIDD Referendum events dashboard > Vote trigger > Citizens (included) on <http://lidd-project.org/data2/> or <https://www.sudd.ch/>, statistics correct as at 15 March 2022.

4.   THE STRUCTURE OF THE BOOK

Following these introductory remarks, the next chapter provides an overview of the referendum authorization procedures for citizen-initiated referendums in the Council of Europe (Chapter 2). This overview is built primarily on the LIDD database, and its aim is to show the general trends in referendum authorization procedures. Subsequently, a brief introduction is provided to the legal provisions that govern referendums in the eight selected states (Chapter 3). Then, the special nature of the referendum authorization procedure is analyzed in more detail (Chapter 4). This part of the book tries to resolve the dualities surrounding the procedure: is the referendum authorization procedure political or legal? Is the review of legal limits abstract or concrete? This chapter also provides an overview of the most common legal limits from a procedural standpoint. Next, I explore how the principles of independence and impartiality of the decision-maker, the right to a reasoned decision, the right to be heard, and the right to an effective remedy shape the referendum authorization practice of the selected states (Chapters 5–9). Each procedural guarantee is evaluated through three questions: (1) What is the function of the procedural guarantee in referendum authorization procedures with regard to the special nature of these procedures? (2) Is the procedural guarantee ensured in the referendum authorization practice of the selected states? (3) How could the procedural guarantee be better incorporated in the referendum authorization procedures of the selected states? Finally, I draw some conclusions based on the comparative analysis and attempt to establish best practices for referendum authorization procedures (Chapter 10).

2. European trends in referendum authorization

A number of online databases are already available to describe the various aspects of direct-democratic instruments. Some data collections have focused on the referendum practice, and the databases list the referendum events per country.[1] In other instances, direct democracy has been analyzed as a segment of broader democracy research, and the databases contain the numerical indicators of direct-democratic instruments, such as signature counts, time-limits, and quorums.[2] Lastly, some of the databases contain the legal provisions applicable to direct-democratic instruments and focus on the classification of the instruments.[3] Even though this last group of databases has touched on the questions of legal limits and referendum authorization, the data collection has not been systematic in this regard.

The findings of this chapter build on the direct democracy database created within the framework of the LIDD project.[4] The LIDD database[5] is the first database which comprehensively contains all the relevant legal rules about direct-democratic instruments with the distinct aim of learning about the legal limits imposed on direct-democratic instruments and their enforcement mechanisms. The database follows a questionnaire format, where each direct-democratic instrument has been assigned between 42 and 75 questions. The questions are grouped according to the various aspects of the direct-democratic process. They are also unified across all instruments to reach comparable results. The LIDD data collection had three phases. First, the members of the LIDD research group filled out questionnaires for all member states of the Council of Europe, which resulted in the first version of the dataset. The questionnaire was then sent out to national experts in each country. In the final phase, the answers of the LIDD dataset and the expert dataset were reconciled by the LIDD researchers, and the final database was

---

[1]   See <https://c2d.ch/> or <https://www.sudd.ch/>, accessed 15 March 2022.
[2]   See Varieties of Democracy dataset <https://www.v-dem.net/en/data/data/v-dem-dataset/>, accessed 15 March 2022.
[3]   See <https://www.direct-democracy-navigator.org/legal_designs> or <https://www.idea.int/data-tools/data/direct-democracy>, accessed 15 March 2022.
[4]   See <http://lidd-project.org/research/>, accessed 15 March 2022.
[5]   See <http://lidd-project.org/data/>, statistics correct as at 15 March 2022.

created. The data collection was carried out when Russia was still a member of the Council of Europe. The figures, charts, and tables illustrating the data collection and analysis incorporate the Russian rules on referendums as well as the practice and the book contain references to this practice.

The final database enables users to view the data on the seven direct-democratic instruments in different configurations. The database offers summaries by country, showing the legal rules governing each direct-democratic instrument in a single country.[6] Alternatively, the data can be viewed by instrument, showing all the countries that allow the use of the given direct-democratic instruments.[7] The collected data can also be explored by instrument, question group, and single question.[8] This configuration has contributed the most to the comparative analysis, because the data is accompanied by legal sources and comments from the experts.

1. CITIZEN-INITIATED REFERENDUMS IN EUROPE

In the LIDD project the direct-democratic instruments are classified into seven categories: agenda initiatives, law-initiated referendums, executive-initiated referendums, legislature-initiated referendums, referendums initiated by subnational entities, proactive citizen-initiated referendums, and rejective citizen-initiated referendums. This classification is based on the initiator of the referendum or agenda initiative, which is understood as the entity that has the power to define the subject of the referendum or agenda initiative. The following definitions are given to each instrument:[9]

Agenda initiative: An instrument that allows a certain number of citizens to put an issue on the agenda of state organs but that does not lead to a referendum (i.e. a popular vote). An agenda initiative mandates the state organ to deal with the proposal: by making a decision about it or at least debating it.

Law-initiated referendum: A referendum that is triggered if certain conditions specified by law (i.e. by the constitution or a legislative act) are met. The law may determine the topic (e.g. transfer of sovereignty) or the type of legal act (e.g. constitutional amendment) that triggers the referendum process. The

---

6   See LIDD data dashboard > Summaries > By Country/Instrument on <http://lidd -project.org/data/>, statistics correct as at 15 March 2022.

7   See LIDD data dashboard > Summaries > By Instrument/Countries on <http:// lidd-project.org/data/>, statistics correct as at 15 March 2022.

8   See LIDD data dashboard > Explore data > By Instrument/Item on <http://lidd -project.org/data/>, statistics correct as at 15 March 2022.

9   See LIDD data dashboard > Get started > Typology on <http://lidd-project.org/ data/>, statistics correct as at 15 March 2022.

law can either directly require the holding of a referendum or require it in case certain additional conditions are not met (e.g. a constitutional amendment is not passed by a supermajority in parliament). In all cases the referendum is triggered by law rather than initiated by a state organ.

Executive-initiated referendum: A referendum that can be initiated by the executive (i.e. by the government (or parts of it)). A referendum is initiated by the executive if the government or other executive actors can start the referendum process by defining the issue for the popular vote.

Legislature-initiated referendum: A referendum that can be initiated by the legislature (i.e. by parliament (or parts of it)). A referendum is initiated by the legislature if the parliament or members of the parliament can start the referendum process by defining the issue for the popular vote.

Referendum initiated by subnational entities: A referendum that can be initiated by (a certain number of) subnational entities (regions, provinces, cantons, municipalities). A referendum is initiated by a subnational entity if it can start the referendum process by defining the issue for the popular vote.

Proactive citizen-initiated referendum: An instrument that allows a certain number of citizens to initiate a referendum and formulate the topic of the referendum.

Rejective citizen-initiated referendum: An instrument that allows a certain number of citizens to initiate a referendum that is aimed at preventing new laws (or parts of them) from being passed or at repealing existing laws (or parts of them).

Out of the member states of the Council of Europe only a handful do not have any of these direct-democratic instruments at national level: Belgium, Bosnia, Cyprus, the Czech Republic, Monaco, and Norway. It is possible to organize ad hoc referendums in these states, but direct-democratic instruments are not part of their constitutional system. All other states have at least one direct-democratic instrument from the seven variants. Two microstates – Liechtenstein and San Marino – lead the list with the most instruments. Neither of them has executive-initiated referendums, but all other instruments are available. Their leading position is not as surprising as the prominent positions of the states that follow: Albania, Armenia, Bulgaria, Montenegro, and Serbia. These states are not well-known for their direct-democratic traditions, and indeed the five of them together have had fewer referendums (25) than San Marino alone (26), which is still far fewer than the number of referendums Liechtenstein has held (41).[10] Interestingly, Figure 2.1 suggests that new democracies are better equipped with direct-democratic instruments than older

---

[10] LIDD Referendum events dashboard > Select country on <http://lidd-project .org/data2/>, statistics correct as at 15 March 2022.

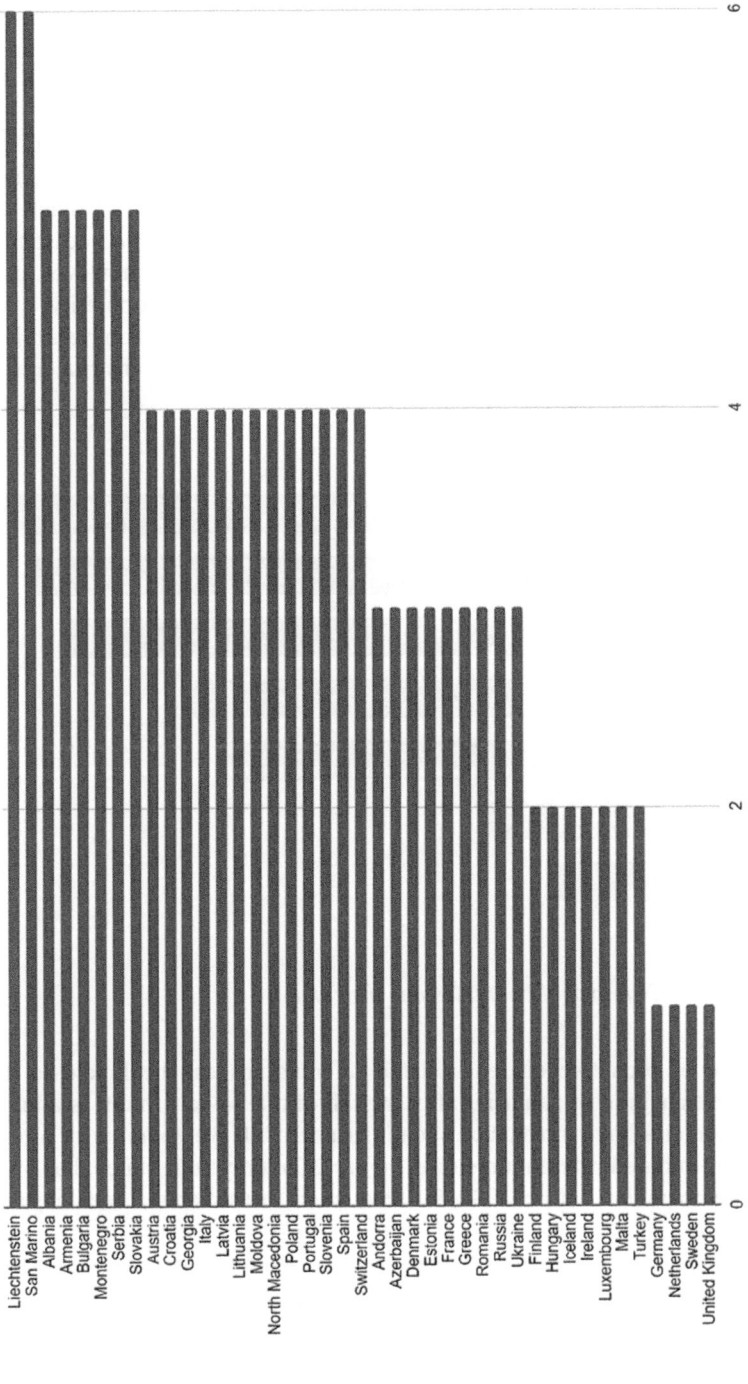

Figure 2.1   Number of instruments per country

ones. However, the examples of the top states show that this does not necessarily mean an active use of these instruments. More often, it was important in
the process of democratic transition to signal the democratization through the
introduction of a broad range of direct-democratic instruments.[11]

Figure 2.2 shows that the most popular direct-democratic instruments are
referendums optionally initiated by the parliament, agenda initiatives, and
law-initiated referendums. This could suggest that most states approach the
introduction of direct-democratic instruments with caution and do not want to
give away too much decision-making authority. Interestingly, however, proactive citizen-initiated referendums also enjoy considerable popularity, even
though they put the most power in the hands on the people. In contrast, rejective citizen-initiated referendums, which are more conservative instruments of
citizen empowerment, are far less popular.

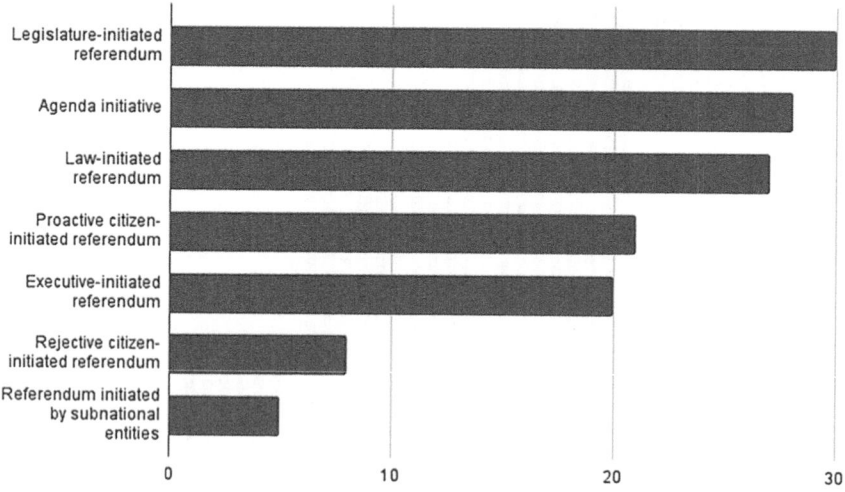

Figure 2.2   Number of countries per instrument

The spread of proactive citizen-initiated referendums can be linked to the
democratic transition of countries after the fall of the Soviet Union, as a lot of
new democracies have introduced such instruments. If we zoom in on proactive citizen-initiated referendums (see Figure 2.3), only four states that were
already democracies before 1989–90 have such instruments: Liechtenstein,

---

[11]   Podolnjak, 'Constitutional Reforms of Citizen-Initiated Referendum: Causes of
Different Outcomes in Slovenia and Croatia' (Ch 1, n 89) 131.

Portugal, San Marino, and Switzerland. The other 17 states that allow proactive initiatives are all new democracies. Meanwhile, the trend is the opposite for rejective citizen-initiated referendums. Older democracies prefer this choice and only two new democracies (Albania, Slovenia) have introduced such instruments.

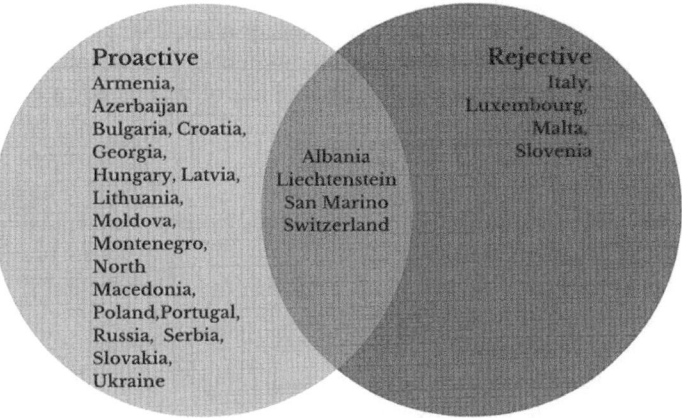

Proactive
Armenia,
Azerbaijan
Bulgaria, Croatia,
Georgia,
Hungary, Latvia,
Lithuania,
Moldova,
Montenegro,
North
Macedonia,
Poland,Portugal,
Russia, Serbia,
Slovakia,
Ukraine

Albania
Liechtenstein
San Marino
Switzerland

Rejective
Italy,
Luxembourg,
Malta,
Slovenia

Figure 2.3   Proactive and rejective citizen-initiated referendums

2.   FORMAL AND SUBSTANTIVE LIMITS

Before turning to the authorization procedures, it is important to give an overview of the legal limits imposed on referendums. Since the referendum authorization procedures are primarily about reviewing the legal limits, the authorization procedures cannot be discussed without giving an overview of the legal limits.

The LIDD database contains data on three formal limits: the clarity of the question, the unity of form, and the unity of substance. These formal limits also appear in the Revised Code of the Venice Commission. The clarity requirement is an integral element of free suffrage, while the unity of form and content are recommended elements of the procedural validity of the texts submitted to referendums.[12]

The questionnaire on substantive limits asks whether referendums are prohibited on:

---

[12]   Revised Code III.2.

(a) constitutional amendments;
(b) international law obligations;
(c) fundamental rights and freedoms;
(d) state structure or form of government;
(e) state symbols;
(f) the official language;
(g) territorial issues or territorial integrity;
(h) state finances (including budget, taxes, or other financial obligations);
(i) national security (including the military, police, and secret services);
(j) emergency powers (including declaration of war, state of emergency) and urgent matters;
(k) pardon or amnesty;
(l) naturalization;
(m) minorities or minority rights;
(n) rules of elections and referendums;
(o) election or appointment of state officials or civil service laws;
(p) legislative competences;
(q) executive competences;
(r) issues related to the judiciary (including competences, independence); or
(s) issues related to local governance.

Some of these limits correspond to the Revised Code, which requires the texts submitted to a referendum to comply with all superior law and not be contrary to international law and the principles of democracy, human rights, and the rule of law.[13] The other limits are formulated based on the national rules on referendums, so that all existing substantive limits could be categorized.

The data collection shows that most states impose a clarity requirement for proactive citizen-initiated referendums, while fewer states specify that the referendum issue should not violate the unity of substance or unity of form requirements. This is not surprising, since the clarity requirement is an overarching principle that is capable of enforcing both other principles. If a referendum question bundles different issues together, then the voters cannot express their preferences on the separate issues, thus the question also violates the clarity requirement. Similarly, if the referendum issue contains both legal texts and general proposals, then the legal consequences of the vote are not clearly determined. Only five states do not impose any formal limits on the proactive citizen-initiated referendums: Azerbaijan, Georgia, Latvia, Montenegro, and Ukraine.

---

[13] Revised Code III.1.

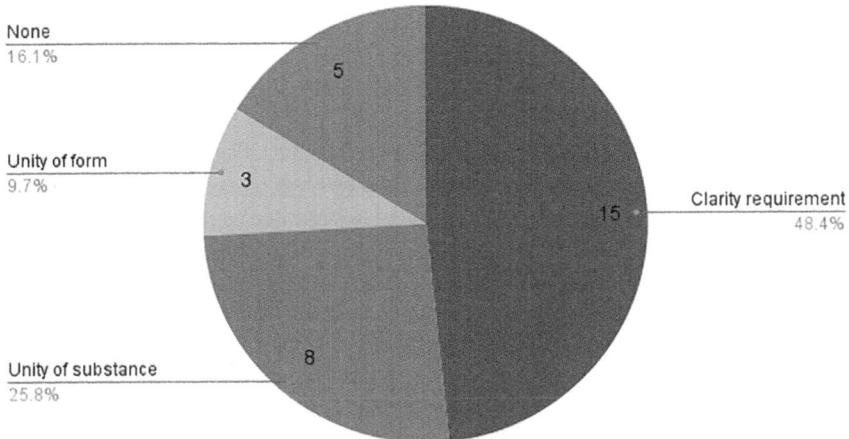

Figure 2.4   Formal limits on proactive citizen-initiated referendums

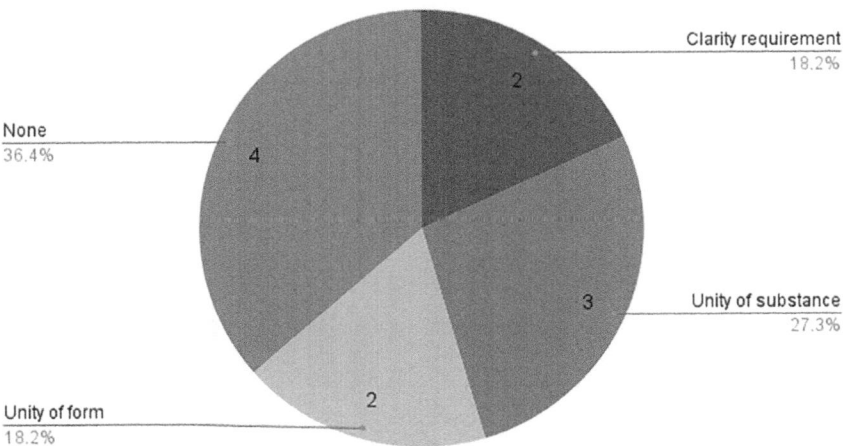

Figure 2.5   Formal limits on rejective citizen-initiated referendums

The regulation of rejective citizen-initiated referendums shows a different picture regarding formal limits. Half of the states that have rejective referendums do not impose any formal limits (Albania, Malta, Luxembourg, and Slovenia). In the other half of the states, the most common formal limit is the unity of substance requirement, which appears in three states (Italy,

Liechtenstein, and Switzerland).[14] The other two formal limits each only appear in two states: the clarity of the referendum issue is required in Italy and San Marino, while the unity of form in Italy and Liechtenstein. Compared to the formal limits on proactive referendums, this difference might be due to the different subject of the referendums, since the subject of rejective referendums is always an official act adopted by state institutions.

The proactive and rejective citizen-initiated referendums show more correlation in terms of the most common substantive limits. The most commonly restricted topic is state finances. Questions about pardon and amnesty, and about emergency powers are also common exceptions from citizen-initiated referendums. Many states do not allow citizen-initiated referendums to take place about fundamental rights (Albania, Armenia, Azerbaijan, Georgia, Hungary, Liechtenstein, Malta, Moldova, San Marino, Serbia, Slovakia, and Slovenia), while prohibitions on minority rights are less common (Hungary, Malta, North Macedonia, and Serbia).

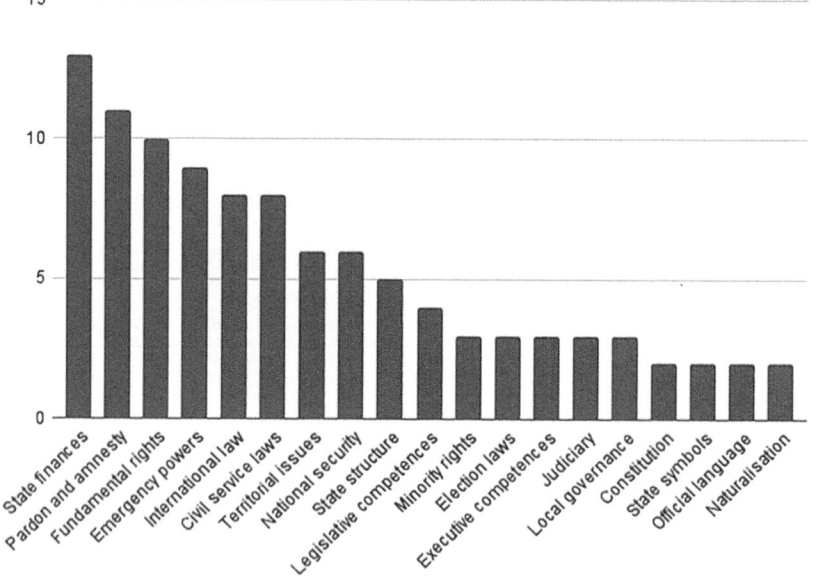

Figure 2.6   Substantive limits on proactive citizen-initiated referendums

---

[14]   It must be noted that the applicability of formal limits to rejective citizen-initiated referendums is contested both in Switzerland and Liechtenstein. Daniel Moeckli, 'Switzerland' in Daniel Moeckli, Anna Forgács, Henri Ibi (eds), *The Legal Limits of Direct Democracy* (Edward Elgar Publishing 2021) 34; Wilfried Marxer, 'Liechtenstein' in Daniel Moeckli, Anna Forgács, Henri Ibi (eds), *The Legal Limits of Direct Democracy* (Edward Elgar Publishing 2021) 55–57.

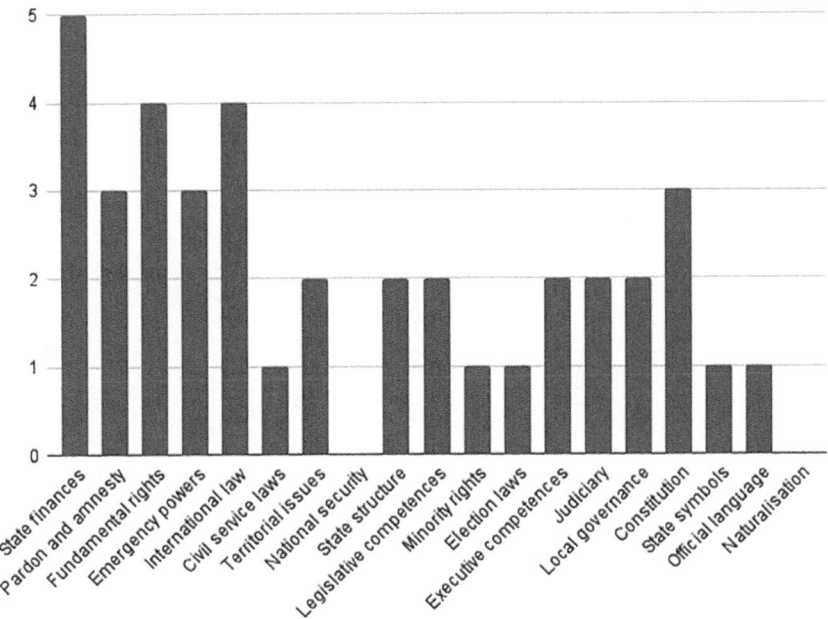

Figure 2.7   Substantive limits on rejective citizen-initiated referendums

The numbers do not suggest that neither new nor old democracies tend to impose more limits than the others. Some older democracies are frontrunners in the number of limits (Portugal, Malta, or San Marino), while Italy is in the middle and Liechtenstein and Switzerland are at the other end of the spectrum. Similarly, some new democracies impose a large number of substantive limits (Hungary, Armenia, Russia, or Serbia), but there are also new democracies with few or no explicit substantive limitations (Slovakia, Ukraine, Croatia, or Lithuania). There are only a few states that do not impose any substantive limits on citizen-initiated referendums: Croatia, Lithuania, Montenegro, Luxembourg, and Switzerland (but only for the rejective instrument).

An anticipated correlation can be seen between the number of legal limits and the use of citizen-initiated referendums. Even though there are states that have had referendum events regardless of the extensive substantive limits imposed on citizen-initiated referendums (Hungary, Malta), the most frequent users of these instruments impose few substantive limits on these instruments (Italy, Liechtenstein, Switzerland[15]).

---

[15]   For Switzerland a random higher number (40) was used to depict the practice, because Switzerland had held 216 citizen-initiated referendums up to 2020.

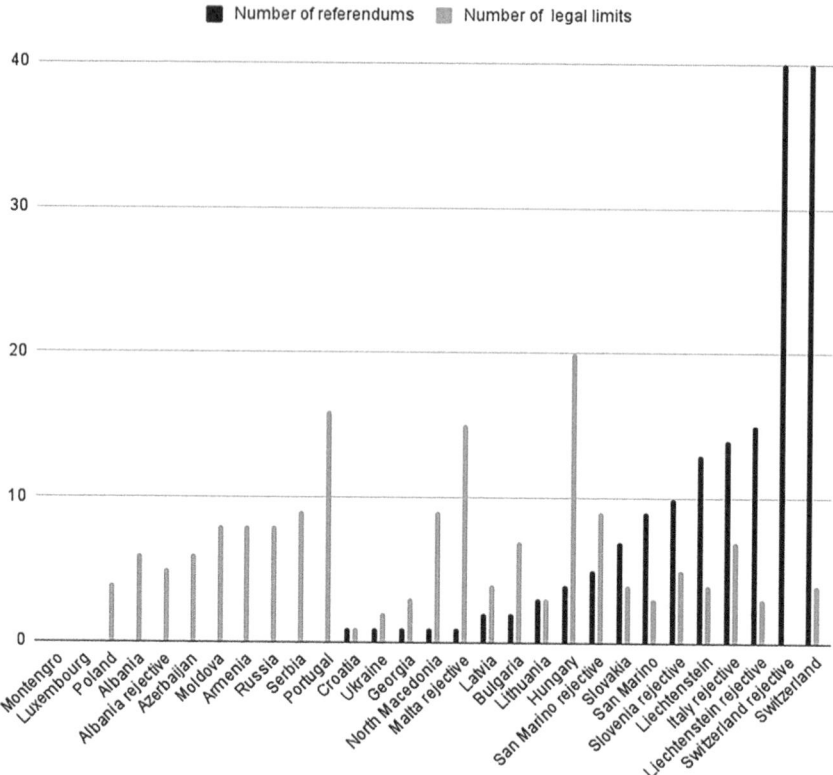

Figure 2.8   Correlation between number of legal limits and use of citizen-initiated referendums

In comparison to citizen-initiated referendums, especially to proactive citizen-initiated referendums, if we look at referendums initiated by executives, we can see that the prevalence of formal limits is not prominent. Similarly, the imposition of substantive limits is not as common as for citizen-initiated referendums. Out of the 20 European states that allow the executives to initiate referendums, only 10 states impose formal and 13 states substantive limits on these referendums.[16] These trends are even more visible for referendums

See LIDD Referendum events dashboard > Select country > Vote trigger > Citizens (included) on <http://lidd-project.org/data2/> and <https://www.bfs.admin.ch/bfs/de/home/statistiken/politik/abstimmungen.html>, accessed 15 March 2022.

[16]   LIDD data dashboard > Explore data > By instrument/item > Executive-initiated referendum on <http://lidd-project.org/data/>, statistics correct as at 15 March 2022.

initiated by legislatures: out of 30 European countries, only 13 states impose formal limits and 15 states substantive limits on these referendums.[17]

3.   REFERENDUM AUTHORIZATION PROCEDURES

The LIDD data on the referendum authorization procedures covers questions about the existence of formal and substantive authorization procedures, the institutional choices for these procedures, the availability of remedy and hearing rights, and the use of evidentiary procedures. Since most states impose legal limits on citizen-initiated referendums, most of them have also created authorization procedures for the enforcement of limits. Authorization procedures are not commonly regulated for referendums initiated by state institutions. Even though 10 states impose formal limits on executive-initiated referendums, only four regulate the corresponding authorization procedure, while 13 states impose substantive limits but only nine have substantive authorization procedures. In case of legislature-initiated referendums, out of the 30 states regulating these instruments, only eight have formal and 12 substantive authorization procedures.

3.1   Choice of State Institutions

The Revised Code of the Venice Commission suggests that the authorization of referendums should be entrusted to a central commission or other impartial authority.[18] Following this recommendation, election commissions can be evident institutional choices for referendum authorizations. However, the data shows that other state institutions are also popular choices among the Council of Europe member states. Some states entrust parliaments or presidents with the referendum authorization competence, while others rely on governments or governmental agencies.

   In the data collection, we use the term *government* to refer to the decision-making both of the government and of administrative authorities in a hierarchical relationship with the government (e.g. a ministry). The term *parliament* refers to the decision-making of unicameral or bicameral parliaments, as well as parliamentary committees. Meanwhile, *president* encompasses the head of state regardless of the actual name of the position or the form of government. *Election commissions* refer to both ad hoc and permanent bodies that

---

[17]   LIDD data dashboard > Explore data > By instrument/item > Legislature-initiated referendum on <http://lidd-project.org/data/>, statistics correct as at 15 March 2022.
[18]   Revised Code II.4.1.

are designed to fulfill functions in relation to voting events and are primarily created to ensure the legality of elections.[19] The referendum authorization competence can also belong to judicial organs, most commonly to constitutional courts and in a few instances to regular courts. In the data collection, *constitutional courts* describes courts with the jurisdiction to review legal acts and invalidate or disregard them if the constitution or the hierarchy of norms is violated, regardless of the institutional constellations.[20] Meanwhile, the term *regular court* is used to describe all courts other than constitutional courts, including civil, administrative, or criminal courts.

In Table 2.1, I make a distinction between technical, formal, and substantive authorization procedures. The technical authorization of citizen-initiated referendums can entail the registration of the initiative group, the verification of the signature collection, and the fulfillment of other technical requirements. The formal and the substantive authorization procedures ensure adherence to the formal limits on the wording of the referendum question, and the substantive limits on the referendum issue.

Overall, the data shows that election commissions are the most popular institutions for authorizing referendums. Parliaments and constitutional courts follow closely, then governments, while the least common institutional choices for the first instance procedures are regular courts (Italy) and presidents (Georgia, Slovakia).

Out of the 25 states that have citizen-initiated referendums, there are some states where one or more types of authorization procedures are not regulated. One reason for this might be the lack of practice in organizing citizen-initiated referendums.

Poland and Montenegro are states that only introduced a technical authorization procedure but have no formal or substantive authorization of referendums.[21] Montenegro has had no practice of direct democracy: no citizen-initiated referendums have been held in the country. In addition, the direct-democratic

---

[19]   Alan Wall et al., *Electoral Management Design: The International IDEA Handbook: Revised Edition* (Stockholm: International Institute for Democracy and Electoral Assistance IDEA, 2014) 5–6.

[20]   Alec Stone Sweet, 'Constitutional Courts and Parliamentary Democracy' (2002) 25 *West European Politics* 77; Víktor Ferreres Comella, *Constitutional Courts and Democratic Values: A European Perspective* (Yale University Press 2009) 6; Leonard F.M. Besselink, 'The Proliferation of Constitutional Law and Constitutional Adjudication, or How American Judicial Review Came to Europe After All' (2013) 9(2) *Utrecht Law Review* 19–35, 20; Tom Ginsburg, Mila Versteeg, 'Why Do Countries Adopt Constitutional Review?' (2014) 30 (3) *Journal of Law, Economics, & Organization* 587–622, 587; de Visser (Ch 1, n 92) 54.

[21]   Switzerland lacks a procedure only for rejective citizen-initiated referendums but has one for the proactive referendums.

Table 2.1   *Technical, formal, and substantive authorization procedures*

Country	Not regulated	Parliament	President	Government	Election commission	Regular court	Constitutional court
Albania proactive					Technical, Formal		Substantive
Albania rejective					Technical, Formal		Substantive
Armenia	Formal				Technical		Substantive
Azerbaijan	Technical, Formal						Substantive
Bulgaria		Formal, Substantive		Technical			
Croatia		Formal, Substantive		Technical			
Georgia			Substantive		Technical, Formal		
Hungary					Technical, Formal, Substantive		
Italy rejective						Technical, Formal	Substantive
Latvia					Technical, Formal, Substantive		
Liechtenstein proactive		Substantive		Technical, Formal			
Liechtenstein rejective	Substantive			Technical, Formal			
Lithuania		Substantive			Technical, Formal		

Country	Not regulated	Parliament	President	Government	Election commission	Regular court	Constitutional court
Luxembourg rejective	Substantive			Technical, Formal			
Malta rejective					Technical		Formal Substantive
Moldova		Substantive			Technical, Formal		
Montenegro	Formal, Substantive				Technical		
North Macedonia		Formal, Substantive			Technical		
Poland	Formal, Substantive				Technical		
Portugal		Formal		Technical			Substantive
Russia					Technical, Formal, Substantive		
San Marino proactive							Technical, Formal, Substantive
San Marino rejective							Technical, Formal, Substantive
Serbia	Formal	Substantive		Technical			
Slovakia			Technical, Formal, Substantive				

Country	Not regulated	Parliament	President	Government	Election commission	Regular court	Constitutional court
Slovenia rejective		Technical, Formal, Substantive					
Switzerland proactive		Formal, Substantive		Technical			
Switzerland rejective	Formal, Substantive			Technical			
Ukraine	Formal				Technical		Substantive

institutions are underregulated and no formal or substantive limits are imposed on the citizen-initiated referendum. Poland is a more interesting case, because it imposes both formal and substantive limits on the proactive citizen-initiated referendum. The referendum is called by the parliament (Sejm), which has a complete discretion in calling the referendum.[22] The Sejm may refuse the initiative based on the limits or based on political considerations. Without any practice to rely on, it is difficult to decide whether the procedure of the Sejm should be considered a substantive authorization procedure.

Azerbaijan regulates only substantive authorization procedures, but the Azeri Election Code only marginally mentions referendums initiated by citizens. The Code does not impose any formal limits, nor does it prescribe how the initiative has to be registered.[23]

Armenia, Serbia, and Ukraine have only technical and substantive authorization procedures for the proactive citizen-initiated referendum, but no formal authorization procedure. In Ukraine, the Constitutional Court has annulled the act on referendums,[24] and a new act has not been adopted yet. Thus, only the constitutional provisions on the referendum are currently in force, and these do not prescribe any formal procedure. In Armenia, there seems to be no separate formal authorization procedure, only a technical registration of initiatives.[25] In the case of Serbia, the state organs do not have to formally register popular initiatives, but instead there is a notification requirement on the side of the initiators. The initiative committee submits the proposal to the body responsible for the subject-matter of the referendum, notifying that the signatures are being collected for the proposal.[26] Since none of these states has developed a practice in citizen-initiated referendums, the need for formal authorization procedures may have not surfaced.

Authorization procedures are also not common for rejective citizen-initiated referendums, as the examples of Liechtenstein, Luxembourg, and Switzerland show. The reason might be that these states impose few limits on these reactive referendums. Despite the differences of rejective citizen-initiated referendums, authorization procedures can take place. If the state excludes certain types of legal acts from consideration by referendum, then it has to be assessed whether the adopted act falls within the exceptions (Slovenia). The formal review of rejective referendum proposals is also possible when the state institutions

---

[22]   Art. 63(1) Act of 14 March 2003 on the nationwide referendum.
[23]   Armenia: Art. 13 Law on Referendum; Azerbaijan: Art. 122.2–123 Election Code.
[24]   Case No. 1–1/2018 (2556/14) of the Constitutional Court of Ukraine.
[25]   Art. 14(6) Law on Referendum.
[26]   See Art. 33–34 Law on Referendum.

decide whether the vote on the legislative act would present clear choices for the voters (Italy).

In most states the technical, formal, and substantive authorization of referendums are not carried out separately from each other. As Figure 2.9 shows, it is common for the formal authorization procedure to be bundled together with the technical authorization or with the substantive authorization. Some states leave all authorization decisions to the same organ.

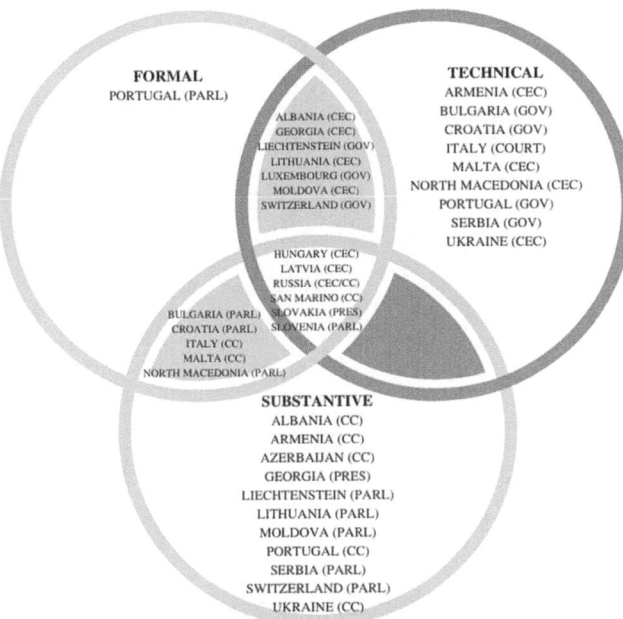

Figure 2.9   Technical, formal and substantive authorization procedures

Table 2.1 and Figure 2.9[27] show that the formal and technical authorization procedures are often entrusted to executive actors such as election commissions and governments, while substantive authorization is mostly left to parliaments and constitutional courts. Presidential decision-making is exceptional and, in both cases, concerns substantive authorization. Governmental bodies are completely excluded from substantive review procedures. Election commissions can only decide about substantive questions when all three kinds

[27]   In Figure 2.9 'PARL' refers to parliament, 'CEC' to central election commission, 'CC' to constitutional court, 'GOV' to government, and 'PRES' to president.

of authorization are carried out in one procedure. This is the case in Hungary, Latvia, and Russia. If the procedures are not completely united, then the substantive authorization is almost exclusively entrusted to parliaments and constitutional courts, regardless of whether the subject of the procedure is both the formal and the substantive limits or only the substantive.

Turning to formal and substantive authorization procedures, which is the narrower focus of the book, this trend is even more visible.

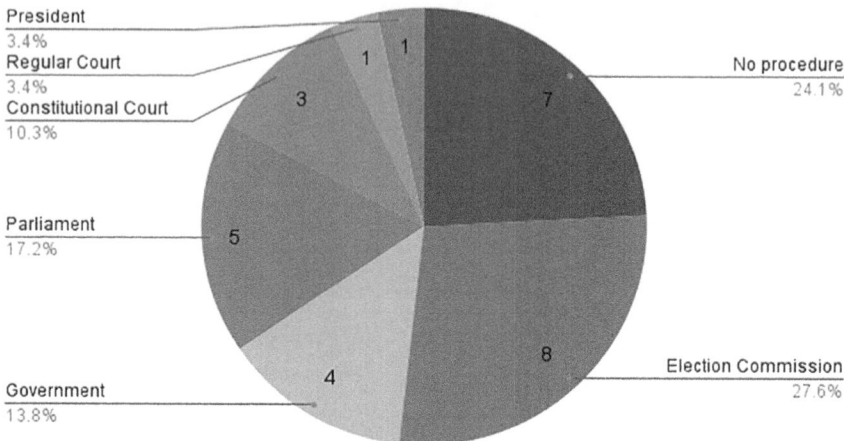

Figure 2.10   Formal authorization

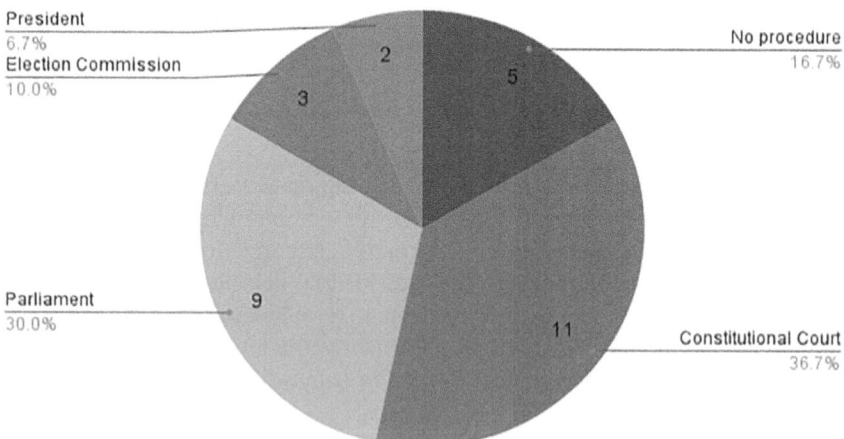

Figure 2.11   Substantive authorization

Comparing the availability of referendum authorization procedures for citizen-initiated referendums with referendums initiated by the executive or the legislature, it is clearly visible that most European states have not created referendum authorization procedures for these instruments.

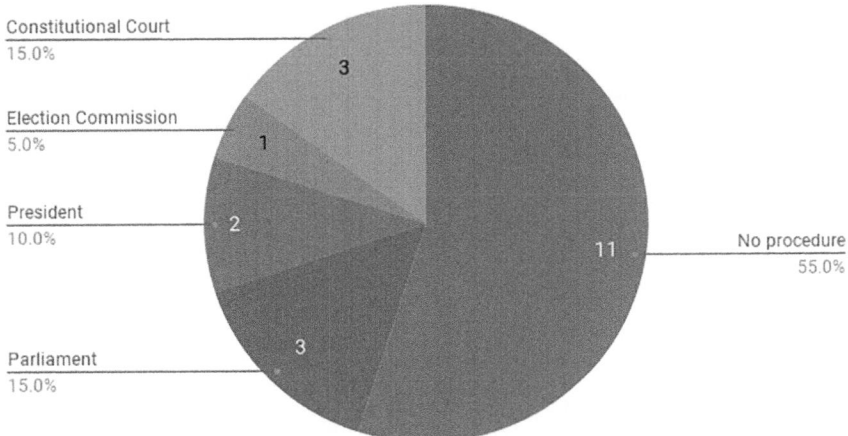

Figures 2.12   Substantive authorization: executive referendum

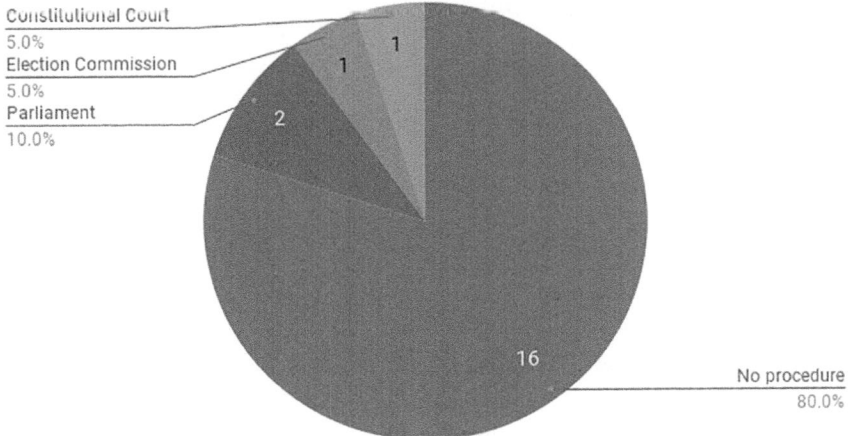

Figure 2.13   Formal authorization: executive referendum

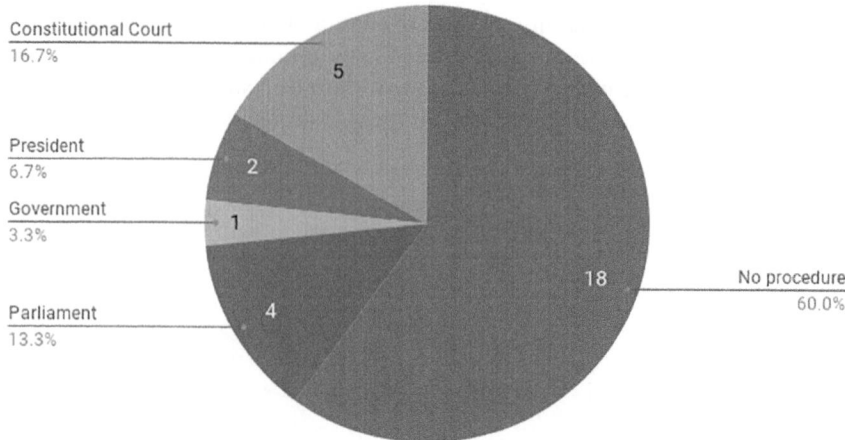

Figure 2.14   Substantive authorization: legislative referendum

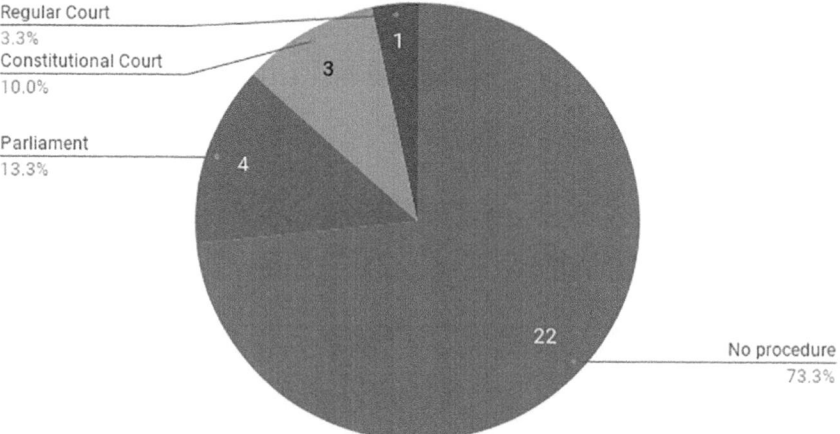

Figure 2.15   Formal authorization: legislative referendum

3.2   Remedies in Referendum Authorization

The Venice Commission recommends that an effective system of appeal should be available in referendum matters, with a final appeal to a court of law.[28] In practice, the availability of remedies largely differs for the different

---

28   Revised Code II.4.3.

institutional settings. An apparent trend for citizen-initiated referendums is that remedies are almost always available against the decisions of election commissions and governments. The only exception is Albania, which does not allow a remedy against the formal-technical authorization decision of the election commission. It is more challenging to draw conclusions about presidential decision-making, as it is underrepresented in the data. While in Slovakia the President can involve the Constitutional Court in the authorization procedure, this is not the case in Georgia. The decisions of parliaments and courts are often final. No state offers remedy against judicial decisions but in most states the highest courts (constitutional courts and supreme courts) are involved in the referendum authorization. More surprisingly, only half of the states allow parliamentary decisions to be challenged. The only states that have remedies against parliamentary decisions are Bulgaria, Croatia, Liechtenstein, Serbia, and Slovenia.

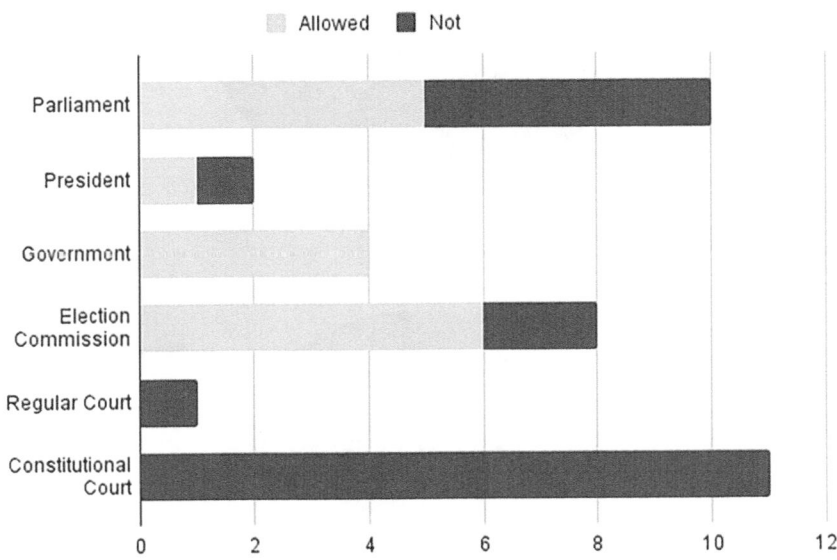

Figure 2.16   Availability of remedies

When looking at the remedy procedures, it is apparent that certain institutional pairings are more common than others. Parliamentary or presidential decisions are almost exclusively reviewed by constitutional courts, if any kind of review is provided at all. The only exception is Serbia, where the substantive authorization decision of the parliament can be challenged at the Supreme Court of Cassation. All the other four states that allow judicial remedies against parliamentary decisions – Bulgaria, Croatia, Liechtenstein, Slovenia – have entrusted this competence to constitutional courts. In contrast, governmental or election commission decisions can only be challenged at regular courts. It follows from this division that formal authorization questions are more commonly decided by regular courts, while substantive authorization questions more often go to constitutional courts.

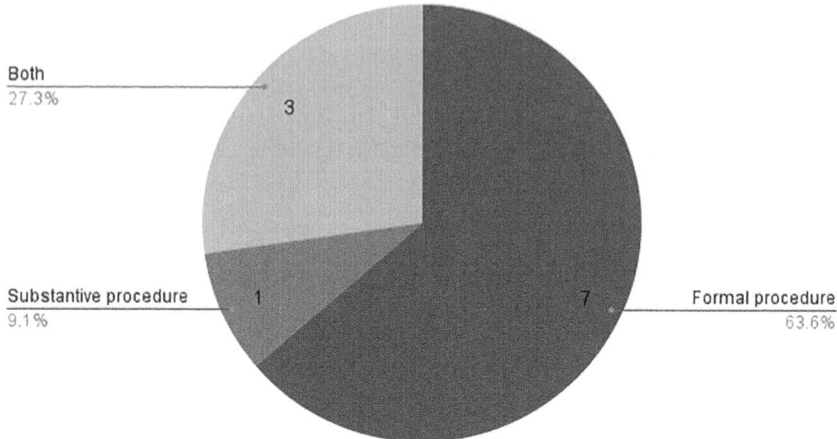

Figure 2.17   Regular court remedy

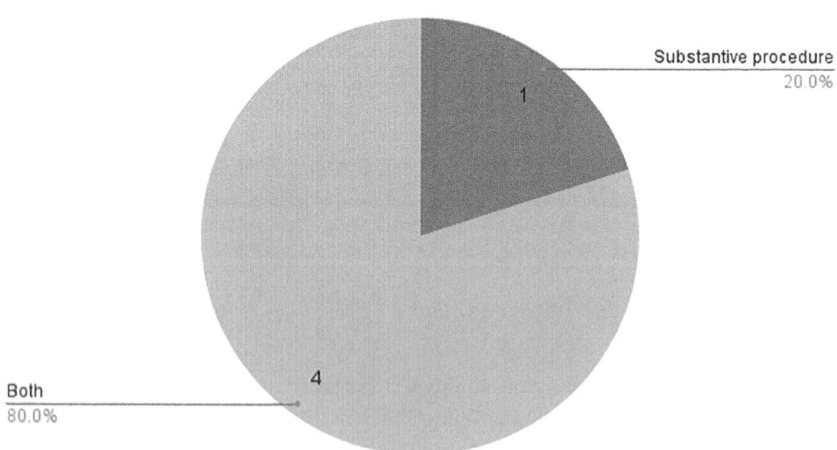

Figure 2.18   Constitutional court remedy

Similar trends can be witnessed in the case of executive- and legislature-initiated referendums, albeit in smaller numbers. For executive-initiated referendums, only Bulgaria, Hungary, and Slovakia allow referendum authorization decisions to be appealed, while only Bulgaria, Denmark, Estonia, Slovakia, and Slovenia do so for legislative-initiated referendums. Parliamentary and presidential decisions can be challenged in constitutional courts (Bulgaria, Slovenia, Slovakia), and governmental and election commission decisions in regular courts (Hungary, Denmark). Estonia is the only exception to this trend, where the parliamentary decision on the initiatives of the parliamentary minority can be challenged at regular courts.

3.3   Procedural Rules of Referendum Authorization

The LIDD database covers certain aspects of the procedural rules governing referendum authorization procedures. Corresponding to the requirements of the Revised Code,[29] the data collection explores the scope of participation rights: whether there is a right to be heard or a right to remedy in the procedure, and who is entitled to challenge the first instance authorization decisions. Hearing rights are not prominent in referendum authorization procedures: half of the states do not allow the interested parties to be heard in either the formal or the substantive authorization of citizen-initiated referendums. The only states that allow hearing rights in both formal and substantive authorization procedures are Malta, North Macedonia, Russia, San Marino, Slovenia, and Slovakia. Meanwhile, some states make it possible for the initiators to participate in at least one of the procedures. Georgia and Portugal provide hearing rights in the formal authorization procedure, while Lithuania, Moldova, and Italy do so in the substantive authorization procedure.

Similarly, hearing rights are limited in procedures authorizing referendums initiated by the executive or the legislature: only Lithuania, Moldova, Slovakia, and Slovenia allow for hearing rights at some stage of the authorization procedure.

Other types of evidentiary procedures, such as those involving expert witnesses, are even less common in referendum authorization procedures than hearing rights. The few states that allow evidentiary procedures are Georgia, Latvia, Lithuania, North Macedonia, Russia, and Slovenia. In some states (Georgia) the evidentiary procedure evolved in practice, in other states (North Macedonia, Russia) it is a feature of the general administrative procedure act, which is also applicable for referendum authorization procedures.[30] Only

---

[29]   Revised Code II.4.3.f, II.4.3.h.
[30]   Russia: Chapter 24 Code of Administrative Procedure of the Russian Federation.

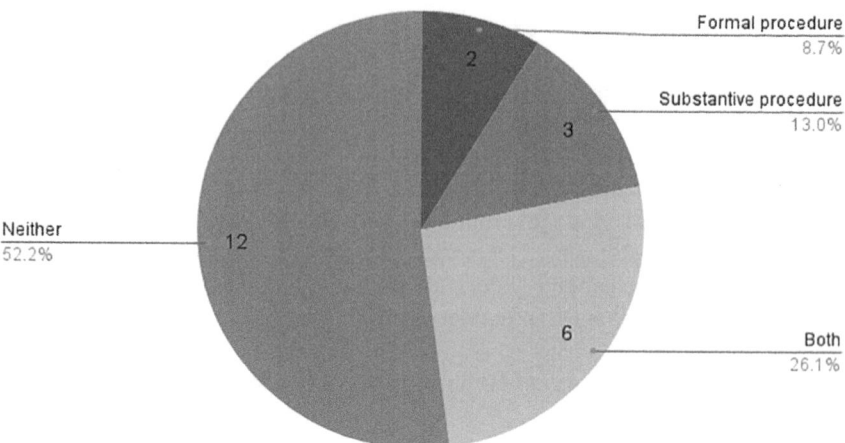

Figure 2.19   Right to be heard

Latvia, Lithuania, and Slovenia regulate the types of evidence specifically among the referendum rules.[31]

The right to an effective remedy is mostly reserved for the initiators of the referendum, while few states allow anyone with voting rights to challenge the first instance decision. Some states allow only the state institutions to initiate a judicial procedure. Out of the 25 states with citizen-initiated referendums only 13 allow remedies against the first instance referendum authorization decisions, and almost two-thirds of them reserve the right to remedy for the initiators (Georgia, Latvia, Liechtenstein, Lithuania, Luxembourg, Moldova, Serbia, Slovenia). Three states allow anyone to challenge the authorization decision (Bulgaria, Hungary, Russia), while Slovakia and Croatia only allow the first instance decision-making body to initiate the judicial review of the referendum question (Figure 2.20).

Another important procedural feature is the timing of the authorization procedure. The member states of the Council of Europe have all opted for a pre-vote authorization procedure. However, in the case of citizen-initiated referendums it can make a difference whether the state intervention takes place before or after the signature collection. In this regard three solutions can be differentiated within the member states of the Council of Europe: some states do not allow the signature collection to start before both the formal and

---

[31]   Latvia: Art. 23 (Art. 6) Law on National Referendum, Legislative Initiative and European Citizens' Initiative. Lithuania: Art. 15(2) Law on Referendum. Slovenia: Art. 21 Referendum and Popular Initiative Act.

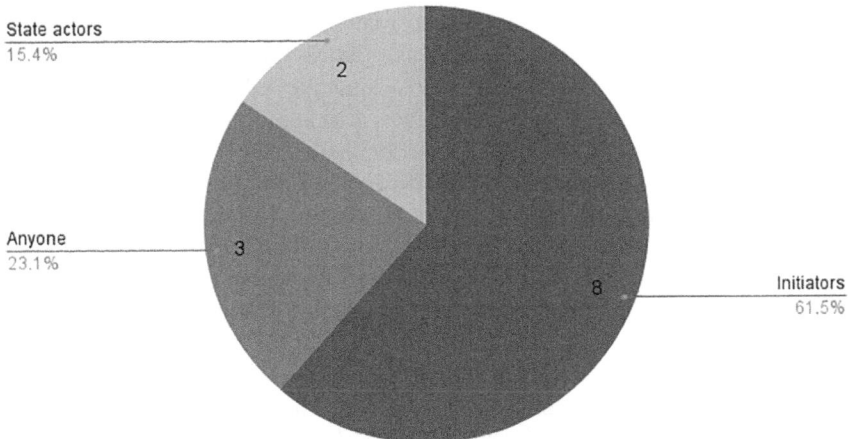

State actors
15.4%

2

Anyone
23.1%

3

8

Initiators
61.5%

Figure 2.20 Right to remedy

the substantive authorization of the referendum proposal; others delay both procedures until the necessary voter support is gathered; while some carry out the formal authorization procedure before the signature collection and leave the substantive authorization until afterward (Figure 2.21).

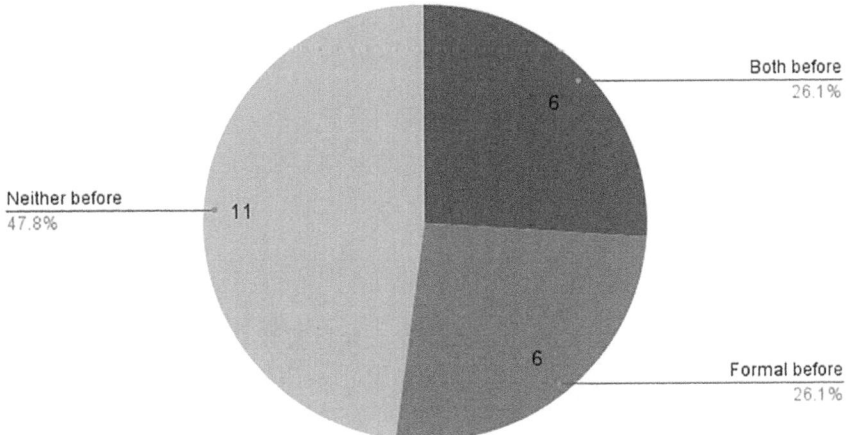

Both before
26.1%

6

Neither before
47.8%

11

6

Formal before
26.1%

Figure 2.21 Timing of formal and substantive procedures

Interestingly, almost half of the states require the collection of signatures before the authorization procedures. This solution is definitely more common than reviewing both the formal and substantive admissibility before the signature collection takes place. Hungary, Liechtenstein, North Macedonia, Russia, San Marino, and Slovenia are the only six states where the substantive admissibility of the question is decided before the initiators can start collecting signatures, while in all other states the substantive review of the question takes place after the referendum request has already gathered public support.

3.4   Institutional Choices and Referendum Practice

There seems to be no clear correlation between the institutional choice for referendum authorization and the actual use of the direct-democratic instrument. If we apply the institutional settings to Figure 2.8 about the number of limits and the number of citizen-initiated referendums, then the frontrunners in referendum practice generally have few limits and no authorization procedure or parliamentary authorization. In states with the least referendum practice, the number of limits is generally higher, but parliamentary authorization procedures are also prevalent. Similarly, constitutional courts and election

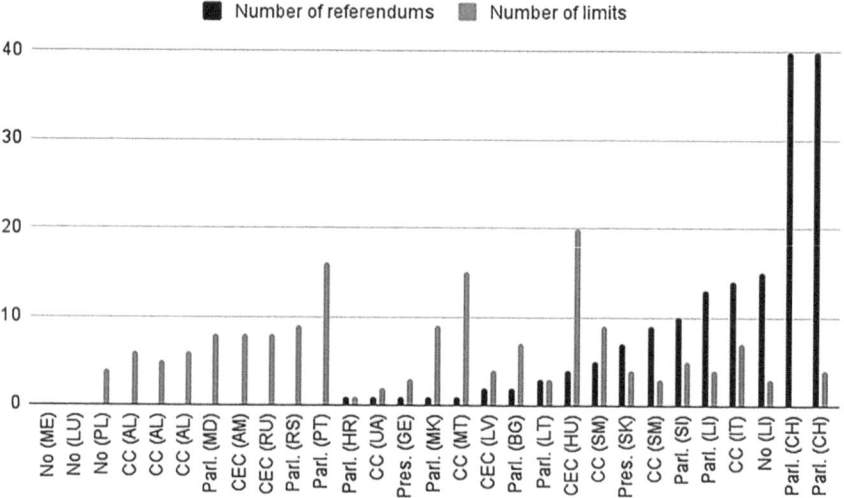

Note: 'No' refers to no authorization procedure, 'Parl.' refers to parliament, 'CEC' to central election commission, 'CC' to constitutional court, and 'Pres.' to president.

Figure 2.22   *Correlation between institutional choice, number of legal limits, and use of citizen-initiated referendums*

commissions can be found among both frequent and infrequent users of citizen-initiated referendums.

Consequently, the determining factor for the (non-)use of citizen-initiated referendums does not seem to be the institutional choice, but rather the number of limits or other factors not visualized here (e.g. the number of required signatures or other technical hurdles). This also suggests that the institutional choice alone does not determine the referendum practice, so theoretically any of these institutions can be an appropriate choice for authorization.

3. The legal rules on referendums in the selected states

Before going into the referendum authorization practice of the selected states, this chapter provides a general overview of the legal rules on citizen-initiated and institution-initiated referendums to help with navigating the rest of the book. The legal rules on popular votes initiated by citizens are described here in greater detail, since these are the focus of the book. The present overview covers the following questions:

(a) the subject of the referendum (whether it is proactive or rejective and the type of legal acts it may affect);
(b) the number of citizens needed to initiate a popular vote;
(c) the time-limit for the collection of signatures;
(d) the formal and substantive limits imposed on the referendum;
(e) the state institutions involved in the authorization procedures;
(f) the timing of the procedures;
(g) the procedural rules of the authorization procedure;
(h) the legal obligation to call the referendum (mandatory or facultative calling of the vote);
(i) the legal effect of the vote (binding or consultative);
(j) the quorum requirements; and
(k) the most important cases of referendums held after 1989/1990.

Following the overview of the selected states, the second part of the chapter highlights some commonalities in the regulation of referendums, and particularly of referendum authorization procedures.

1. OVERVIEW OF THE SELECTED STATES

1.1   Croatia

Croatia introduced the legal rules for citizen-initiated referendums in 2000:[1] 10 per cent of the citizens (approximately 430,000 voters[2]) can initiate a referendum on a proposal for the amendment of the Constitution; on a bill; or on any other issue within the competence of the Parliament.[3] Thus the people can use the instrument for both initiating change and abrogating existing rules. For the collection of this relatively high number of signatures, the citizens have only 15 days.[4] The Croatian Parliament and the President of the Republic may also call a referendum on important issues.[5]

The Referendum Act lays down one formal limit: the request must contain a clearly worded question, so only a clarity requirement is prescribed for the referendum question.[6] Although no explicit substantive limits are prescribed, the Constitutional Court can review the constitutionality of citizen-initiated referendum proposals.[7] This way the competence of the Constitutional Court has created an implicit substantive limit for citizen-initiated referendums. The same limitation does not apply to state institution-initiated referendums. After the signatures have been collected, the initiative has to be submitted to the Parliament, which decides about the authorization of the referendum. The Parliament can choose to refer the initiative to the Constitutional Court to establish its constitutionality.[8] Thus the involvement of the Constitutional Court depends on the Parliament. Nevertheless, in the recent defense of marriage referendum case, the Constitutional Court has issued opinions even without referral, *ex officio*.[9] The parliamentary rules and the Constitutional

---

[1]   Čepo, Čakar (Ch 1, n 90) 31.

[2]   Hrvoje Butković, 'The Rise of Direct Democracy in Croatia: Balancing or Challenging Parliamentary Representation?' (2017) 23(77) *Croatian International Relations Review* 39, 58.

[3]   Art. 87(3) Constitution.

[4]   Art. 8b(2) Law on Referendum and Other Forms of Personal Participation in the Exercise of State Power and Local and Regional Self-Government.

[5]   Art. 87(1)–(2) Constitution.

[6]   Art. 8b Law on Referendum and Other Forms of Personal Participation in the Exercise of State Power and Local and Regional Self-Government.

[7]   Art. 95 Constitutional Law on the Constitutional Court of the Republic of Croatia.

[8]   Art. 95 Constitutional Law on the Constitutional Court of the Republic of Croatia.

[9]   Warning of the Constitutional Court of the Republic of Croatia No. U-VIIR-5292/2013 of 28 October 2013, Official Gazette 131/2013, 2869.

Act on the Constitutional Court do not specify that participation rights shall be allowed in the authorization procedure.

Prior to Croatia's accession to the European Union, the quorum rules for referendums were changed and the turnout quorum was abolished.[10] According to the current regulation, the referendum is adopted if it is supported by the majority of voters taking part in the vote.[11] The decision made at the referendum is binding.[12]

To date, only one citizen-initiated referendum has been held in Croatia and a number of initiatives have failed to reach a vote. In some cases, the failed initiative lacked the necessary number of signatures. In other cases, the Parliament adopted the proposed change and preempted the referendum. Lastly, in some instances, the Constitutional Court found the initiative unconstitutional.[13] The only successful citizen-initiated referendum was the initiative of the 'In the Name of the Family' association in 2013. This initiative aimed to add a constitutional provision stating that marriage is the union of a man and a woman.[14] The defense of marriage initiative not only reached the polls by collecting over 600,000 signatures but also was supported by 65.8 per cent of the votes with a turnout of 37.8 per cent.[15]

The Constitutional Court has so far refused the authorization of three citizen-initiated referendums based on their unconstitutionality. In 2014, the Constitutional Court held that the initiative of the 'Committee for defense of Croatian Vukovar' to increase the threshold for the official use of minority languages was inadmissible.[16] Then in the following year, the Court rejected two initiatives that aimed to prevent the outsourcing of non-core services in the public sector and the monetization of motorways.[17] To this date, two referendums have been triggered by the President: on the independence of the country

---

[10]   Butković (n 2) 55; Čepo, Čakar (Ch 1, n 90) 32; Robert Podolnjak, 'Croatia' in Daniel Moeckli, Anna Forgács, Henri Ibi (eds), *The Legal Limits of Direct Democracy* (Edward Elgar Publishing 2021) 175.

[11]   Art. 87(4) Constitution.

[12]   Art. 87(5) Constitution.

[13]   Butković (n 2) 62–63; Podolnjak, 'Croatia' (n 10) 161–162.

[14]   Đorđe Gardašević, 'Constitutional Interpretations of Direct Democracy in Croatia' (2015) 12 *Iustinianus Primus Law Review* 1–50, 7.

[15]   Ibid.

[16]   Decision of the Constitutional Court of the Republic of Croatia No. U-VIIR-4640/2014 of 12 August 2014, Official Gazette 104/14. See also Endre Dudás, 'Croatian Constitutional Court: The Referendum on the Cyrillic Script' (2015) 9(1) *Vienna Journal on International Constitutional Law* 126, 126–133.

[17]   Decision No. U-VIIR-1159/2015 of 8 April 2015 of the Constitutional Court and Decision of the Constitutional Court of the Republic of Croatia No. U-VIIR-1158/2015 of 21 April 2015, Official Gazette 46/2015, 919. See also Podolnjak, 'Croatia' (n 10) 161–162.

and on remaining part of Yugoslavia, while the referendum on the accession to the European Union was mandatory.[18]

1.2　Hungary

Similar to Croatia, one set of legal rules apply to citizen-initiated referendums in Hungary, which can be used both in a proactive and in a rejective way.[19] Constitutional amendments are excluded from the scope of referendums, so only legislative changes can be initiated. Citizens have to collect 200,000 signatures (2.41 % of the electorate) for the referendum to be mandatory. In cases where only 100,000 signatures are collected, the parliament (National Assembly) is not obliged to call the referendum (facultative referendum).[20] The initiators have 120 days to collect the necessary number of signatures following the authorization of the initiative by the National Election Commission.[21]

Article 8(2)–(3) of the constitution (Fundamental Law) contains the substantive limits of referendums, which consist of the positive scope of referendums and the prohibited subjects. These limits apply to both citizen-initiated and institution-initiated referendums. National referendums may be held about any matter falling within the functions and powers of the National Assembly, while no national referendum may be held on:

(a)　any matter aimed at the amendment of the Fundamental Law;
(b)　the content of the Acts on the central budget, the implementation of the central budget, central taxes, duties, contributions, customs duties, or the central conditions for local taxes;
(c)　the content of the Acts on the elections of Members of the National Assembly, local government representatives and mayors, or Members of the European Parliament;
(d)　any obligation arising from international treaties;
(e)　person- and organization-related matters falling within the competence of the National Assembly;
(f)　the dissolution of the National Assembly;

---

[18]　See <http://lidd-project.org/data2/> Select country > Croatia.

[19]　Most recently Decision 15/2017 (VI. 30.) of the Constitutional Court clarified that the Fundamental Law does not limit the aim or form of the referendum initiative. It can be aimed to amend, abrogate or create a legislative act or other legislative decision; the question can be the summary of its content, an actual legislative provision or a reference to a legal act or proposed legal act: Decision 15/2017. (VI. 30.) of the Constitutional Court, Official Gazette of the Constitutional Court 19/2017, 966.

[20]　Art. 8(1) Fundamental Law.

[21]　Art. 19 Act CCXXXVIII of 2013 on Initiating Referendums, the European Citizens' Initiative and Referendum Procedure.

(g)   the dissolution of a representative body;
(h)   the declaration of a state of war, state of national crisis, and state of emergency; furthermore, on the declaration and extension of a state of preventive defense;
(i)   any matter related to participation in military operations;
(j)   the granting of amnesty.

The Referendum Act contains the relevant provisions on formal limits. The question proposed for referendum shall be worded in such manner that it allows a straightforward response and permits the National Assembly to decide – based on the outcome of the referendum – whether it has an obligation to make a law, and if so, what kind of law.[22]

The referendum question must be formulated by the initiators and submitted to the National Election Commission, which reviews its compliance with the formal and substantive limits. The National Election Commission decides about the authorization of the question within 30 days of its submission, preliminary to signature collection.[23] The Commission meetings are open to the public, so the initiators can participate in the meeting. However, the Commission is free to decide what kind of evidence it uses to support its decision. The Commission may – on request – allow the applicant to present an oral statement.[24] Anyone affected by the decision can apply for a remedy at the supreme court (Curia) within 15 days of the publication of the resolution.[25] The Curia decides without holding a trial, based on written submissions. Interestingly, the same referendum authorization procedure applies for citizen-initiated and referendums initiated by the government or the President.

The decision made in a referendum is always binding.[26] The majority of people with voting rights must participate in the referendum, and the majority of participants have to approve the referendum question in order for it to be valid and have binding legal effects.[27]

Since 1989, Hungary has held four votes on citizen-initiated referendums with ten referendum questions in total, meanwhile the government has initiated

---

[22]   Art. 9 Act CCXXXVIII of 2013 on Initiating Referendums, the European Citizens' Initiative and Referendum Procedure.
[23]   Art. 11 Act CCXXXVIII of 2013 on Initiating Referendums, the European Citizens' Initiative and Referendum Procedure.
[24]   Art. 43 Act XXXVI of 2013 on Electoral Procedure.
[25]   Based on Art. 1 and Art. 29 Act CCXXXVIII of 2013 on Initiating Referendums, the European Citizens' Initiative and Referendum Procedure, and Art. 222 Act XXXVI of 2013 on Electoral Procedure.
[26]   Art. 8(1) Fundamental Law.
[27]   Art. 8(4) Fundamental Law.

two referendums on five questions in the recent years.[28] Two citizen-initiated referendums were held about the different aspects of the democratic transition in 1989/90, then two further referendums in the 2000s.[29] Government-initiated referendums have been held on migration in 2016 and on questions affecting the LGBTQ community in 2022, all of which show the marks of populist referendums. Hungary is also a very interesting case for failed citizen-initiated referendums. Since 2006 the number of initiatives submitted by citizens has risen rapidly and has remained at a high level ever since.[30] In the last 30 years, Hungarian citizens have initiated over 2,000 referendums, but the election commissions and courts have rejected over 90 per cent of the initiatives.[31] Some recent examples of rejected citizen-initiated referendums include the initiatives on abolishing the legal provisions on higher education that have led to the move of the Central European University from Hungary, initiatives on imposing a term limit on the re-election of the prime minister, and initiatives about joining the European Prosecutor's Office.[32]

1.3   Italy

Citizens in Italy can only initiate referendums for the rejection of laws and constitutional amendments.[33] Referendums on constitutional reforms can also be initiated by the parliamentary minority. A legislative referendum may be held to repeal, in whole or in part, a law or a measure having the force of law, when so requested by 500,000 voters (1.07 % of the electorate).[34] The electorate are able to initiate a referendum on whole legal acts in force, on specific articles of the legal acts, or on even just words of the regulation. By allowing the abrogation of one or more articles or words, the legislative referendum is

---

[28]   László Komáromi, 'Milestones in the History of Direct Democracy in Hungary' (2013) 9(4) *Iustum Aequum Salutare* 49–56.

[29]   László Komáromi, 'Popular Rights in Hungary: A Brief Overview of Ideas, Institutions and Practice from the Late 18th Century until Our Days' (C2D Working Paper Series. 35/2010) 16–17; Zoltán Tibor Pállinger, 'Potentials of Direct Democracy in an Extremely Majoritarian System: The Case of Hungary' (2016) *Andrássy Working Papers zur Demokratieforschung* 1/2016, 1–20.

[30]   On the political background, see Pállinger (n 29) 17.

[31]   For the statistical overview see: <https://www.valasztas.hu/documents/20182/305738/Statisztik%C3%A1k+az+elb%C3%ADr%C3%A1lt+n%C3%A9pszavaz%C3%A1si+kezdem%C3%A9nyez%C3%A9sekr%C5%91l.pdf/a0655454-ecd7-412f-ab08-8a23dc419f5e>, accessed 15 March 2022.

[32]   See the analysis of some of the recent cases in Anna Forgács, 'Hungary' in Daniel Moeckli, Anna Forgács, Henri Ibi (eds), *The Legal Limits of Direct Democracy* (Edward Elgar Publishing 2021) 201–206.

[33]   Art. 75 and Art. 138 Constitution.

[34]   Art. 75(1) Constitution.

also able to serve proactive purposes, because the referendum can change the meaning of the remaining provisions.[35] In contrast, constitutional referendums are confirmatory in their nature, as the amendment submitted to a referendum can only be promulgated if approved.[36] A constitutional amendment is submitted to a referendum when, within three months of its publication, such request is made by 500,000 voters.[37]

Both types of rejective referendums require the same number of signatures and the same three-month time-limit applies for the signature collection.[38] One difference between the two types is in the scope of substantive limits: the Constitution excludes laws regulating taxes, the budget, amnesty or pardon, or laws ratifying international treaties from being the subject of a legislative referendum.[39] However, such restrictions do not apply to constitutional referendums. The only limit for these referendums is that the republican form of government shall not be the subject of a constitutional amendment.[40] Formal limits are not present in the regulation. However, the Italian Constitutional Court has introduced some formal requirements: the question must be formulated in simple and clear terms and a plurality of issues must be avoided.[41]

The authorization procedures are left entirely to judicial organs. The technical admissibility is assessed by the Central Office established in the Court of Cassation (supreme court). The technical authorization procedure takes place after the signature collection, and the signatures are checked at the same time.[42] There is no legal remedy against the decision of the Central Office, but the initiators are given a chance to correct any irregularities of the referendum request.[43] In the case of legislative referendums, the Constitutional Court reviews whether the referendum request is in violation of the formal and substantive limits.[44] The procedure is automatic once the Central Office has

---

[35]   Pier Vincenzo Uleri, 'On Referendum Voting in Italy: YES, NO or Non-vote? How Italian Parties Learned to Control Referendums' (2002) 41 *European Journal of Political Research* 863–883, 869–870.

[36]   Art. 138(2) Constitution.

[37]   Ibid.

[38]   Art. 28 Law no. 352 of 25 May 1970 and Art. 138(2) Constitution.

[39]   Art. 75(2) Constitution.

[40]   Art. 139 Constitution.

[41]   Judgment no. 16 of 1978 of the Constitutional Court, Official Gazette, 1st Special Series no. 39 of 8 February 1978. See also Uleri, 'Institutions of Citizens' Political Participation in Italy: Crooked Forms, Hindered Institutionalization' (Ch 1, n 82) 76–77; Henri Ibi, 'Italy' in Daniel Moeckli, Anna Forgács, Henri Ibi (eds), *The Legal Limits of Direct Democracy* (Edward Elgar Publishing 2021) 78–79.

[42]   Art. 12 and Art. 32 Law no. 352 of 25 May 1970.

[43]   Ibid.

[44]   Art. 33 Law no. 352 of 25 May 1970.

accepted the request. Legal remedy is not provided against the judgment. The Constitutional Court can order a hearing of the parties.[45] There is no formal or substantive authorization procedure for constitutional referendums, including the referendums initiated by the parliamentary minority.

Once a referendum request has fulfilled all the legal requirements, it is mandatory to call the referendum, and the referendum results are binding. One exception exists for constitutional referendums: a referendum shall not be held if the constitutional law has been approved in the second voting by each House of Parliament by a majority of two-thirds of the members.[46] A legislative referendum is successful if the majority of voters participate in the vote and the majority of the valid votes are in favor of the referendum.[47] In contrast, there is no turnout quorum for the validity of a constitutional referendum: the amendment submitted to referendum shall not be promulgated if not approved by a majority of valid votes.[48]

Italy is a frequent user of referendums.[49] Fifty-five citizen-initiated referendums have been held since 1990.[50] Since the legislative referendum has a turnout quorum requirement, it is common to campaign for abstention instead of a 'no' vote, which leads to a high number of unsuccessful referendums.[51] Multiple referendums have aimed to introduce changes to the election laws, but questions of morals and ethics such as reproduction rights have also been the subject of referendums.[52] The Constitutional Court has been active in forming the practice: the Court has authorized 79 referendums and rejected 69 between 1970 and 2011, which shows a restrictive practice with almost every second referendum declared inadmissible.[53]

1.4   Latvia

Latvia has a proactive citizen-initiated referendum and a special shared initiative that is rejective. The parliamentary majority can also initiate a ref-

---

[45]   See in Judgment no. 16 of 2008 of the Constitutional Court, Official Gazette, 1st Special Series no. 6 of 2 May 2008.

[46]   Art. 138(3) Constitution.

[47]   Art. 75(4) Constitution.

[48]   Art. 138(2) Constitution.

[49]   Morel, 'Types of Referendums, Provisions and Practice at National Level Worldwide' (Ch 1, n 72) 52–53.

[50]   LIDD Referendum events dashboard > Select Country > Vote trigger > Citizens (included) on <http://lidd-project.org/data2/>, accessed 15 March 2022.

[51]   Uleri, 'Institutions of Citizens' Political Participation in Italy: Crooked Forms, Hindered Institutionalization' (Ch 1, n 82) 80–81.

[52]   Ibid 84–85.

[53]   Ibid 77.

erendum on the substantial changes regarding the membership of Latvia in the European Union.[54] Under Articles 65 and 78 of the Constitution, one-tenth of the electorate (approximately 150,000 voters) have the right to submit a fully elaborated draft constitutional amendment or a draft law to the President, who shall present it to the parliament (Saeima). If the Saeima does not adopt the draft without any changes, it shall then be submitted to national referendum. This instrument can be used in a proactive or a rejective manner, as the draft law can be formulated to abrogate legal provisions.[55]

There is also a genuine rejective direct-democratic instrument under Article 72 of the Constitution. This veto referendum is not triggered by citizens per se, it is a shared initiative between the President, the Saeima, and the citizens. The President has the right to suspend the proclamation of a law for a period of two months if so requested by not less than one-third of the members of the Saeima. Then, the suspended law shall be put to a national referendum if so requested by not less than one-tenth of the electorate. If no such request is received during the two-month period, the law shall be promulgated.[56] This reactive instrument is not a genuine citizen-initiated instrument, because it requires both the parliament and the President to create the conditions in which the popular vote can be initiated.[57]

The substantive limits on referendums are listed in the Constitution:

(a)   the budget and laws concerning loans, taxes, customs duties, railroad tariffs;
(b)   military conscription;
(c)   declaration and commencement of war and peace treaties;
(d)   declaration of a state of emergency and its termination;
(e)   mobilization and demobilization; as well as
(f)   agreements with other nations

may not be submitted to national referendum.[58]

When the Russian language referendum was initiated in 2012, the Constitutional Rights Commission of the President issued a non-binding opinion, suggesting the prohibition of referendums that would violate the *inviolable core of the Constitution*.[59] The Constitutional Court has started to

---

[54]   Art. 68 Constitution.
[55]   Martins Birgelis, 'Latvia' in Daniel Moeckli, Anna Forgács, Henri Ibi (eds), *The Legal Limits of Direct Democracy* (Edward Elgar Publishing 2021) 220.
[56]   Art. 72 Constitution.
[57]   It can also be classified as a semi-plebiscite, see Somer (Ch 1, n 87) 33.
[58]   Art. 73 Constitution.
[59]   Opinion of the Constitutional Rights Commission of 17 September 2012 <http://blogi.lu.lv/tzpi/files/2017/03/17092012_Viedoklis_2.pdf>, accessed 15 March 2021.

use this unwritten substantive limit and has also deduced additional formal and substantive limits from wording of the Constitution declaring that the initiators must submit a *fully elaborated* draft.[60] According to the Court, a draft is not fully elaborated if it violates the Constitution or the international commitments of Latvia.[61] In addition, a draft law can only be considered fully elaborated if it is clearly and precisely formulated and fits into the Latvian legal system.[62]

The technical, formal, and substantive limits are evaluated in one authorization procedure. The initiative group must register the popular initiative with the Central Election Commission. The Commission can return the initiative for the elimination of its flaws. The Commission rejects the initiative if the initiative group does not conform to the statutory requirements or if the draft law or constitutional amendment is not fully elaborated in its form or content.[63] The registration decision can be appealed by the initiators at the Department of Administrative Cases of the Senate of the Supreme Court.[64] Hearing rights are provided only in the judicial procedure.

If the popular initiative is registered, then the citizens have a year for the collection of signatures.[65] The initiative is then submitted to the Saeima, which has to decide the request. If the Saeima does not adopt the initiative without changes, it must be submitted to a popular vote.[66] The quorum requirements are different for constitutional amendments and draft laws: an amendment to the Constitution is adopted if at least half of the electorate votes in favor. For a successful vote on a draft law, it is necessary that at least half of the number of electors who participated in the previous Saeima election participate in the referendum and that the majority of votes are in favor of the draft law.[67] The results of the referendum are binding.

---

[60] Art. 78 Constitution.

[61] Judgment No. 2012-03-01 of 19 December 2012 of the Constitutional Court, Official publication No. 2012/200.22 and Judgment No. 2013-06-01 of 18 December 2013 of the Constitutional Court, Official publication No. 2013/250.67. See also Kristīne Jarinovska, 'Popular Initiatives as Means of Altering the Core of the Republic of Latvia' (2013) 20 *Juridica International* 152–159, 154; Birgelis (n 55) 227–228.

[62] Judgment No. 2013-06-01 of 18 December 2013 of the Constitutional Court, Official publication No. 2013/250.67, para 13.2. See also Birgelis (n 55) 226–227.

[63] Art. 23 Law On National Referendum, Legislative Initiative and European Citizens' Initiative.

[64] Art. 23 (1 prim) Law On National Referendum, Legislative Initiative and European Citizens' Initiative.

[65] Art. 22 Law On National Referendum, Legislative Initiative and European Citizens' Initiative.

[66] Art. 78 Constitution.

[67] Art. 79 Constitution.

Since 1989–90 only three citizen-initiated referendums have been held in Latvia, all unsuccessful.[68] In 2008 two popular votes were held: one on the dissolution of parliament and one on increasing public pensions. Then, the Russian minority promoted a citizen-initiated referendum in 2012 to introduce Russian as a second official language, which also failed at the ballots.[69] The rejective referendum has been triggered four times, while mandatory and institution-initiated referendums have also been held on the independence of the country, on accession to the European Union, and on the dissolution of parliament. Latvia also has some examples of rejected citizen-initiated referendums. After the failed language referendum, the Russian minority proposed a referendum to automatically naturalize all Latvian non-citizens.[70] The Central Election Commission refused to authorize the referendum pro-posal because it would violate the doctrine of state continuity and the invio-lable core of the Constitution.[71] The Supreme Court upheld the refusal.[72] The Commission and the Court also refused to authorize a popular initiative against the introduction of the euro because it would violate international agreements, as well as an initiative for an educational reform due to unclear formulation.[73]

1.5   Liechtenstein

Liechtenstein allows for both proactive and rejective referendums that can be initiated by citizens. A proactive initiative may seek the enactment or amend-ment of a law, the enactment of a constitutional amendment, or the enactment of a new constitution that abolishes the monarchy.[74] For legislative initiatives, 1,000 citizens (5.05% of the electorate) are enough to start the procedure, while constitutional initiatives require 1,500 citizens. The time-limit for the

---

[68]   LIDD Referendum events dashboard > Select Country > Vote trigger > Citizens (included) on <http://lidd-project.org/data2/>, accessed 15 March 2022. See also Birgelis (n 55) 221.

[69]   David Lublin, 'The 2012 Latvia Language Referendum' (2013) 32 *Electoral Studies* 385–387, 387; Ina Druviete and Uldis Ozolins, 'The Latvian Referendum on Russian as a Second State Language' (2016) 40(2) *Language Problems & Language Planning* 121–145, 121.

[70]   Ivars Ijabs, 'After the Referendum: Militant Democracy and Nation-Building in Latvia' (2016) 30(2) *East European Politics and Societies and Cultures* 288–314, 305.

[71]   Decision No. 6 of 1 November 2012 of the Central Election Commission, Official publication No. 2012/175.7.

[72]   Judgment No. SA-1/2014 of 12 February 2014 of the Supreme Court on the citi-zenship referendum.

[73]   Judgment No. SA-3/2014 of 28 March 2014 of the Supreme Court on the rejec-tion of the euro, and Judgment No. SA-1/2020 of 2 March 2020 of the Supreme Court on the education reform.

[74]   Art. 64(2), Art. 64(4), and Art. 113(1) Constitution.

collection of signatures is six weeks.[75] The majority of the Parliament can also initiate referendums on laws, financial resolutions, and international treaties. These types of institution-initiated referendums are not limited in any way, and referendum authorization procedures do not apply.

A citizens' initiative can either be a formulated request or an unformulated proposal: in the first case the initiators present a draft law, while in the second case a generally phrased question is submitted.[76] The formal limits imposed on initiatives include a unity of form and a unity of substance requirement.[77] The substantive limits are not extensive, but the initiative must comply with the Constitution and the existing international treaties.[78]

The initiative is first assessed by the government, which checks both the formal and substantive admissibility requirements and compiles a report which is forwarded to the Parliament.[79] The formal and substantive authorization is carried out by the Parliament. If the Parliament finds that the initiative request does not comply with the Constitution and the existing international treaties, it is declared null and void. The initiators can submit a complaint to the constitutional court (State Court) against the rejection decision.[80] The authorization procedure takes place before the signature collection.[81]

If an initiative fulfills all the legal requirements, then the Parliament must decide on it. Here, there are differences between a formulated initiative and an unformulated proposal. If the initiative is an unformulated proposal, then the Parliament may decide to adopt the necessary legal changes, or it may refuse it. In this case the initiative lapses, unless the Parliament decides to call a referendum.[82] Meanwhile, if the initiative is formulated, then the Parliament either adopts it or is obliged to order a referendum.[83]

For an initiative to be adopted in a referendum only a majority of valid votes is required, the legal acts do not prescribe any minimum participation.[84] The results of a referendum are binding on the Parliament, which has to adopt the relevant decision. However, the decision must be sanctioned by the Prince Regnant, thus the Prince can veto the referendum decision.[85]

---

[75]   Art. 70(1)(b) People's Rights Act.
[76]   Art. 80(2) People's Rights Act.
[77]   Art. 69(5) People's Rights Act.
[78]   Art. 70b(1) and Art. 85 People's Rights Act.
[79]   Art. 69, Art. 70, and Art. 71 People's Rights Act.
[80]   Art. 70 and Art. 70b People's Rights Act.
[81]   Art. 70, Art. 70b, and Art. 71 People's Rights Act.
[82]   Art. 81 People's Rights Act.
[83]   Art. 82 People's Rights Act.
[84]   Art. 78(1) and Art. 84 People's Rights Act.
[85]   Art. 66(6) Constitution; Art. 78(1) People's Rights Act.

The rejective citizen-initiated referendums have slightly different rules. The subject of a rejective referendum can be a law, a financial resolution, a constitutional amendment, or an international treaty.[86] A referendum on a law or on a financial resolution needs the support of 1,000 citizens, while 1,500 citizens are needed for a referendum on a constitutional amendment or on an international treaty. A rejective referendum can take place before the Act enters into force (i.e. before it is sanctioned by the Prince Regnant).[87]

The applicable limits are somewhat different from the proactive initiative. It must be clear against which parliamentary decision the referendum is aimed, and the same formal limits apply.[88] Meanwhile, the only substantive limit is that laws and financial resolutions that are declared urgent cannot be the subject of a referendum.[89]

The authorization procedure is also more lenient for the rejective referendum than for the proactive one. Once the Act has been published, the signature collection can begin, with a 30-day time-limit.[90] The government checks the signatures along with the legality of the submission.[91] Thus, the government checks the technical and formal admissibility requirements, and its decision can be appealed at a regular court. However, the Parliament does not carry out a substantive authorization procedure.

If a rejective referendum request fulfills all legislative requirements, then the government must order the referendum.[92] The same quorum provisions apply as to proactive referendums.[93] The binding effect of a referendum is different for international treaties and other acts: in the case of laws, financial resolutions, and constitutional amendments, the Prince Regnant must sanction the referendum decision.[94] Meanwhile, a referendum decision adopted on an international treaty is always binding.[95]

Liechtenstein is also a frequent user of direct-democratic instruments. Since 1989/90, Liechtenstein has held 30 citizen-initiated referendums: 14 of these

---

[86]   Art. 66 and Art. 66bis Constitution.
[87]   Art. 66(5) Constitution.
[88]   Art. 69(5) People's Rights Act. Even though the legal provisions mandate the application of formal limits, it is contested. See Marxer, 'Liechtenstein' (Ch 2, n 14) 55–57.
[89]   Art. 66(1) Constitution.
[90]   Art. 66 and Art. 66bis Constitution; Art. 70(1)(a), Art. 70a(1), and Art. 75(1)(b) People's Rights Act.
[91]   Art. 71 People's Rights Act.
[92]   Art. 66 and Art. 66bis Constitution; Art. 72 and Art. 77(1) People's Rights Act.
[93]   Art. 78(1) People's Rights Act.
[94]   Ibid.
[95]   Art. 78a People's Rights Act.

were proactive, while 16 were rejective.[96] The citizen-initiated referendums included a proactive initiative on the rules governing termination of pregnancy, a rejective referendum on the act on partnership of same-sex couples, as well as a number of referendums on pension and health insurance.[97] Despite the large number of referendums held, the State Court has only been petitioned in a handful of cases to reach a final decision on the referendum authorization.[98]

1.6   Slovakia

Citizens or the parliament (the National Council) may initiate a referendum in Slovakia on important issues of public interest.[99] The legal rules do not differentiate between proactive and rejective referendums, and no separate rules apply for referendums initiated by the parliament. A petition requesting a referendum must be signed by at least 350,000 people (7.89% of the electorate).[100] There is no time-limit for the collection of signatures.

The Constitution of Slovakia excludes basic rights and freedoms, taxes, levies, and the state budget from being the subject of a referendum.[101] The Constitutional Court has interpreted the limits in such a way that basic rights and freedoms may be the subject of a referendum, but only in order to extend the rights and without diminishing other rights and freedoms.[102] In a recent decision, the Court has also introduced an implicit substantive limit for referendums: they cannot violate the *material core of the Constitution*, including the principles of rule of law, democracy, and separation of powers.[103] The proposal has to be formulated in such a way that it can be unambiguously answered by 'yes' or 'no', and multiple proposals cannot be conditional on each other.[104]

---

[96]   LIDD Referendum events dashboard > Select Country > Vote trigger > Citizens (included) on <http://lidd-project.org/data2/>, accessed 15 March 2022.

[97]   Wilfried Marxer, 'Minorities and Direct Democracy in Liechtenstein' in Wilfried Marxer (ed), *Direct Democracy and Minorities* (Springer 2012) 156–180, 176.

[98]   Marxer, 'Liechtenstein' (Ch 2, n 14) 54–55.

[99]   Art. 93(2) Constitution.

[100]   Art. 95(1) Constitution.

[101]   Art. 93(3) Constitution.

[102]   Decision PL. ÚS 24/2014 of 28 October 2014 of the Constitutional Court. See also Marián Sekerák, 'Same-Sex Marriages (or Civil Unions/Registered Partnerships) in Slovak Constitutional Law: Challenges and Possibilities' (2017) 13(1) *Utrecht Law Review* 34–59, 49.

[103]   Judgment PL. ÚS 7/2021 of 7 July 2021 of the Constitutional Court, Collection of Laws 280/2021, paras 111–112.

[104]   Art. 202(3) Act no. 280/2014 Coll. on the exercise of election rights.

The President decides about the formal and substantive authorization of an initiative.[105] However, the President may decide to file a petition about the constitutionality of the initiative to the Constitutional Court.[106] The procedure of the President does not offer participation rights, but the Constitutional Court is obliged to hold a hearing in its procedure.[107]

If the legal requirements are met, then the President must call the referendum within 30 days.[108] The results of the referendum are binding; the proposals adopted in the referendum will be promulgated by the parliament in the same way as it promulgates laws.[109] The results of the referendum are valid if more than half of eligible voters participate in the vote and if the decision is endorsed by more than half of the participants.[110]

Slovakia has held seven referendum events initiated by citizens since 1989/90, but the last two voting events contained multiple questions.[111] Two of the seven referendums have been on calling early elections, which should be classified as recalls based on their content. In 2014, the 'Alliance for the Family' civil organization initiated a vote on defining marriage as a union of a man and a woman, on prohibiting the adoption for same-sex couples, on opting out of sexual education in schools, and on providing legal protection to the institution of marriage.[112] The referendum was authorized on the first three questions in 2015, but it was invalid due to the low turnout: only 21 per cent of the voters participated in the vote.[113] The parliament has initiated referendums on three issues: the deployment of nuclear weapons; the creation of military bases; and the accession to the European Union. The President has so far utilized its prerogative to ask the Constitutional Court for its opinion only twice: first in the case of the defense of marriage referendum[114] and then, more recently, in relation to an initiative about early elections.[115] While in the

---

[105] Art. 95(1) Constitution; Art. 203 Act no.180/2014 Coll. on the conditions of exercise of the election rights.

[106] Art. 95(2) and Art. 125b Constitution.

[107] Art. 58 (1)(c) Act no. 314/2018 on the Constitutional Court of Slovak Republic.

[108] Art. 95(1) Constitution.

[109] Art. 98(2) Constitution.

[110] Art. 98(1) Constitution.

[111] LIDD Referendum events dashboard > Select Country > Vote trigger > Citizens (included) on <http://lidd-project.org/data2/>, accessed 15 March 2022.

[112] Daniel Krošlák, 'The Referendum on the So-called Traditional Family in the Slovak Republic' [2015] 1 *Central and Eastern European Legal Studies* 149–167, 150; Marek Rybar, Anna Sovcikova, 'The 2015 Referendum in Slovakia' (2016) 44(1–2) *East European Quarterly* 79–88, 80; Sekerák (n 102) 34–59.

[113] Krošlák (n 112) 163.

[114] Sekerák (n 102) 36.

[115] Šimon Drugda, 'The People v Their Representatives: The Slovak Constitutional Court Blocks Referendum on Early Election' (Verfassungsblog 14 September 2021)

defense of marriage referendum case the Court only declared the question on the legal protection of marriage unconstitutional,[116] the more recent decision blocked the early election referendum from going forward.[117]

1.7   Slovenia

Similarly to Italy, Slovenia has only rejective citizen-initiated referendums: the parliament (the National Assembly) shall call a referendum on the entry into force of a law if so required by at least 40,000 voters (2.34% of the electorate).[118] Prior to 2013, the parliamentary minorities also had the right to initiate referendums, which was frequently used by the opposition.[119] However, under the current regulation, the parliament is only allowed to initiate referendums on ratifying international treaties.[120] The citizens decide on the legislative act before it is promulgated, thus the referendum is confirmatory.[121] The request for the referendum must be submitted within seven days of the adoption of the law, while 35 days are provided for the collection of signatures.[122]

Before 2013 the Constitution did not contain any substantive limits on referendums, but the Constitutional Court assessed the possible *unconstitutional consequences* of the referendum.[123] Since a 2013 constitutional amendment, the Constitution excludes certain legal acts from being the subject of a referendum. A referendum may not be called:

(a)   on laws on urgent measures to ensure the defense of the state, security, or the elimination of the consequences of natural disasters;

(b)   on laws on taxes, customs duties, and other compulsory charges, and on the law adopted for the implementation of the state budget;

<https://verfassungsblog.de/the-people-v-their-representatives/>, accessed 15 March 2022.

[116]   Decision PL. ÚS 24/14 of the Constitutional Court.

[117]   Judgment PL. ÚS 7/2021 of 7 July 2021 of the Constitutional Court, Collection of Laws 280/2021.

[118]   Art. 90 Constitution.

[119]   Podolnjak, 'Constitutional Reforms of Citizen-Initiated Referendum. Causes of Different Outcomes in Slovenia and Croatia' (Ch 1, n 89) 129–149.

[120]   Art. 3a Constitution.

[121]   Art. 90(1) Constitution; Art. 9 Referendum and Popular Initiative Act.

[122]   Art. 12a Referendum and Popular Initiative Act.

[123]   Podolnjak, 'Constitutional Reforms of Citizen-Initiated Referendum. Causes of Different Outcomes in Slovenia and Croatia' (Ch 1, n 89) 129–149; Ciril Ribičič, Igor Kaučič, *Referendum and the Constitutional Court of Slovenia* (Entwicklung im Europäischen Recht Vol. 11. Universitätsverlag Regensburg 2016) 68; Bruna Žuber, Igor Kaučič, 'Slovenia' in Daniel Moeckli, Anna Forgács, Henri Ibi (eds), *The Legal Limits of Direct Democracy* (Edward Elgar Publishing 2021) 142.

(c)   on laws on the ratification of treaties;
(d)   on laws eliminating an unconstitutionality in the field of human rights and fundamental freedoms, or any other unconstitutionality.[124]

Formal limits are not imposed on the initiative, but the wording of the question is prescribed by law.[125]

The correctness of the wording and the substantive limits are checked by the National Assembly.[126] If the parliament finds that the wording of the referendum question does not follow the legal requirements, then the initiators are given an opportunity to correct the request within three days. If the parliament rejects the initiative, the initiators can appeal to the Constitutional Court.[127] Participation rights are not provided either in the parliamentary procedure or in the judicial procedure, but the President of the Court can call a public hearing.[128]

If the initiative does not violate any legislative requirement, it is mandatory for the National Assembly to call the referendum.[129] The results of the vote are binding.[130] The referendum is valid and the law is rejected, if the majority of the participating voters vote against the law, provided that at least one-fifth of all qualified voters vote against the law.[131]

Since 1990 Slovenia has held 11 referendums initiated by citizens, most recently in 2021 on water laws.[132] The Constitutional Court has also been active in forming the referendum practice,[133] although since the constitutional amendment in 2013 only two cases have reached the Court.[134] Regarding a referendum request on the Defense Act, the Court upheld the parliamentary rejection of the referendum due to the violation of the limit on urgent meas-

---

[124]   Art. 90 (2) Constitution.
[125]   Art. 16c Referendum and Popular Initiative Act.
[126]   Art. 20 and Art. 21 Referendum and Popular Initiative Act. See also Igor Luksic, Andrej Kurnik, 'Slovenia' in Andreas Auer and Micheal Bützer (eds), *Direct Democracy: The Eastern and Central European Experience* (Ashgate 2001) 198.
[127]   Art. 5 Referendum and Popular Initiative Act.
[128]   Art. 35 Constitutional Court Act; Art. 47(3) and Art. 51 Rules of Procedure of the Constitutional Court.
[129]   Art. 90(1) Constitution.
[130]   Ibid.
[131]   Art. 90(4) Constitution.
[132]   LIDD Referendum events dashboard > Select Country > Vote trigger > Citizens (included) on <http://lidd-project.org/data2/> accessed 15 March 2022.
[133]   Ciril Ribičič, Igor Kaučič, 'Constitutional Limits of Legislative Referendum: The Case of Slovenia' (Ch 1, n 90) 902; Ribičič, Kaučič, *Referendum and the Constitutional Court of Slovenia* (n 123) 66–67.
[134]   Bruna Žuber, Igor Kaučič, 'Referendum Challenges in the Republic of Slovenia' (2018) 24 *Białostockie Studia Prawnicze* 137–150, 144.

ures.[135] In the same year, the Court reversed the parliamentary rejection of the Slovene defense of marriage referendum.[136] The referendum on the legislative act regulating the rights of same-sex couples took place in 2015, with 36 per cent of registered voters participating and 63 per cent of the voters rejecting the legal act.[137]

1.8   Switzerland

Switzerland is such an active user of direct democracy that it is sometimes described as a 'half-direct democracy'.[138] Not surprisingly, Switzerland has both proactive and rejective citizen-initiated referendums. A proactive referendum may be requested with the support of 100,000 citizens (1.83% of the electorate). Its subject can only be a complete constitutional revision or a constitutional amendment.[139] The initiative can take the form of a draft law or a general proposal.[140] In contrast, state institutions cannot initiate optional referendums.

The limits imposed on popular initiatives are even narrower than in Liechtenstein. The Constitution declares that the initiative has to comply with the requirements of consistency of form and subject-matter and that it may not infringe the mandatory provisions of international law.[141] The Federal Act on Political Rights offers some explanation for the formal limits. There is consistency of subject-matter in a popular initiative when there is an intrinsic connection between the individual parts of the initiative. Meanwhile, there is consistency of form in a popular initiative when the initiative is worded exclusively in the form of a general proposal or of a specific draft provision.[142] The

---

[135]   Decision No. U-II-2/15 of 3 December 2015 of the Constitutional Court, Official Gazette of the Republic of Slovenia No. 98/2015. See also Žuber, Kaučič, 'Slovenia' (n 123) 145.

[136]   Decision No. U-II-1/15 of 28 September 2015 of the Constitutional Court, Official Gazette Republic of Slovenia No. 80/15. See also Žuber, Kaučič, 'Referendum Challenges in the Republic of Slovenia' (n 134) 146.

[137]   Małgorzata Podolak, 'Rights of Sexual Minorities as the Subject of Referenda in the Republic of Slovenia' (2018) 24 *Białostockie Studia Prawnicze* 45–56, 53.

[138]   Walter Haller, 'Das schweizerische System der halbdirekten Demokratie' [1994] *Zeitschrift für Verwaltung* 613; Wolf Linder, *Schweizerische Demokratie: Institutionen, Prozesse, Perspektiven* (Bern: Verlag Paul Haupt 2012) 236.

[139]   Art. 138–139 Constitution.

[140]   Art. 139(2) Constitution.

[141]   Art. 139(3) Constitution.

[142]   Art. 75 Federal Act on Political Rights.

practice has developed a fourth limit: the initiative must not be impossible to implement.[143]

The technical registration of the initiative is carried out by a governmental body (Federal Chancellery), which ensures that the signature list corresponds to the form prescribed by law, that the translations into the official languages correspond to each other, and that the title is not misleading and does not contain commercial advertising or personal publicity, or give rise to confusion.[144] The initiators can appeal the decision of technical authorization at the Federal Supreme Court.[145] After the registration process, the citizens have 18 months to collect the necessary number of signatures.[146]

The formal and substantive authorization takes place after the signature collection and is entrusted to the parliament (Federal Assembly).[147] Similarly to Liechtenstein, the government (Federal Council) prepares a report for the parliamentary decision that contains a detailed socio-economic and legal analysis of the initiative. Participation or remedy rights are not provided in the authorization procedure.

A proactive proposal is accepted in the popular vote if the majority of the participants approve it. However, the legal provisions also foresee a territorial approval quorum: the majority of the cantons must support the referendum proposal.[148] The decisions approved in the referendum are binding.

A rejective referendum can be initiated by 50,000 citizens. Its subject can be a federal Act; an emergency federal Act whose term of validity exceeds one year; or a federal decree, if so required by the Constitution or an Act. An international treaty can also be the subject of a rejective referendum if the treaty is for unlimited duration, or for accession to an international organization, or if it contains important legislative provisions or its implementation requires the enactment of federal legislation.[149] Thus, constitutional amendments are excluded from this list, but they are subject to law-initiated referendums.[150]

The citizens have 100 days from the official publication of the enactment to collect the signatures. The referendum takes place before the legal Act enters into force, except in case of emergency federal Acts.[151]

---

[143]   Keller, Lanter, Fischer (Ch 1, n 12) 137; Biaggini (Ch 1, n 12) 329–330; Moeckli, 'Switzerland' (Ch 2, n 14) 32.
[144]   Art. 69 Federal Act on Political Rights.
[145]   Art. 80(3) Federal Act on Political Rights.
[146]   Art. 138(1) and Art. 139(1) Constitution.
[147]   Art. 139(3) Constitution; Art. 75 Federal Act on Political Rights.
[148]   Art. 139(5) and Art. 142(2) Constitution.
[149]   Art. 141 Constitution.
[150]   Art. 140 Constitution.
[151]   Art. 141 Constitution; Art. 59a Federal Act on Political Rights.

No explicit substantive or formal limits are imposed on rejective referendums, and no authorization procedure is prescribed for this instrument. If the signatures are collected, the Federal Council shall order the popular vote.[152] The vote is successful if the majority of participants support it.[153] For this type of vote neither a turnout quorum nor a territorial approval quorum applies. The decisions approved in the referendum are binding.

Switzerland organizes citizen-initiated referendums multiple times a year. Between 1990 and 2021 there were 231 federal referendums held at the initiation of citizens.[154] Some of the more controversial citizen-initiated referendums have included initiatives banning the building of minarets,[155] or mandating the automatic expulsion of convicted foreign criminals or the lifelong custody of non-treatable, extremely dangerous sexual and violent offenders.[156] The Swiss parliamentary practice is very lenient towards proactive citizen-initiated referendums. So far it has declared only four popular initiatives partially or fully invalid.[157] Nevertheless, this does not mean that popular initiatives are particularly successful. Due to the double majority requirement of voters and cantons, only 14 proactive citizen-initiated referendums have been adopted at the polls since 1991.[158] In contrast, rejective citizen-initiated referendums are much more successful: 71 optional referendums have been successful since 1991.[159]

2. COMMONALITIES IN REGULATING REFERENDUMS

The right to initiate a referendum and to participate in a popular vote represents the direct exercise of popular sovereignty. Therefore, it is important how these rights are regulated. In the Revised Code, the Venice Commission highlights that the rules of referendums should not be ad hoc for a specific referendum

---

[152] Art. 59c of the Federal Act on Political Rights.

[153] Art. 141(1) and Art. 142(1) Constitution.

[154] For the complete list, see: LIDD Referendum events dashboard > Select country > Vote trigger > Citizens (included) on <http://lidd-project.org/data2/> (up to 2020), and <https://www.bfs.admin.ch/bfs/de/home/statistiken/politik/abstimmungen.html>, accessed 15 March 2022.

[155] Biaggini (Ch 1, n 12) 325–343.

[156] For an overview of some of the controversial cases, see Keller, Lanter, Fischer (Ch 1, n 12) 121–154; Moeckli, 'Of Minarets and Foreign Criminals: Swiss Direct Democracy and Human Rights' (Ch 1, n 12) 774.

[157] Keller, Lanter, Fischer (Ch 1, n 12) 126; Biaggini (Ch 1, n 12) 329–330; Moeckli, 'Switzerland' (Ch 2, n 14) 29–35.

[158] See https://www.bfs.admin.ch/bfs/de/home/statistiken/politik/abstimmungen .html, accessed 15 March 2022.

[159] Ibid.

and should be regulated at the rank of a statute.[160] The stability, clarity, and pre-dictability of the referendum rules are also important features of legal certainty and the rule of law.[161]

All selected states lay down the basic rules of referendums at constitutional level, while the details of the referendum process are usually left to statutes. A common feature is that the authorization procedures are not regulated extensively, and the rights of the initiators and voters are usually limited.

2.1   Legal Rules on the Basic Conditions and Limits of Referendums

Most states regulate the conditions for initiating a popular vote and the substantive legal limits imposed on referendums in constitutions. All eight selected states lay down the right to initiate a referendum and its basic conditions at constitutional level. This solution is common overall in Europe, although in some states the legal basis of referendums is contained 'only' in statutes.[162]

The constitution usually determines the available types of referendums and other direct-democratic instruments, the conditions of the initiation, and the subject of the referendum (the type of issues or legal sources). Most states regulate the substantive legal limits also in their constitutions. Lastly, the turnout and approval quorums for adopting a referendum decision are also mostly contained in the constitutions. The provisions on referendums either prescribe the same rules for all direct-democratic instruments or differentiate between referendums initiated by citizens and by state institutions. As the examples of the selected states show, only Hungary and Slovakia prescribe the same limits and authorization procedures for all direct-democratic instruments. Meanwhile, in other states where both types of referendums are available, the requirements for initiating referendums by citizens are usually more stringent. In Croatia, Italy, Latvia, Liechtenstein, and Slovenia (at least some of) the legal limits and the corresponding authorization procedures apply only for citizen-initiated referendums.

The Italian Constitution serves as an example for laying down the basic rules. It first states that the referendum is rejective and then determines the potential initiators: 'a general referendum may be held to repeal, in whole or in part, a law or a measure having the force of law, when so requested by

---

[160]   Revised Code II. 3.

[161]   Lon L. Fuller, *The Morality of Law* (Yale University Press 1964) 162.

[162]   Bulgaria: Art. 10(1)(5) and Art. 10(2) Law on the Direct Participation of Citizens in the Public Power and Local Self-Governance; Macedonia: Art. 154, Art. 155, and Art. 163 Election Code; San Marino: Art.2 (2) Qualified Law on referendum and citizens' popular initiative.

five hundred thousand voters or five Regional Councils'.[163] Then it restricts the scope of the referendum by listing the substantive limits: 'no referendum may be held on a law regulating taxes, the budget, amnesty or pardon, or a law ratifying an international treaty'.[164] Lastly, it determines the quorum requirements: 'the referendum shall be considered to have been carried if the majority of those eligible has voted and a majority of valid votes has been achieved'.[165]

Regulating the basic conditions of initiating a referendum at constitutional level has a further implication. All selected states and most of the European states acknowledge that not only the right to vote in a referendum but also the initiation of the referendum is a constitutional right of voters. This is an important point for the referendum authorization procedures because it elevates the position of the initiators by specifically mentioning the constitutional right to initiate referendums. It follows that if either of these constitutional rights are restricted, then (procedural) safeguards should be available.

The formal limits on the wording of the referendum proposal are mostly regulated in statutes. These provisions are more technical than substantive prohibitions on the subject of the referendum. Some states do not just impose the requirements of clarity, unity of form, and unity of substance but also regulate the content and form of the ballot paper,[166] or prescribe the exact wording of the referendum question.[167] The only state from the selected eight that prescribes the formal limits at constitutional level is Switzerland.[168] Out of all the member states of the Council of Europe, Switzerland and Portugal[169] are the only ones regulating formal limits in constitutions.

In some states, the legal practice of referendum authorization has led to the introduction of implicit legal limits that have no, or at least no explicit, foundation in written law. One example is Italy, where the Constitutional Court has declared that the referendum request must be formulated in simple and clear terms and the plurality of issues must be avoided.[170] Neither the Constitution nor the referendum law contains any formal limits. Instead, the Court has deduced these limits from the purpose of the abrogative referendum as an instrument of genuine manifestation of popular sovereignty.[171] In Latvia,

---

[163] Art. 75(1) Constitution (Official translation).

[164] Art. 75(2) Constitution (Official translation).

[165] Art. 75(4) Constitution (Official translation).

[166] Slovakia: Art. 204 Act no. 180/2014 Coll. on the exercise of election rights; Slovenia: Art. 16c Referendum and Popular Initiative Act.

[167] Slovenia: Art. 16c Referendum and Popular Initiative Act.

[168] Art. 34(2) and Art. 139(3) Constitution.

[169] Article 115(6) Constitution.

[170] Judgment no. 16 of 1978 of the Constitutional Court, Official Gazette, 1st Special Series no. 39 of 8 February 1978, Legal considerations, para 3.

[171] Ibid, Legal considerations, paras 2–3.

the legal rules for referendums already contain some substantive legal limits, but the Constitutional Court has added implicit limits based on the requirement that the initiators must submit a *fully elaborated* draft. The Court interpreted this term not only to contain formal limits on the wording of the draft, but that the draft law must comply with the Constitution and with Latvia's international commitments.[172] In Slovakia, the Constitutional Court pronounced a limit on referendums violating the *material core of the Constitution*.[173] The use of implicit legal limits to reject citizen-initiated referendums raises concerns about legal certainty. Even though these implicit limits can protect important constitutional values that may not be explicitly covered by the legal limits, they introduce uncertainty to the procedure and can lead to the arbitrary restriction of the exercise of popular sovereignty. All the examined constitutions – including the constitutional monarchy of Liechtenstein – derive the powers of the state from the people and recognize the people as the ultimate source of power, thus it seems vital that all limits on the exercise of popular sovereignty are laid down in the constitutions or at least in statutes.

2.2   Legal Rules on Referendum Authorization Procedures

The institutional and procedural configurations of referendum authorization are mostly left to statutes. The institutional competence for authorizing referendums appears explicitly only in the Swiss Constitution.[174] In Liechtenstein and Slovenia, it is clear that the referendum request must be submitted to the parliaments, although the constitutions do not explicitly state that the limits imposed on referendums are evaluated by the legislatures.[175] In Croatia and Slovakia, the constitutions establish only the parliamentary and presidential rights to request the opinion of the constitutional courts.[176] Meanwhile, in Italy, Latvia, and Hungary, the competences of the courts and election commissions are laid down in the referendum acts along with the procedural rules.[177]

The procedural rules of referendum authorization are the most sporadically regulated parts of the referendum process. The referendum authorization is

---

[172]   Judgment No. 2012-03-01 of 19 December 2012 of the Constitutional Court, Official publication No. 2012/200.22, para 18.3.

[173]   Judgment PL. ÚS 7/2021 of 7 July 2021 of the Constitutional Court, Collection of Laws 280/2021.

[174]   Art. 139(3) Constitution.

[175]   Slovenia: Art. 90(2) Constitution; Liechtenstein: Art. 64 Constitution.

[176]   Croatia: Art. 125 Constitution; Slovakia: Art. 95(2) and Art. 125b Constitution.

[177]   Italy: Art. 33 Law no. 352 of 25 May 1970; Hungary: Art. 11 Act CCXXXVIII of 2013 on Initiating Referendums, the European Citizens' Initiative and Referendum Procedure; Latvia: Art. 23 Law on National Referendum, Legislative Initiative and European Citizens' Initiative.

never the core constitutional function of the state institution entrusted with the decision. It is always an ancillary function, which may be one reason for the lack of extensive regulation. The constitutions do not contain any procedural provisions for referendum authorization, while the statutes regulating referendums often only state the competence of the first instance decision-maker, the possibility of a remedy, and the time-limits for rendering a decision.[178] Some procedural rules are contained in the organizational statutes of state institution,[179] or can be derived from references to other procedural regimes.[180]

The most unregulated procedure is presidential decision-making, which is rarely regulated in general. It is mostly discretionary both in its outcome and in its procedure.[181] Thus, for instance, no procedural rules exist for the referendum authorization of the President of Slovakia.

In case of parliamentary decision-making, referendum authorization procedures are integrated into the ordinary decision-making procedures of these organs. However, the parliamentary acts mostly regulate the debate, the voting process, and the rights of the members of parliament but not the individual procedural rights of voters. For instance, the Swiss Federal Act on the Federal Assembly contains a whole chapter on popular initiatives, but it predominantly regulates how the two houses have to conduct the debate of the draft, and what deadlines apply for the procedure.[182] The only reference to individual procedural rights is that the parliamentary Drafting Committee shall give the initiative group the opportunity to express its opinion when it corrects obvious translation errors or makes formal adjustments to the proposed constitutional amendment.[183]

The procedures of constitutional courts are also not extensively regulated; the procedural rules are largely contained in statutes on the organization of the court. These legislative acts only regulate few procedural aspects of the referendum authorization procedure. For instance, hearing rights are provided

---

[178] Croatia: Art. 49 Law on Referendum and Other Forms of Personal Participation in the Exercise of State Power and Local and Regional Self-Government; Liechtenstein: Art. 70b (1), Art. 71 People's Rights Act.

[179] Slovakia: Art. 58 Act no. 314/2018 Coll. on the Constitutional Court of the Slovak Republic; Croatia: Art. 95 Constitutional Law on the Constitutional Court of the Republic of Croatia.

[180] Hungary: Art. 1 and Art. 29 Act CCXXXVIII of 2013 on Initiating Referendums, the European Citizens' Initiative and Referendum Procedure, and Art. 222 Act XXXVI of 2013 on Electoral Procedure.

[181] Héctor Fix-Fierro, Pedro Salazar-Ugarte, 'Presidentialism' in Michel Rosenfeld and András Sajó (eds), *Oxford Handbook of Comparative Constitutional Law* (Oxford University Press, 2012) 628.

[182] Title 5 Chapter 3 Federal Act on the Federal Assembly.

[183] Art. 99(2) Federal Act on the Federal Assembly.

for the initiators in Slovakia, but the statute of the Constitutional Court does not contain any other procedural rules or guarantees.[184]

The procedural rules are more detailed for the procedures of election commissions and governmental bodies. Interestingly, only Switzerland has integrated its technical authorization procedure into administrative procedures.[185] Latvia and Hungary have not chosen this path for the procedures of the election commissions, thus emphasizing the special nature of referendum authorization. Hungary has even explicitly exempted referendum authorization from administrative procedures.[186] In Hungary, the procedural rules for referendum authorization refer back to the rules of electoral complaint procedures.[187] In Latvia, the rules on institutional competence and procedure have been incorporated in the referendum act, after the competence of the Central Election Commission was challenged at the Constitutional Court.[188] In both states, the remedy against the first instance decision is entrusted to administrative law judges[189] operating under extensive procedural provisions.[190]

Consequently, the procedural rules of referendum authorization are rather ad hoc and rarely extensive. Referendum authorization procedures are in most states regulated as *sui generis* procedures in the referendum acts or in the statutes of the decision-making body, which results in fragmented procedural rules. In comparison to administrative procedures – as a prototype of extensively regulated public law procedures – referendum authorization procedures are underregulated and offer only few clear procedural guarantees for the participants. With the scarce procedural regulation, it is mostly up to the practice to determine the actual extent of procedural rights.

---

[184] Art. 58 Act no. 314/2018 Coll. on the Constitutional Court of the Slovak Republic.

[185] Art. 69(1) Federal Act on Political Rights; Art. 1–5 Federal Act on Administrative Procedure.

[186] Art. 8.(1)(b) Act CL of 2016 on the Code of General Administrative Procedure.

[187] Art. 1 and Art. 29 Act CCXXXVIII of 2013 on Initiating Referendums, the European Citizens' Initiative and Referendum Procedure, and Art. 222 Act XXXVI of 2013 on Electoral Procedure.

[188] Judgment No. 2012-03-01 of 19 December 2012 of the Constitutional Court, Official publication No. 2012/200.22.

[189] Latvia: Art. 23 (1 prim) Law On National Referendum, Legislative Initiative and European Citizens' Initiative; Hungary: Art. 1 and Art. 29 Act CCXXXVIII of 2013 on Initiating Referendums, the European Citizens' Initiative and Referendum Procedure, and Art. 222 Act XXXVI of 2013 on Electoral Procedure.

[190] Latvia: Part C Law on Administrative Procedure; Hungary: Chapter XXI Act I of 2017 on the Code of Administrative Court Procedure.

4.   The nature of the referendum authorization procedure

In order to assess the institutional and procedural configurations for authoriz-ing referendums, it is necessary to analyze the nature of referendum disputes. I define referendum authorization procedures as procedures for reviewing the technical, formal, and substantive legal limits imposed on referendums. According to the type of legal limit that the referendum has to comply with, the authorization procedure can be categorized into three types. In the *tech-nical authorization procedure*, the competent state institutions ascertain that the necessary number of signatures have been gathered and other technical requirements (e.g. formation of an initiative group) are fulfilled. In the *formal authorization procedure*, the state institutions review the formulation of the referendum proposal. Meanwhile in the *substantive authorization procedure*, the decision-makers review whether the referendum proposal falls into one of the prohibited subjects.[1] I focus on the formal and substantive authorization procedures.

The first part of the chapter explores the legal nature of the authorization procedures despite the presence of political elements. Then the next part investigates whether the authorization procedure necessitates an abstract or a concrete review by the decision-maker. The last part of the chapter takes a closer look at the most common formal and substantive legal limits. Since the referendum authorization procedure centers around the legal limits, it is important to understand the functions of these restrictions. By identifying the public interests protected by the limits, their domain of interpretation can be determined. In turn, the domain of interpretation indicates the level of dis-cretion the decision-maker exercises, which is telling about the interpretative methods and the expertise necessary to review the limit.

The expectation is that a better understanding of the nature of referendum authorization procedures, as well as a closer look at the legal limits, can help with identifying some minimum requirements for the institutional and proce-dural settings of referendum authorizations.

---

[1]   See Chapter 1, section 3 on the topical scope of the book.

1.   THE LEGAL NATURE OF THE REFERENDUM AUTHORIZATION PROCEDURE

Referendums offer a channel for voters to take some power back from the elected representatives and directly decide about the important questions of the country.[2] Referendums limit the decisional competences of parliaments and governments by allowing citizens to decide policy ideas or legislative solutions that would otherwise be decided by these state institutions. The aim of a referendum proposal is to facilitate political events and the direct participation of citizens in politics. Thus, a claim can be made that the whole referendum process is political in nature.

However, if legal limits are imposed on referendums, then the review of these limits cannot be deemed political. The existence of legal limits – that is also a defining element of authorization procedures – turns the referendum authorization procedure into a legal procedure. The legal limits represent the legal standards that guide the decision-maker.[3] Even though the initiators of the referendum submit a legislative or general proposal, the competent state institution does not decide about the general desirability or feasibility of the proposal but about its legality. This applies for citizen-initiated referendums as well as referendums initiated by state actors. If no legal limits are imposed on referendums, which is more often the case for state institution-initiated referendums, then the whole referendum process is political and at the discretion of the state institution initiating the referendum. However, once legal limits are imposed, then the authorization procedure is a legal procedure. Using the analogy of the *political question doctrine*, it can be seen that the referendum authorization actually involves legally resolvable issues. The political question doctrine bars the justiciability of certain discretionary and political decisions. It is present in several administrative law systems.[4] The theoretical ground for exempting political decisions from judicial review is that they represent

---

[2]   Alber (Ch 1, n 30) 76; Matsusaka, *Let the People Rule: How Direct Democracy Can Meet the Populist Challenge* (Ch 1, n 27) 155.

[3]   Anna Christmann, *Die Grenzen direkter Demokratie: Volkentscheide im Spannungsverhältnis von Demokratie und Rechtsstaat* (Nomos Verlag 2012) 155.

[4]   See also 'prerogative power', 'actes de gouvernement', 'justizfreie Hoheitsakte': Günter Sczostak, 'Zur Problematik der gerichtsfreien Hoheitsakte' [1958] 12 *Juristische Rundschau* 445; Margit Cohn, 'Form, Formula and Constitutional Ethos: The Political Question/Justiciability Doctrine in Three Common Law Systems' (2011) 59(3) *The American Journal of Comparative Law* 675–713; János Fazekas, 'Local Governments and Political Question Doctrine in Hungary' (2019) 17(3) *Lex Localis: Journal of Local Self-Government* 809–819; Jackson A. Myers, 'Comment: Transatlantic Perspectives on the Political Question Doctrine' (2020) 106 *Virginia Law Review* 1007.

the exercise of sovereignty,[5] while the practical reason is that there are no legal standards to evaluate such decisions.[6] The popular vote itself indeed represents the exercise of sovereignty and the referendum proposal might be a clear political question. However, the existence of legal limits ensures that the decision-maker has manageable legal standards for resolving the case. The assessment of whether the referendum proposal violates the formal or substantive limits requires the *legal* interpretation of the limits and an assessment of whether the proposal falls within the scope of them.

In theory, the legal limits also curb the discretion of the decision-maker by determining the only conditions for rejecting a referendum. Ideally, the decision-maker should not consider any other aspect of the referendum proposal beyond its compliance with the legal limits. So, for instance the political impacts or economic feasibility of the proposal should not come into question in the authorization procedure. This requirement of legal assessment follows from the imperative wording of the legal limits imposed on referendums: the constitutions or statutes list the cases when the referendum cannot be authorized, meaning also that additional − non-legal − reasons should not warrant the rejection of the referendum. If the competent state institution considers other, non-legal reasons in deciding about the legal limits, then it should be considered a malfunction.

This does not mean that the consideration of non-legal (political, economic, moral, etc.) questions cannot play a role in the referendum process as a whole. These considerations, however, do not belong in the review of legal limits, so ideally the authorization procedure should be isolated from non-legal questions and another procedure should be provided for the non-legal considerations. The Revised Code of the Venice Commission mentions that the parliament should be able to provide a non-binding opinion or a counterproposal in the citizen-initiated referendum process,[7] which can be one way to evaluate the non-legal implications of the referendum before the vote. The Code regulates the parliamentary opinion separately from the assessment of the *validity* of the referendum proposal. There are examples from state practice of when parliaments can submit counterproposals or debate the referendum proposal before calling a vote. For instance, in Switzerland, the Federal Assembly can submit a counterproposal to the vote along with the referendum proposal.[8] In Latvia and Liechtenstein, the authorized referendum proposals are submitted to the

---

[5]   Jesse H. Choper, 'The Political Question Doctrine: Suggested Criteria' (2005) 54 *Duke Law Journal* 1457, 1513.

[6]   *Baker v. Carr* 369 U.S. 186, 217 (1962).

[7]   Revised Code III.6.

[8]   Art. 139(5) Sentence 3 Constitution.

parliaments, which either adopt the proposal or call the vote.[9] However, these procedures are not linked to the review of legal limits and are separate from referendum authorization procedures.

There are some legislative solutions that derogate the legal nature of referendum authorization procedures by conflating the review of legal limits and the discretionary powers of state institutions to call the referendum. In Serbia and Poland, the legal limits imposed on citizen-initiated referendums are reviewed by the parliaments. In addition, the final decision on calling the referendum is also left to the discretion of the parliaments and they are not obliged to call a referendum even if the statutory conditions are fulfilled.[10] The same applies for Georgia, with the difference that the President has to review the legal limits and decide on calling the referendum.[11] In these combined procedures, the ultimate decision on calling the referendum is not dependent on its adherence to legal limits. The legal standards are only advisory in the procedure, thus the decision can be deemed political in nature.[12]

Alternatively, in other states, the referendum authorization procedure is carried out based on legal considerations, but another state institution can override the decision based on non-legal considerations. In Hungary, if the election commission authorizes the referendum proposal but the citizens collect only 100,000 signatures instead of 200,000, then the National Assembly is not obliged to call the referendum.[13] This solution does not derogate the legal nature of the referendum authorization itself because the procedures are not combined. However, it derogates the power of the citizens to take competences back from the elected government. Nonetheless, in most European states the authorization procedure is ultimately decisive for the fate of the referendum, thus the adherence to the legal limits is decisive for the permissibility of the referendum.

The fact that the competent state institution must interpret the legal limits in the referendum authorization procedure already implies that state institutions with the core function of deciding legal disputes are better suited to decide about referendum authorization than state institutions normally fulfilling other constitutional functions. Courts or administrative authorities that routinely decide legal disputes and interpret and apply legal provisions are considerably

---

[9]   Latvia: Art. 78 Constitution; Liechtenstein: Art. 82 People's Rights Act.

[10]   Poland: Art. 63(1) Act of 14 March 2003 on the nationwide referendum; Serbia: Art. 40 Law on Referendum and People's Initiative. See also LIDD data dashboard > Explore data > By Instrument/Item > Theme: Referendum related on <http://lidd -project.org/data/>, accessed 15 March 2022.

[11]   Art. 178(1) Organic Law of the Election Code of Georgia.

[12]   Cohn (n 4) 686.

[13]   Art. 8(1) Fundamental Law.

better equipped to review referendum proposals than parliaments or governments that primarily decide policy and political questions.

2. THE DUALITY OF ABSTRACT AND CONCRETE REVIEW IN THE REFERENDUM AUTHORIZATION PROCEDURE

The referendum authorization procedure is atypical in several respects. It is decisive for the exercise of popular sovereignty, but it is also a future-oriented dispute about a legislative proposal or policy question. The state institution has to carry out both an abstract and a concrete review when deciding about the authorization. The review of the referendum proposal is abstract in the sense that it does not relate to a dispute about the implementation of the proposed legal change. The referendum proposal has not yet affected individual rights or caused individual injuries. It is reviewed in its totality without being attached to an individual dispute. At the same time, the state institution decides whether a popular vote can take place. In this sense, the decision-maker has to decide a concrete controversy. Referendum authorization procedures can be captured in this duality: the state institution must reach a decision on both the right to vote and the legality of the proposal, thus carrying out a concrete and an abstract review.

2.1 Abstract Review

The term *abstract review* is borrowed from constitutional adjudication.[14] Constitutional adjudication is used here as a reference to the jurisdiction to review legal acts and to invalidate or disregard them if the constitution or the hierarchy of norms is violated.[15] In constitutional adjudication, abstract review means that the court 'measures the text of a statute as *is* against the constitution, that is, without the need for and separate from any actual and individualized legal dispute'.[16] In contrast, a *concrete review* requires that there is an individual case in which the incompatibility of a legal provision with the constitution or other higher-ranking law is challenged.[17]

The initiators of the referendum – be it citizens or state institutions – propose a change in the legal system. This can be direct, in the case of a formulated proactive initiative or the request to abrogate a provision, or indirect, in the

---

[14] Comella (Ch 2, n 20) 7; de Visser (Ch 1, n 92) 2.
[15] Stone Sweet (Ch 2, n 20) 77; Comella (Ch 2, n 20) 6; Besselink (Ch 2, n 20) 20; Ginsburg, Versteeg (Ch 2, n 20) 587; de Visser (Ch 1, n 92) 54.
[16] de Visser (Ch 1, n 92) 97.
[17] Comella (Ch 2, n 20) 67.

form of a generally worded proposal. For citizen-initiated referendums, the citizens formulate the referendum proposal, which may involve the creation of a draft legal act (formulated proactive initiative) or the formulation of a question (rejective initiative or unformulated proactive initiative). State institutions initiating referendums can also either submit formulated legislative proposals or generally worded questions. The authorizing state institution evaluates this proposal before the referendum (and thus before it could become part of the legal system). Thus, it is an *a priori* review of a proposal not yet in force. In constitutional adjudication, the *a priori* review is 'of necessity abstract, as a law that has not yet entered into force cannot have triggered constitutional doubts in the context of an individual case'.[18]

In referendum authorization procedures, the abstract nature can be captured at the review of the substantive limits. The review of the substantive limits shows the most similarities to an *a priori* abstract constitutional review of legislation, when a judicial body determines the compatibility of a legal act or a legal norm with the constitution, with international law, or with other higher-ranking norms.[19] In a substantive referendum authorization procedure, the compatibility of the proposal is measured against the substantive limits. This can show similarities to constitutional adjudication, especially when states prohibit referendums that would violate the constitution or the international law commitments of the state. In these cases, the state institution carries out an *a priori* abstract constitutional review of the referendum proposal. Other substantive limits carve out certain issues from the direct exercise of popular sovereignty. Reviewing these limits requires the legal interpretation whether the issue falls within one of the topical restrictions. Thus, in the substantive authorization procedure, the state institution evaluates how the proposal fits into the legal system and whether it is in line with the topical restrictions imposed on popular votes. This analysis is detached from both the initiators' and voters' political rights: the analysis of the proposal does not require the legal interpretation of the right to initiate a referendum or the right to vote, but instead interprets the proposal vis-à-vis the substantive limits.

The abstract dimension of the referendum authorization procedure would suggest that – like the abstract review of legislation – the procedure is separate from any individualized legal dispute.[20] In cases about the abstract review of legislation, all citizens have a legal interest in preserving the constitutional order, but citizens rarely participate in the procedure. Some states allow

---

[18]   de Visser (Ch 1, n 92) 97.
[19]   Sadurski (Ch 1, n 104) 13; Comella (Ch 2, n 20) 6; Christmann, *Die Grenzen direkter Demokratie: Volkentscheide im Spannungsverhältnis von Demokratie und Rechtsstaat* (n 3) 180; de Visser (Ch 1, n 92) 97.
[20]   de Visser (Ch 1, n 92) 97.

citizens to initiate the review in the form of *actio popularis*,[21] but this is not common in Europe.[22] One possible stance about the referendum authorization procedure could be to emphasize that it is an abstract review and claim that the involvement of voters is redundant, because the dispute is about the legality of the proposal. However, this argument is not viable. Even if the subject of the procedure is the proposal, the aim of the procedure is to decide whether a popular vote can take place or not. Therefore, the referendum authorization is not completely removed from an individual legal dispute.

2.2   Concrete Review

In constitutional adjudication, concrete review means that the 'constitutional issue presents itself to the judge within the context of a specific controversy'.[23] The compatibility of the legal provision with the constitution or higher-ranking laws must be decided before the individual dispute can be resolved. In referendum authorization procedures, the underlying concrete question is whether the proposal can reach the ballots.

Ultimately, it is a decision on whether the right to vote can be exercised or not. This element gives the procedure its concreteness: it is not only about the review of the proposal, but also about the rights of the initiators and the voters. The authorization procedure is decisive for a submission of the initiators and determines whether voters can go to the ballots or not.

One difference in regard to concrete constitutional review is that the initiators formulate the proposal and promote it, thus their legal interests lie in the proposal not violating the legal limits. So, they bring an application to the state institution to validate the proposal, instead of challenging a legal act to have it declared invalid as is the case in concrete constitutional review. In this regard, the authorization procedure is more akin to administrative procedures.[24] The state institution authorizing a referendum provides a 'permit' for the initiators and the voters to continue the referendum process. The state institution is in a hierarchical relationship to the parties, and it reaches an authoritative and final decision on the legality of the proposal. In practice, the authorizing state institution is not necessarily an administrative authority, but the relationship

---

[21]   de Visser (Ch 1, n 92) 99.
[22]   Sadurski (Ch 1, n 104) 6; de Visser (Ch 1, n 92) 99.
[23]   de Visser (Ch 1, n 92) 97.
[24]   Peter L. Strauss (ed), *Gellhorn and Byse's Administrative Law: Cases and Comments* (New York: Foundation Press 2011) 51; Paul Craig, *Administrative Law* (8th edn., London: Sweet & Maxwell Thomson Reuters 2016) 335; Vincenzo De Falco, *Administrative Action and Procedures in Comparative Law* (Eleven International Publishing 2018) 8.

between the decision-maker and the applicants is similar to administrative procedures.

The other major difference in regard to concrete constitutional review is that in referendum authorization procedures the content of the referendum proposal and the concrete question about the exercise of the right to vote are not connected. In a concrete constitutional review case, the applicants have an individual legal dispute on a certain issue and challenge a legal act that guides decision-makers on that issue.[25] For instance in a dispute about the prohibition of a demonstration, the organizers challenge a legal act that regulates some aspect of the right to protest. In referendum authorization procedures, the proposal submitted by the initiators does not – in most cases – have any topical connection to the right to vote.

The authorization procedure itself creates the connection between the proposal and the right to vote when the state institution assesses the formal limits that ensure the free will-formation of the voters and protect the freedom of vote. In the formal authorization procedure, the state institution analyzes the right to vote by reviewing whether the proposal is sufficiently clear and formulated in a manner that allows for a free vote. Thus, the referendum proposal is assessed from the standpoint of the right to vote if formal limits exist in the state. Otherwise – as mentioned above – the substantive review of the referendum proposal is detached from the right to vote and is an abstract review by its nature.

The duality of the abstract and concrete review in referendum authorization procedures has implications for the procedural and institutional settings. The abstract dimension of the procedure suggests that state institutions with competences in constitutional adjudication have the most expertise to carry out the substantive referendum authorization procedures. Meanwhile, the concrete dimension of the procedure and its attachment to the right to vote is an indication that the rights and legal interests of the initiators and voters should be translated into procedural rights.

2.3   The Particularities of Institution-Initiated Referendums

When state institutions initiate referendums, then two alternative solutions exist for integrating this power in the constitutional order: either it is approached as a pure political action or the initiating institution is regarded similarly to any other initiator. Under the first option, no legal limits are imposed on the substance or the wording of the referendum initiated by state actors. The state institution is free to initiate a referendum on any question

---

[25]   Comella (Ch 2, n 20) 7.

that is deemed important. Other state institutions do not have the power to authorize or block the referendum. Deference is shown to the initiating state institution because there is a presumption that the state institution will not act against the rights and interests of its citizens and will not propose an unconstitutional or unlawful referendum. Meanwhile, under the second option, either some legal limits are imposed on referendums initiated by state actors, or the same legal limits apply as for citizens' initiatives. In this case a referendum authorization procedure must be devised to not let the legal limits become dead letters. If this is the case, then all the above-mentioned arguments about the legal nature of referendum authorization and the duality of abstract and concrete review apply for institution-initiated referendums. It is presumed that state institutions may also initiate unlawful referendums, thus the referendum authorization procedure is integrated into the system of checks and balances. Consequently, if legal limits are imposed on institution-initiated referendums, then the authorizing state institution should ideally have competence in constitutional adjudication, and the rights of the voters should be translated into procedural rights.

3. VARIATIONS AND FUNCTIONS OF LEGAL LIMITS

In establishing the requirements for an authorization procedure, a more nuanced approach is warranted which takes into consideration the types of legal limits the state institutions review. Understanding the variations and functions of the legal limits is crucial to evaluate the institutional and procedural configurations of referendum authorization. The functions of the legal limits, the constitutional values, and the public interests they protect show the domain of interpretation for the authorizing institution. The decision-making process may require different levels of discretion, special expertise, or particular modes of legal interpretation according to the different limits. Such variations have implications for the institutional and procedural settings. Only a few limits do not confer any discretion on the decision-maker and can be decided through a straightforward grammatical analysis of the proposal or question. In most cases, the legal limits are broadly worded prohibitions without detailed regulation. Consequently, the competent state institution has considerable leeway in drawing the margins of the limits. Parallel to the level of discretion, the required legal expertise can also change with each legal limit. The review of all legal limits requires a certain level of legal expertise, but the more broadly the limit is worded and the more discretion it confers, the more thoroughly the proposal has to be analyzed.

3.1   The Abstract Review of Substantive Limits

Substantive limits exclude issues from being the subject of the referendum. Multiple and varied objectives lie behind substantive restrictions on direct democracy.[26] Without analyzing the legitimacy of substantive restrictions, the following pages map the functions of the most common limits to an extent that is necessary to understand how they affect the nature of authorization procedures. The classification of substantive limits follows the categories used during the data collection for the LIDD database.[27]

On a general level, substantive limits either (1) exclude issues that are incompatible with the current constitutional order or even more generally with the rule of law[28] or (2) reserve issues for the representative government.[29] The first group contains limits that go to the core of the constitutional democracy. The underlying reason for the prohibition is that the referendum decision could violate higher-ranking norms (the constitution or international law) and/or the fundamental principles of the constitutional democracy (e.g. fundamental rights or democratic elections).[30] Depending on the rules of constitutional adjudication, these decisions may not only be off-limits for the people, but also for the representative government.[31] Within this first group of substantive limits, three types of limits are looked into that – to some extent – protect the constitutional order and the rule of law: limits on the constitutionality of the proposal; limits on fundamental rights and freedoms; and limits on international law obligations.

The second group of substantive limits bars the people from deciding about certain policies or laws, but not the representative organs. Examples of these limits are substantive restrictions on state finances, civil service rules, or elec-

---

[26]   John Gildersleeve, 'Editing Direct Democracy: Does Limiting the Subject Matter of Ballot Initiatives Offend the First Amendment?' (2007) 107(6) *Columbia Law Review* 1437–1481; Shaun Bowler, 'When is it OK to Limit Direct Democracy?' (2013) 97(5) *Minnesota Law Review* 1780–1803.

[27]   LIDD data dashboard > Explore data > By Instrument/Item > Theme: Substantive limit on <http://lidd-project.org/data/>, accessed 15 March 2022.

[28]   Moeckli, 'Referendums: Tyranny of the Majority?' (Ch 1, n 50) 340.

[29]   Louis J. Sirico Jr., 'Constitutionality of the Initiative and Referendum' (1980) 65 *Iowa Law Review* 637, 663.

[30]   Christmann, *Die Grenzen direkter Demokratie: Volkentscheide im Spannungsverhältnis von Demokratie und Rechtsstaat* (n 3) 23; Moeckli, 'Referendums: Tyranny of the Majority?' (Ch 1, n 50) 340; Žuber, Kaučič, 'Referendum Challenges in the Republic of Slovenia' (Ch 3, n 134) 144.

[31]   Andreas Auer, Nicolas von Arx, 'Direkte Demokratie ohne Grenzen? Ein Diskussionsbeitrag zur Frage der Verfassungsmässigkeit von Einbürgerungsbeschlüssen durch das Volk' [2000] *Aktuelle Juristische Praxis* 923, 925.

tion laws. Even though the elected bodies must also adhere to the constitutional order of the state, they have a great leeway in adopting different policies in these fields. The reasons for reserving these decisions to the representative organs can be various. In the following pages, these limits are grouped into two broad categories: substantive limits that protect the stability of the state organization (e.g. limits on the judiciary, election laws), and limits that ensure the adequate functioning of the state (e.g. emergency powers, budgetary and financial questions).

3.1.1 Limits on the constitutionality of the proposal
Several substantive limits aim to ensure that the proposal is not in violation of the constitution. The objective behind these types of limits is to avoid a situation where the popular vote would lead to a conflict with the constitution, and the will of the people would have to be declared invalid or could not be implemented.[32] In a way, these limits protect the voters from the frustration of a decision that is impossible to implement. At the same time, they confine the exercise of popular sovereignty within the current constitutional order and take the opportunity away from citizens to initiate – at least fundamental – changes in the constitutional system. The Venice Commission highlights that 'under the principle of rule of law, the people are not exempt from compliance with the law',[33] which is clearly reflected in these limits. These types of limits represent a substantive understanding of rule of law and take a stance in the rivalry between rule of law and popular sovereignty on the side of the former.[34] Some limits spell out general limits on the constitutionality of the proposal, while others exclude specific elements of the constitutional order.[35]

The broadest version of these limits is to exclude all proposals that would amend the constitution from being the subject of referendums. This solution confines referendums to legislative acts and reserves the initiation of constitutional change to the representative organs. It is still possible that the citizens are involved in the constitutional amendment process through mandatory or ad hoc referendums; however, the formulation of the constitutional amendment is taken out of their hands. For instance, the Hungarian Fundamental Law explicitly excludes 'any matter aimed at the amendment of the Fundamental Law' from being the subject of a referendum.[36]

---

[32]   Fatin-Rouge Stefanini (Ch 1, n 26) 380–381.
[33]   Original Code, Explanatory Memorandum, para 32.
[34]   Comella (Ch 2, n 20) 88; Žuber, Kaučič, 'Referendum Challenges in the Republic of Slovenia' (Ch 3, n 134) 144.
[35]   Fatin-Rouge Stefanini (Ch 1, n 26) 380–381.
[36]   Art. 8(3) Fundamental Law.

A less sweeping, but still broad restriction is to prohibit unconstitutional proposals. This is the case in Liechtenstein, where the initiative must comply with the constitution.[37] This option measures all proposals against the current constitutional provisions but does not close out the option to add to the constitution provisions that fit in the constitutional order.[38]

A third general option is to exclude only some parts of the constitution that are deemed essential, without specifically naming the provisions. For instance, in Latvia, the referendum shall not violate the *inviolable core of the Constitution*,[39] or in Slovakia the *unamendable material core of the Constitution*.[40] This solution confers wide discretionary powers to the state institutions to determine the essential parts of the constitution.

Lastly, it is possible that substantive limits do not pronounce a general constitutionality requirement but exclude specific elements of the constitution from referendums. This solution is similar to prohibiting referendums on the essential elements of the constitution, but instead of leaving the definition of the essential elements to legal interpretation, the legal provisions specify the essential parts. These substantive limits can include limits on proposals violating fundamental rights and freedoms or on amending state structure or form of government, the state symbols, or the official language. For instance in Slovenia 'laws eliminating an unconstitutionality in the field of human rights and fundamental freedoms or any other unconstitutionality' are excluded from being the subject of a rejective referendum.[41] In Azerbaijan and Armenia, the constitutions list the articles that cannot be amended by referendum.[42] It is certainly a solution that is more in line with the formal requirements of rule of law and confines the discretion of the decision-maker in interpreting the limits. Nevertheless, the legal interpretation of such specific substantive limits on constitutionality also allows for the exercise of discretion.

Reviewing limits on state symbols or on the official language is quite straightforward and does not require any special expertise. However, all other limits on the constitutionality of the proposal require expertise in constitutional

---

[37]   Art. 70b(1) and Art. 85 of the People's Rights Act.
[38]   Wilfried Marxer, *Direkte Demokratie in Liechtenstein: Entwicklung, Regelungen, Praxis* (Bendern: Verlag der Liechtensteinischen Akademischen Gesellschaft 2018) 143–144.
[39]   Opinion of the Constitutional Rights Commission of 17 September 2012 <http://blogi.lu.lv/tzpi/files/2017/03/17092012_Viedoklis_2.pdf>, accessed 15 March 2022. See also Jarinovska (Ch 3, n 61) 152–159.
[40]   Judgement PL. ÚS 7/2021 of 7 July 2021 of the Constitutional Court, Collection of Laws 280/2021, para 111. See also Drugda (Ch 3, n 115).
[41]   Art. 90(2) Constitution.
[42]   Azerbaijan: Article 155 Constitution, Armenia: Article 5(1), (2) Law on Referendum.

adjudication and confer wide discretion on the decision-maker.[43] It is impossible to determine their violation without dissecting the content of the proposal and the legal consequences arising from it. When such limits are imposed, then the referendum authorization procedures can be seen as *a priori* constitutional review in constitutional adjudication.[44] The similarities to constitutional adjudication are especially apparent with formulated proposals. But a generally worded referendum proposal also has to be integrated into the legal system in the case of a successful referendum, thus the decision-maker also has to evaluate how it fits into the constitutional order. It follows that constitutional courts (or general courts that regularly assess the constitutionality of the legal acts they apply) are best equipped to carry out such a review of referendums.

3.1.2   Limits on fundamental rights and freedoms

The prohibition of holding referendums on fundamental rights and freedoms is also mentioned as a limit on the constitutionality of the proposal, as it can contribute to shielding parts of the constitutional order from a popular vote. It is, however, important to mention that the exclusion of fundamental rights and freedoms, along with minority rights, serves the primary aim of protecting the rights of individuals or minorities from majoritarian decisions.[45] These limits are crucial in countering the threat of the 'tyranny of the majority' because they directly exclude issues that could harm vulnerable minorities. The importance of the protection of fundamental rights in referendums also appears in the Code of the Venice Commission.[46]

These limits prohibit either any questions that touch upon fundamental rights and freedoms or only proposals restricting them. For instance, the Slovak Constitution states that basic rights and freedoms cannot be the subject of a referendum,[47] while in Albania the Constitution only prohibits referendums on the 'limitations of fundamental rights and freedoms'.[48] The first option excludes any proposal on these issues, including those that try to expand the scope of these rights. Such an approach indirectly protects the constitutional status quo by reserving all decisions about fundamental rights to

---

[43]   Fatin-Rouge Stefanini (Ch 1, n 26) 380–381.

[44]   Comella (Ch 2, n 20) 47.

[45]   Christmann, *Die Grenzen direkter Demokratie: Volkentscheide im Spannungs-verhältnis von Demokratie und Rechtsstaat* (n 3) 99; Fatin-Rouge Stefanini (Ch 1, n 26) 380–381.

[46]   Revised Code II.2, III.1.

[47]   Art. 93(3) Constitution. It must be mentioned that the Constitutional Court interpreted this limit to prohibit only referendums restricting fundamental rights in the defense of marriage referendum case (Decision PL. ÚS 24/2014 of 28 October 2014 of the Constitutional Court).

[48]   Art. 151(2) Constitution.

the elected organs. In contrast, prohibiting referendums that negatively affect the already existing level of rights protection allows the expansion of rights.

Reviewing a proposal for its potential violation of fundamental rights and freedoms requires an in-depth analysis of the possible legal consequences of the decision. It is a constitutional review of the content of the proposal but with the specific aim of reviewing the proposal against the constitutionally guaranteed fundamental rights and freedoms, and not the constitution in general. Referendum proposals on minority rights also require an extensive legal analysis, especially if they are formulated in a seemingly neutral way, where the discrimination against the minority is not instantly apparent. The legal analysis can unveil that the proposal would affect the minority disproportionately more than the majority. Similar to other limits on the constitutionality of the proposal, these limits confer wide discretion on the decision-maker and require expertise in constitutional adjudication.[49]

3.1.3   Limits on international law

Similar to the previous limits, the substantive limit on the violation of international law also appears in the Code of the Venice Commission.[50] The Explanatory Memorandum emphasizes that the text put to a referendum must not be contrary to international law regardless of the relationship between international and domestic law.[51]

The substantive limits on international law can have multiple functions. They can overlap with the functions of the constitutionality limits. These limits prevent referendums that would violate the international commitments to protect human rights or the peremptory norms of international law. This aspect also shows a commitment to a substantive understanding of rule of law that cannot be overridden by popular will.[52] For instance the Swiss Constitution prohibits referendums on the 'mandatory provisions of international law', which is interpreted to include the core principles of international humanitarian law, the non-derogable guarantees of the European Convention on Human

---

[49]   de Visser (Ch 1, n 92) 143.
[50]   Revised Code III.1.
[51]   Original Code, Explanatory Memorandum para 33.
[52]   Robert Baumann, 'Völkerrechtliche Schranken der Verfassungsrevizion' (2007) 108 *Schweizerisches Zentralblatt für Staats- und Verwaltungsrecht* 181, 182; Christmann, *Die Grenzen direkter Demokratie: Volkentscheide im Spannungsverhältnis von Demokratie und Rechtsstaat* (n 3) 23; Tobias Naef, 'Popular Initiatives Contrary to International Law – A Swiss Dilemma' in Andreas Kellerhals, Tobias Baumgartner (eds), *Rule of Law in Europe – Current Challenges: 8th Network Europe Conference, Moscow, 10th–13th July 2016* (Zürich: Schulthess Verlag 2016) 241–242.

Rights (ECHR), the prohibition on torture and slavery, the prohibition of aggression, the prohibition of genocide, and the principle of non-refoulement.[53]

However, the limits on international law obligations also reserve the traditional royal or executive prerogatives of forming foreign policy to the representative organs. These limits can prevent the expression of popular will on a wide range of economic, trade, or environmental issues that are regulated by international agreements. For instance, Italy and Slovenia exclude laws ratifying international treaties from being the subject of a legislative referendum.[54] Similarly, the Latvian Constitution states that agreements with other nations may not be submitted to a national referendum.[55]

The limit on international law obligations can completely exclude citizens from foreign affairs if the limit includes both current and future international law commitments of the state. Alternatively, it can be limited to the already existing obligations and allow popular votes on any new accession to international treaties or organizations. This is the case in Hungary, where the Fundamental Law only prohibits referendums on obligations arising from international treaties but does not explicitly exclude referendums on new international commitments.[56] The limits on existing international law obligations prevent situations in which the outcome of the popular vote would oblige the state to withdraw from international agreements or organizations. Meanwhile, also precluding future international law commitments is more about reserving prerogatives in foreign affairs. A differentiation can also be made regarding traditional international law obligations and EU law where the sovereignty transfer to the EU institutions can warrant a different approach to the exercise of popular sovereignty.[57]

When looking at the necessary expertise to decide whether a referendum proposal violates international law, it is important to differentiate between limits on already existing international law obligations and limits on future ones. In the first case, the state institution authorizing referendums must assess the proposal for its compatibility with international treaties ratified by the state and other sources of international law. This requires a similar review process as the constitutional review of legislation, with a difference in the higher-ranking norms against which the proposal is measured. Similarly, the

---

[53] Keller, Lanter, Fischer (Ch 1, n 12) 124; Moeckli, 'Switzerland' (Ch 2, n 14) 30.

[54] Italy: Art. 75(2) Constitution; Slovenia: Art. 90(2) Constitution.

[55] Art. 73 Constitution.

[56] Art. 8 (3) Fundamental Law. See also László Komáromi, 'A népszavazásra vonatkozó szabályozás változásai az Alaptörvényben és az új népszavazási törvényben' (2014) 35 *MTA Law Working Papers* 6; Pállinger (Ch 3, n 29) 11.

[57] Tierney, *Constitutional Referendums: The Theory and Practice of Republican Deliberation* (Ch 1, n 6) 155.

assessment of a proposal against EU law already in force requires an in-depth legal interpretation of the proposal. In contrast, the assessment whether the proposal requests an accession to an international agreement or organization does not necessitate such a thorough analysis: a simple grammatical interpretation of wording should be enough to decide. While judicial bodies – constitutional and regular courts – are best equipped to conduct the review of already existing international law obligations, the review of accession requests does not necessitate judicial decision-making.

3.1.4   Limits on the stability of the state organization

There are various substantive limits that exclude questions about the current state organization from referendums. Such limits may prohibit initiating referendums on legislative or executive competencies, on issues surrounding the judiciary or local governments, and on election and referendum laws. For instance, Hungary and Portugal exclude issues on the content of the election laws,[58] while Moldova prohibits referendums on issues pertaining to the jurisdiction of the courts and the prosecutor's office.[59]

The functions of these limits show similarities to constitutionality limits. Most of the above-mentioned issues – for example, legislative competencies or the fundamental features of the judiciary – are regulated in constitutions. Consequently, the exclusion of these issues may also aim to protect the current constitutional order and the institutional balance enshrined in the constitutions. The limits on the judiciary can protect judicial independence that is central to the rule of law.[60] Limits on local governments protect the autonomy of these subnational entities and the rights of the local communities to self-govern. Limits on election laws aim to protect the stability of the government as well as the freedom of vote.[61] Meanwhile, the exclusion of referendum laws can prevent a situation where the voters would decide about the scope of their own rights.

Even though the objectives behind excluding these subjects seem similar to the imposition of constitutionality limits, the assessment of these limits does not require such extensive review. Proposals that violate these limits can mostly be identified by looking into what legal provisions the proposals aim

---

[58]   Hungary: Art. 8(3) Fundamental Law; Portugal: Art. 164 Constitution, Art. 3(d) Referendum Legal Framework.

[59]   Art. 158 Election Code.

[60]   Albert Venn Dicey, *Introduction to the Study of the Law of the Constitution* (originally published 8th edn., London: Macmillan 1915; Liberty Classics Reprint 1982) 110; Joseph Raz, *The Authority of Law: Essays on Law and Morality* (2nd edn, Oxford University Press 2009) 216.

[61]   Ibi (Ch 3, n 41) 77.

to amend. If the proposal aims to introduce or abrogate provisions of an Act on parliamentary elections and a substantive limit on election laws exists, it is a straightforward invalidation decision. Be that as it may, the margins of these limits may not be so clean cut in practice. The authorizing state institution has discretion in deciding whether all proposals touching on the legal framework of these issues are excluded from the referendum or only those that are actually connected to the functions of the limits. For instance, a law on creating more transparency in the public administration may change the rules on publishing official documents but does not necessarily amend executive competencies. In this case the decision-maker has some leeway in interpreting whether a substantive limit on executive competencies includes procedural and technical changes or only substantive changes. Consequently, the review of these limits does require interpretation and legal expertise, but it does not necessitate expertise in constitutional adjudication.

3.1.5   Limits on the functioning of the state
There are several substantive limits that can be loosely grouped together based on their broad objective to protect the functioning of the state.[62] Nonetheless, the more concrete reasons for excluding these topics are various. These limits include the substantive limits on emergency powers or on national security; limits on budget, taxes, and state finances; limits on civil service laws or individual appointments of state officials; and limits on pardon and amnesty. A common feature of these state powers is that the states do not only regulate them in statutes but also adopt individual acts and decisions using these powers (e.g. an emergency measure, an individual civil service appointment or a pardon granted to an individual). Thus, it is always a question when these issues are excluded from direct democracy whether referendums are prohibited only on the individual acts, or the regulatory framework is also beyond the reach of the voters.

Limits on emergency powers are one of the most common substantive limits. The limit may only exclude individual acts, as for instance in Latvia, which has placed a substantive limit on the 'declaration of a state of emergency and its termination'.[63] The individual acts of the exercise of emergency powers may be excluded to allow for an immediate response to crisis situations, which would be impossible through a lengthy referendum process.[64] An additional reason for prohibiting referendums on the individual measures can be that finding the adequate response may require special expertise or restrict the

---

[62]   Gildersleeve (n 26) 1452–1453.
[63]   Art. 73 Constitution.
[64]   Sirico Jr. (n 29) 663.

fundamental rights of citizens. It is, however, a separate question whether legislative provisions regulating emergency decision-making are also excluded from referendums. Slovenia, for instance, excludes all laws 'on urgent measures to ensure the defense of the state, security, or the elimination of the consequences of natural disasters'.[65] Legal provisions may be excluded from popular decision-making to ensure the adequate conditions for handling crisis situations,[66] although it is a question of interpretation whether all parts of such laws should be exempt to fulfill this objective.

Similarly, the aim of excluding issues on national security or policing is also to ensure the security of citizens and to respond swiftly to internal or external threats. These issues can also affect the fundamental rights of citizens. In addition, some information necessary for decision-making may be classified, which can hinder informed popular decision-making. Nevertheless, it requires a careful deliberation on the side of the authorizing body to decide which proposals would actually limit the responsiveness and proper functioning of the security bodies and which ones are not linked to the fulfillment of these functions.

Substantive limits on taxes, budgets, and other financial matters are also among the most common restrictions. Italy and Slovakia exclude laws regulating taxes and the budget from the referendum.[67] Latvia imposes a limit on the budget and laws concerning loans, taxes, customs duties, and railroad tariffs.[68] Slovenia has a limit on the laws on taxes, customs duties, and other compulsory charges, and on the law adopted for the implementation of the state budget.[69] In Hungary the content of the Acts on the central budget, the implementation of the central budget, central taxes, duties, contributions, customs duties, or the central conditions for local taxes are excluded.[70] Such restrictions

---

[65]   Art. 90(2) Constitution. See also Decision No. U-II-2/15 of 3 December 2015 of the Constitutional Court, Official Gazette of the Republic of Slovenia No. 98/2015.

[66]   This was the argument of the Constitutional Court of Slovenia for upholding a parliamentary decision rejecting a referendum. The Court stated that without the statutory basis, it would be impossible to carry out the urgent measures. Thus the statutory regulation which entails the basis for the implementation of urgent measures for ensuring security corresponds to the notion of a law on urgent measures referred to in the first indent of Art. 90(2) of the Constitution: Decision No. U-II-2/15 of 3 December 2015 of the Constitutional Court, Official Gazette of the Republic of Slovenia No. 98/2015, para 17–18.

[67]   Italy: Art. 75(2) Constitution; Slovakia: Art. 93(3) Constitution.

[68]   Art. 73 Constitution.

[69]   Art. 90(2) Constitution.

[70]   Art. 8(3) Fundamental Law.

aim to protect the financial stability of the state.[71] Similar to the restrictions on emergency matters, there is a paternalistic element in the exclusion of financial matters: the idea that citizens would not be able to decide in a responsible way about questions that affect their own financial situation.[72] Reviewing these limits also requires defining the outer margins of these limits, as almost all referendum proposals have implications on the state finances.[73]

The exclusion of pardon and amnesty decisions from popular vote is also a common restriction.[74] Granting amnesty or pardon is a traditional prerogative of the sovereign, mostly entrusted to the head of the state. It is a decision about the forgiveness of guilt for individuals or groups, thus it directly affects the rights of people. The exclusion of amnesty and pardon from popular vote ensures the exceptional use of these powers and the integrity of the criminal justice system. This way it also contributes to the functioning of the state.

A commonality of these limits is that reviewing proposals to hold referendums on individual acts (e.g. the termination of state emergency) is quite straightforward and does not require extensive legal or constitutional expertise. The authorizing state institution cannot exercise much discretion if the individual measures are targeted by the referendum. It is, however, a question of legal interpretation to what extent the regulatory framework is shielded from referendums. It involves the exercise of discretion to decide what parts of the regulatory framework are necessary to fulfill the functions of these limits. Similar to the substantive limits on the stability of the state organization, these decisions require legal interpretation, but they may not necessitate expertise in constitutional adjudication.

3.2   The Concrete Review of Formal Limits

The review of formal limits is concrete in the sense that it is connected to the voting event. The state institution must assess how the voters can perceive and understand the referendum proposal. The common aim of these limits is to

---

[71]   Slovakia: Decision PL. ÚS 24/2014 of 28 October 2014 of the Constitutional Court, para 105.

[72]   Sirico Jr. (n 29) 663.

[73]   Hungary: Decision 51/2001 (XI. 29.) of the Constitutional Court defined the fiscal limit to exclude referendums that would oblige the National Assembly to amend the current annual Acts on the central budget or the Acts on the implementation of the central budget, or that would aim to precisely determine single fiscal expenditures of future Acts on the central budget. see Decision 51/2001 (XI. 29.) of the Constitutional Court, Official Gazette of the Constitutional Court 134/2001, 9411.

[74]   See Hungary: Art. 8(3) Fundamental Law; Italy: Art. 75(2) Constitution.

avoid popular votes on unclear, confusing, or misleading proposals.[75] These limits generally ensure that the voters understand the referendum proposal as well as the legal consequences of the referendum. They can develop a position on the referendum issue and are able to express their position in the vote. Thus, the formal limits ensure that the referendum does not violate the right to vote, which is a fundamental political right in all selected states.[76]

3.2.1   Unity of form

The unity of form requirement is the most technical limit among the formal limits. It prohibits mixing generally worded proposals with formulated legislative proposals. The unity of form is not a common limit in Europe. In Switzerland proactive citizens' initiatives must comply with the consistency of form, meaning that the initiative must be drafted either exclusively in the form of a general proposal or that of a specific draft provision.[77] In Liechtenstein and Lithuania this limit also precludes mixing constitutional and legislative amendments (or, in the case of Liechtenstein, financial resolutions).[78]

This limit contributes to the clarity of the referendum proposal and aims to prevent confusion in the implementation stage of the referendum. While formulated proposals can enter into force automatically, a generally worded proposal has to be turned into legal provisions that require implementation measures. The Explanatory Memorandum of the Code highlights that when formulated and non-formulated proposals are combined, then the voters are not able to clearly foresee the actual legal consequences of the vote and the confusion distorts the right to a free vote.[79]

Reviewing the unity of form requirement mostly requires a textual-grammatical interpretation of the proposal. The review does not usually necessitate an in-depth legal interpretation of the text. Some referendum proposals

---

[75]   Tierney, *Constitutional Referendums: The Theory and Practice of Republican Deliberation* (Ch 1, n 6) 227–228; François Rocher, André Lecours, 'The Correct Expression of Popular Will. Does the Wording of a Referendum Question Matter?' in Laurence Morel and Matt Qvortrup (eds), *The Routledge Handbook to Referendums and Direct Democracy* (Routledge 2018) 227–228.

[76]   Croatia: Art. 45 Constitution; Hungary: Art. XXIII Fundamental Law; Italy: Art. 48 Constitution; Latvia: Art. 8 Constitution; Liechtenstein: Art 29 Constitution; Slovakia: Art 30 Constitution; Slovenia: Art 43 Constitution; Switzerland: Art 136 Federal Constitution.

[77]   Art. 139(3) Federal Constitution, Art. 75(3) Federal Act on Political Rights. See also Pierre Tschannen, 'Die Formen der Volksinitiative und die Einheit der Form' (2002) 103 *Schweizerisches Zentralblatt für Staats- und Verwaltungsrecht* 2–29, 18.

[78]   Liechtenstein: Art. 69(5) and Art. 70(3) People's Rights Act; Lithuania: Article 7(1) Law on Referendum.

[79]   Original Code, Explanatory Memorandum, III.2.29.

might be controversial, if their formulation does not make it clear whether their direct enforcement is possible or further implementation measures are needed. For instance, an initiative to reduce the use of fossil fuels by 40 per cent can be interpreted as a question of principle, where the implementation requires legislative action to determine the timeline and conditions for the reduction or as a formulated proposal that can be directly enforced. Thus, the review of this formal limit does confer some discretionary powers on the state institution and require some expertise in legal interpretation.

3.2.2 Unity of substance

When the referendum proposal consists of multiple parts, then the voters may support one part of the proposal, but not others. By requiring voters to express their opinion in a single vote about different issues, the results may not reflect the actual preferences of the voters.[80]

One solution is to allow referendums on multiple issues but require separate votes on all components. For example, in Portugal each referendum may only address one matter.[81] In Serbia or North Macedonia, if multiple issues are decided in a referendum, then each question must be formulated separately.[82] However, this is not always feasible with complex proposals where the parts of the proposal depend on each other and represent one elaborate solution for a problem.

The unity of substance limit guarantees that the voters are able to express their preferences by requiring that in a case where multiple issues are put to a single vote, then an inherent link should connect the parts of the proposal.[83] One example is the Swiss Constitution, which allows multiple proposals but the individual parts of the initiative must be connected by an intrinsic link.[84] The unity of substance requirement aims to confine proposals to one larger issue or goal that creates a connection between the parts of the proposal. Requiring that the parts of the proposal are connected, reduces the chance that voters cannot formulate a stance on the issue. The unity of substance requirement is supposed to ban proposals that cover multiple issues when the link between them is not apparent. In addition, it can also prevent cases where separate issues are bundled together intentionally to gain support for the less

---

[80] Original Code, Explanatory Memorandum, III.2.30; See also Laurence Morel, 'The Democratic Criticism of Referendums. The Majority and the True Will of the People' (Ch 1, n 23) 164.

[81] Art. 115(6) Constitution.

[82] Serbia: Art. 15(3) Law on Referendum and Other Forms of Direct Expression of Citizens; North Macedonia: Art. 19 Referendum and People's Initiative Law.

[83] Revised Code, III.2.

[84] Art. 139(3) Federal Constitution, Art. 75(2) Federal Act on Political Rights.

popular part of the proposal by building on the popularity of the other part.[85] The unity of substance limit is crucial for ensuring that the referendum is a vehicle for the genuine, democratic will-formation of the people.

Reviewing the unity of substance requirement requires extensive contextual and teleological interpretation of the proposals. It also confers a wide discretionary power on the decision-maker. Finding a link between separate issues can largely depend on the abstraction level on which the decision-maker defines the 'common aim' or 'connection' between the issues.[86] Seemingly connected issues can be interpreted as distinct legal institutions if the level of abstraction is low and, vice versa, seemingly unconnected issues can be grouped together through a broad common aim.[87] Reviewing the unity of substance limit clearly requires legal expertise. However, any state institution that is accustomed to deciding legal disputes and using the traditional methods of legal interpretation can develop legal standards for assessing the connection between issues.

3.2.3   Clarity

The clarity requirement is the broadest formal limit. It ensures that the referendum proposal is not confusing or misleading but is formulated clearly and precisely. Most variations of the clarity requirement contain the elements listed in the Revised Code. This definition states that 'the question put to the vote must be clear and comprehensible; it must not be misleading; it must be unbiased, not suggesting an answer; voters must be informed of the effects of the referendum; voters must be able to answer the questions asked solely by yes, no or a blank vote'.[88] In Hungary, the question proposed for referendum shall be worded in such manner that it allows a straightforward response, and permits the National Assembly to decide – on the basis of the outcome of

---

[85]   Gildersleeve (n 26) 1450; Robert D. Cooter, Michael D. Gilbert, 'A Theory of Direct Democracy and the Single Subject Rule' (2010) 110(3) *Columbia Law Review* 687–730, 689.

[86]   Robert Hurst, 'Der Grundsatz der Einheit der Materie' (DPhil thesis, University of Zurich 2002) 3, <https://doi.org/10.5167/uzh-70565>; Cooter, Gilbert (n 85) 690; Andreas Kley, 'Die Einheit der Materie bei Bundesgesetzen und der Stein der Weisen' (2019) 120 *Schweizerisches Zentralblatt für Staats- und Verwaltungsrecht* 3, 10.

[87]   For example, the Swiss parliamentary debate about the 'Ecopop' initiative, which aimed to limit immigration to Switzerland to no more than 0.2% of its permanent resident population and to provide international aid for birth control and family planning in developing countries. See National Council debate 2014 summer 6th session 10.06.14, Official Bulletin 2014, 951–962. See also Daniel Moeckli, 'Die Teilungültigerklärung und Aufspaltung von Volksinitiativen' (2014) 115 *Schweizerisches Zentralblatt für Staats- und Verwaltungsrecht* 579–599, 580.

[88]   Revised Code, I.3.1.c.

the referendum – whether it has the obligation to make a law, and if so, what kind of a law.[89] In Croatia, the request for a referendum must contain a clearly formulated issue.[90] In Russia, the question submitted to the referendum should be formulated in such a way as to exclude the possibility of multiple interpretations and to exclude the uncertainty of the legal consequences of the decision taken at the referendum.[91]

The aim of this limit is to guarantee the freedom of vote and the free will-formation of voters.[92] As the Venice Commission's definition shows, the clarity requirement can have different layers.[93] On the first and most basic level, the proposal has to be understandable for the voters, which encompasses that the proposal is grammatically comprehensible. The second level is that the voters must be able to understand the legal consequences of the vote, thus the legal surroundings of the proposal and the changes it promotes. The proposal must also be clear so that the voters understand it to mean the same thing. Otherwise, the popular vote cannot be a vehicle of democratic will-formation. In addition, the requirement of clarity can also encompass other formal limits. Proposals that violate the unity of form may be deemed confusing for the voters in their legal consequences. In a case where the proposal contains multiple unrelated issues, the voters cannot express their clear preferences.[94]

Reviewing the clarity limit confers wide discretion on the decision-maker. One reason for this is the broad interpretation domain of the term *clarity*. The term 'clarity' is not an exact legal term, it can be interpreted to cover a formalistic-grammatical requirement or a more in-depth condition. In addition, the decision-maker has to evaluate the formulation of the proposal against the assumed mindset of the voters.[95] This requires creating a standard for the comprehension of a 'general voter' or a similar abstract construct. In a sense, the decision-maker creates an irrebuttable legal presumption about the understanding of the voters. Thus, the decision-maker not only has discretion

---

[89]   Art. 9 Act CCXXXVIII of 2013 on Initiating Referendums, the European Citizens' Initiative and Referendum Procedure.

[90]   Art. 8b Law on Referendum and Other Forms of Personal Participation in the Exercise of State Power and Local and Regional Self-Government.

[91]   Art. 6(7) Federal Constitutional Law of June 28, 2004 N 5-FKZ on the Referendum of the Russian Federation.

[92]   Tierney, *Constitutional Referendums: The Theory and Practice of Republican Deliberation* (Ch 1, n 6) 227–228.

[93]   Ibid.

[94]   Ibid.

[95]   The Curia of Hungary regularly refuses to authorize referendums because the proposed questions would require voters to have such a deep understanding of complex legal issues that only experts or directly affected persons could have. See Decisions Knk.IV.37.425/2017/3 and Knk.IV.37.426/2017/3 of the Curia.

in interpreting such a broadly worded principle as clarity, but also in determining the level of comprehension of the voters. Similar to the unity of substance requirement, reviewing the clarity of the proposal requires legal expertise but any state institution that regularly decides legal disputes may be able to develop a consistent practice about clarity.

3.3   The Particularities of Rejective Referendums

In case of rejective referendums, the initiators formulate a referendum request about a legal act adopted by the representative organs. The subject of the referendum authorization procedure is the referendum request and not the adopted legal act itself.[96] This means that the authorization procedure focuses on slightly different questions than in case of proactive referendums.

The review of substantive limits is similar to that of proactive referendums in most respects. One important difference is that the constitutional review of the legal act subject to a referendum request is usually separate from the authorization procedure.[97] The constitutionality of the legal act is usually decided according to the regular constitutional remedies of the given state. Naturally, it is feasible to construct an authorization procedure that combines the review of the referendum proposal and the legal act. However, it would necessitate placing the competence of referendum authorization with the same state institution that is entrusted with the constitutional adjudication competence. A composite procedure would also entangle the legal limits imposed on referendums with the constitutional principles that guide the constitutional review of legislation.

Nevertheless, it is not out of the question that rejective referendum proposals can be reviewed for their constitutionality or for their compliance with other higher-ranking norms. The rejective referendum either prevents new legal provisions or legal acts from entering into force or abrogates existing legal provisions or legal acts. In the second case, it is possible that the result of a referendum would create an unconstitutional situation, because the legal order would lack a rule that is crucial for its proper functioning.[98] In this

---

[96] For example in Slovenia, the Constitutional Court carries out a preliminary review of the referendum request, which is separate from the constitutional review of the legislation. Žuber, Kaučič, 'Referendum Challenges in the Republic of Slovenia' (Ch 3, n 134) 142.

[97] Auer, von Arx (n 31) 923.

[98] This problem has appeared in both Slovenia and Italy. The Slovene Constitutional Court developed its practice on the 'unconstitutional consequences' of the referendum in Decision U-II-1/09 of 5 May 2009 of the Constitutional Court, Official Gazette of the Republic of Slovenia No. 35/2009; Decision U-II-2/09 of 9 November 2009 of the

case the subject of the review is not the legal act or legal provision that is the subject of the referendum but the remainder of the legal order. This type of review is similarly complex and extensive as the review of proactive initiatives against limits protecting the constitution, fundamental rights and freedoms, or international law. The state institution requires expertise in constitutional adjudication to determine whether an unconstitutional situation would emerge following a successful referendum.

The review of formal limits is also distinct in the case of rejective referendums. The formal limits apply somewhat differently because formulation of the subject of the referendum is in the hands of the representative organs. Thus, the formal defects of the referendum – its lack of clarity, or the combination of multiple issues or text styles – can either be inherent flaws of the legal act submitted to a referendum or flaws of the referendum proposal. An inherent flaw of the legal act is for instance if the legislature deliberately joins together seemingly unrelated policy decisions in one statute.[99] Similarly, if the newly adopted legal act submitted to a referendum contains incomprehensible provisions, then the clarity problem derives from the legal act itself. Alternatively, the defect of the referendum proposal can come from the way the initiators formulate it. For instance, if the initiators do not aim to abrogate one legal act in its entirety, but instead propose the abrogation of multiple provisions from one legal act, then it can cause a concern about clarity as well as about the unity of substance.[100] The clarity requirement can also be crucial to assess whether the voters understand the consequences of a legal provision or a legal act disappearing from the legal system. Ideally, all of the above-mentioned defects should prevent the authorization of referendum. However, the decision-maker might not have the competence or the willingness to reject a referendum based on the inherent flaws of the legal act, because it would conflate the review of the legal act and the referendum proposal.

Constitutional Court, Official Gazette of the Republic of Slovenia No. 91/2009; and Decision U-II-1/10 of 10 June 2010 of the Constitutional Court, Official Gazette of the Republic of Slovenia No. 50/2010. See also Žuber, Kaučič, 'Referendum Challenges in the Republic of Slovenia' (Ch 3, n 134) 144; Žuber, Kaučič, 'Slovenia' (Ch 3, n 123) 142. Similarly, the Italian Constitutional Court had to devise practice on referendums abrogating only words or small parts of the legislative act and changing the meaning of the whole regulation. Uleri, 'Institutions of Citizens' Political Participation in Italy: Crooked Forms, Hindered Institutionalization' (Ch 1, n 82) 83–84; Ibi (Ch 3, n 41) 76–77.

[99] For instance in a 2019 Swiss referendum the voters approved a legal act that contained a corporate tax reform and a pension reform. See: Moeckli, 'Switzerland' (Ch 2, n 14) 34.

[100] Uleri, 'Institutions of Citizens' Political Participation in Italy: Crooked Forms, Hindered Institutionalization' (Ch 1, n 82) 83–84.

Even though rejective referendums have some special features compared to proactive ones, when the legal limits are applied to the referendum proposals, the review of the limits necessitates the same legal expertise and confers the same level of discretion to the decision-maker as in case of proactive referendums.

4.   CONCLUSIONS

Even though the competent state institution authorizes a political event, the referendum authorization procedure is a legal procedure. As defined here, it is inherently linked to the existence of legal limits: the state institution has to decide on the compliance of the referendum proposal with the legal limits. The referendum authorization procedure has elements of both the abstract and concrete review of constitutional adjudication. The review of the proposal vis-à-vis the substantive limits is abstract in the sense that it does not arise from a challenge against the application of the proposed legal change. The proposal has not yet affected individual rights or caused individual injuries, but it is reviewed in its totality without an attachment to a concrete legal question. At the same time, referendum authorization is decisive for the referendum event and for the initiators' and the voters' right to vote. In this sense it is a concrete procedure. The difference from concrete constitutional review is that initiators promote the proposal, and their legal interests lie in the proposal not violating the legal limits. In addition, the proposal itself may not be connected to the right to vote: the formal authorization procedure creates the topical connection between the proposal and the right to vote. Referendum authorization procedures can be captured in this duality: the state institution must reach a decision on both the right to vote and the legality of the proposal, thus carrying out a concrete and an abstract review. Regarding the institutional and procedural settings, the concrete nature of the procedure and its attachment to the right to vote implies that the rights and legal interests of the initiators and voters should be translated into procedural rights. The abstract nature of the procedure suggests state institutions with expertise in constitutional adjudication are best suited for these procedures. However, a closer look at the limits shows that such expertise is only crucial for reviewing some of the substantive limits.

Looking into the variations and functions of the most common legal limits helps to understand the decision-maker's domain of interpretation and the necessary expertise to review the limits. The overview of the most common formal and substantive limits shows that from a procedural perspective the limits can be grouped into three categories. There are very few legal limits whose review does not require the exercise of discretion and can be assessed without extensive legal expertise. The most straightforward limits are the substantive limits on state symbols or official language, on future international law obligations, and the formal limit on the unity of form. The assessment of whether a referendum proposal violates these limits does not necessarily require in-depth legal analysis and, in most cases, a grammatical interpretation of the referendum proposal suffices. At the other end of the spectrum are the substantive limits on the constitutionality of the proposal, on fundamental rights and freedoms, and on existing international obligations. These are all broadly worded limits that confer a considerable amount of discretion and require a very thorough legal analysis of the referendum proposal as well as expertise in constitutional adjudication. Between these two poles are the substantive limits on the state organization and on the functioning of the state as well as the formal limits on unity of substance and clarity. These limits do provide some level of discretion to the decision-maker and may involve an extensive legal analysis of the proposal, but do not necessitate expertise in constitutional adjudication.

If the state imposes legal limits beyond the few straightforward limits – which is the case in most European states – then the state institution authorizing referendums must have expertise in deciding legal disputes. Moreover, if limits on the constitutionality of the referendum, on fundamental rights and freedoms, or on international law obligations are imposed, then the state institution must have expertise in constitutional adjudication. Without such expertise, the state institution will not be able to devise a practice that balances popular sovereignty and rule of law.

Referendum authorization procedures are always an ancillary task for state institutions.[101] Even in states that have multiple referendums a year, such as Switzerland or Liechtenstein, the number of referendum authorization cases does not warrant the establishment of a specialized state institution. Thus, this competence is always an additional task for the state institution that has other constitutional functions, and these other functions can be deemed their core functions. In a very simplistic understanding, parliaments primarily adopt legislation, governments prepare legislative proposals and execute parliamentary decisions, regular courts adjudicate individual legal disputes, and constitutional courts review legislation.[102] Even election commissions that are designed to fulfill functions relating to voting events are primarily created to

---

[101] Comella (Ch 2, n 20) 6; Tom Ginsburg, 'Constitutional Court in East Asia: Understanding Variation' in Andrew Harding, Peter Leyland (eds), *Constitutional Courts: A Comparative Study* (Wildy, Simmonds and Hill Publishing 2009) 309.

[102] Comella (Ch 2, n 20) 55; Roderick A. Macdonald, Hoi Kong, 'Judicial Independence as a Constitutional Virtue' in Michel Rosenfeld, András Sajó (eds), *Oxford Handbook of Comparative Constitutional Law* (Oxford University Press 2012) 832; Philip Norton, 'Referendums and Parliaments' in J. Smith (ed), *The Palgrave Handbook of European Referendums* (Cham: Palgrave Macmillan 2021) 91–108, 91.

ensure the legality of elections.[103] Thus, referendum authorization procedures are ancillary tasks for any of these state institutions.

Nonetheless, when providing this competence to a state institution it is crucial to select a state institution which has similar functions. In practice this means that constitutional courts and regular courts should participate in the decision-making either as first-instance forums or as appellate bodies. Administrative authorities with adjudicatory functions or election commissions are also prudent institutional choices since they are experienced in adjudication. In addition, a judicial remedy is provided against their decisions in all selected states. For parliaments, governments, and presidents, the application of legal limits to individual cases is an atypical function compared to their core functions. The existence of remedies against their decisions may alleviate this concern to some extent. Nevertheless, it seems to be a better solution to involve these organs in a way that is in line with their core functions. Instead of the legal authorization of referendums, their role should be limited to the assessment of the social, political, and economic implications of referendums.

The most common institutional choices for referendum authorization in Europe and in the eight selected states do not necessarily ensure the legal expertise of the decision-maker. Focusing on the eight selected states, Italy is the only state that exclusively involves judicial bodies in the referendum authorization procedure, while four states (Hungary, Latvia, Liechtenstein, and Slovenia) provide judicial remedies against the first instance decisions. Election commissions decide about referendum authorization in Hungary and Latvia. Meanwhile, parliaments and presidents are entrusted with deciding about the formal and substantive legal limits in five states: Croatia, Liechtenstein, Slovakia, Slovenia, and Switzerland.

In the next chapter I investigate how these state institutions fare in providing some basic procedural guarantees to the participants in the procedure. Based on the special nature of referendum authorization procedures, some procedural guarantees seem indispensable. The concrete review dimension of the referendum authorization warrants some form of participation rights for the initiators and voters. Meanwhile, the wide discretionary powers that the state institutions exercise in reviewing most of the substantive and formal limits necessitate procedural guarantees to hinder the chance of arbitrary decision-making.

---

[103]   Wall et al. (Ch 2, n 19) 5–6.

5. Procedural guarantees in referendum authorization

This chapter introduces the procedural guarantees that I analyze in relation to the referendum authorization practice of the selected eight states. In Chapters 6 to 9, I focus on both authorized and rejected referendums to evaluate the procedural rights in referendum authorization procedures. Some examples include the referendums in Croatia, Slovakia, and Slovenia that aimed to prohibit the marriage of same-sex couples,[1] the referendum proposal to provide citizenship to all non-citizens in Latvia,[2] the referendum requests on reproduction rights in Italy,[3] and on pension reform in Liechtenstein.[4] Immigration referendums are chosen to illustrate the practice of Switzerland, such as the 'Ecopop' initiative and the initiative about the expulsion of foreign criminals,[5] while Hungary provides examples of initiatives on immigration, fiscal matters, and constitutional reforms.[6] Most of the selected cases concern referendums initiated by citizens, although Hungary also offers some interesting examples of government-initiated referendums. The reason for selecting mostly cases of citizen-initiated referendums is prosaic: with the exception of Hungary, the selected states have published authorization decisions only about citizen-initiated referendums.

The main question posed in Chapters 6 to 9 is how the practice of the eight selected states complies with four procedural guarantees: the independence and impartiality of the decision-maker, the right to a reasoned decision, the right to be heard, and the right to an effective remedy. This chapter provides some background on the selection of these procedural guarantees. In the next chapters, each procedural guarantee is analyzed by posing three questions: (1) What is the function of the procedural guarantee in referendum authorization procedures with regard to the special nature of these procedures? (2) Is the procedural guarantee ensured in the referendum authorization practice of the

---

[1] Kużelewska (Ch 1, n 10) 13–27.
[2] Jarinovska (Ch 3, n 61) 152–159.
[3] Uleri, 'Institutions of Citizens' Political Participation in Italy: Crooked Forms, Hindered Institutionalization' (Ch 1, n 82) 71–88.
[4] Marxer, 'Liechtenstein' (Ch 2, n 14) 54–55.
[5] Keller, Lanter, Fischer (Ch 1, n 12) 121–154.
[6] Forgács (Ch 3, n 32) 202–206.

selected states? (3) How could the procedural guarantee be better incorporated in the referendum authorization procedures of the selected states based on the comparative analysis?

The four procedural guarantees are selected based on the fair trial rights guaranteed by international treaties, on the procedural understanding of rule of law, and on the procedural recommendations of the Venice Commission's Revised Code on the Holding of Referendums.

These procedural guarantees mirror some of the most important fair trial rights appearing in international law.[7] All the selected states have ratified the ICCPR, which requires that 'everyone shall be entitled to a fair and public hearing by a competent, independent and impartial tribunal established by law'[8] in the determination of their rights and obligations in a suit at law. The ICCPR also obliges states to offer an effective remedy against the violation of the rights enshrined in the Covenant.[9] The right to participate in a referendum is protected under the right to vote.[10] The Human Rights Committee has found the right to an effective remedy applicable for referendum cases.[11] Meanwhile, the right to a fair trial has been applied in election cases, suggesting that it could also be applicable in the referendum context.[12]

All the eight states selected are members of the Council of Europe and have ratified the European Convention on Human Rights (ECHR).[13] The four procedural guarantees chosen for the analysis are integral elements of the right to a fair trial under Article 6 and the right to an effective remedy under Article 13 of the ECHR.[14] Nonetheless, the applicability of fair trial rights to referendum

---

[7]   See Art. 6 and Art. 13 European Convention for the Protection of Human Rights and Fundamental Freedoms, as amended by Protocols Nos. 11 and 14 [1950] 4 November 1950, ETS 5 (ECHR); Art. 47 Charter of Fundamental Rights of the European Union [2012] OJ C 326/391; Art. 2(3)(a), Art. 14 ICCPR.

[8]   Art. 14 ICCPR.

[9]   Art. 2(3)(a) ICCPR.

[10]   Art. 25 ICCPR. See also UN Human Rights Committee CCPR General Comment No. 25 [1996] CCPR/C/21/Rev.1/Add.7 (General Comment No. 25) para 6.

[11]   *Mario Staderini and Michele De Lucia v Italy*, UN Human Rights Committee, No. 2656/2015.

[12]   *Burgoa v Bolivia*, UN Human Rights Committee, No. 2628/2015; *Iporre v Bolivia*, UN Human Rights Committee, No. 2629/2015. See also Daniel Moeckli, 'Völkerrechtliche Vorgaben für den Rechtsschutz in Wahlsachen' in Andreas Glaser, Lorenz Langer (eds), *Das Parlamentswahlrecht als rechtsstaatliche Grundlage der Demokratie* (Dike Verlag, 2020) 191.

[13]   European Convention for the Protection of Human Rights and Fundamental Freedoms, as amended by Protocols Nos. 11 and 14 [1950] 4 November 1950, ETS 5.

[14]   Bernadette Rainey, Elizabeth Wicks, Clare Ovey (eds), *Jacobs, White, and Ovey: The European Convention on Human Rights* (7th edn, Oxford University Press 2017) 274–368.

procedures is not provided under the ECHR. According to the judgments of the European Court of Human Rights (ECtHR), referendum procedures do not fall under the scope of Article 3 of Protocol No. 1 on the right to free elections.[15] The ECtHR has noted that the scope of the right to free elections is more narrowly drafted in the Convention than in the ICCPR, because only regular elections concerning the choice of legislature fall within it.[16] Referendums are not held at regular intervals and are usually not organized as a means of electing citizens to certain posts.[17] It follows that the violation of the right to an effective remedy cannot be claimed in referendum procedures in conjunction with the right to free elections.[18] The ECtHR has not established the applicability of fair trial rights for referendum procedures either. Be that as it may, the provisions of the ECHR and practice of the ECtHR have largely influenced the interpretation of fair trial rights in the Council of Europe member states. Thus, the practice of the ECtHR cannot be disregarded when analyzing these rights in the eight selected states, and it influences how the four procedural guarantees are defined in this chapter.

Beyond the international treaties, the chosen procedural guarantees also appear as part of the procedural understanding of rule of law. Procedural components of the rule of law appear in several foundational works. John Rawls states that the rule of law requires some form of due process: a process reasonably designed to ascertain the truth. For this, judges need to be independent and impartial, and trials need to be fair and open, but not prejudiced by public clamor.[19] Joseph Raz highlights that beyond the independence of the judiciary, the principles of natural justice require an 'open and fair hearing, absence of bias and the like', and the easy accessibility of courts.[20] The most comprehensive account of the procedural understanding of rule of law stems from Jeremy Waldron. He argues that the formal view of rule of law is not complete without a more extensive list of procedural requirements.[21] According to Waldron, the

---

[15] See *X v UK* (1975) 3 DR 165 para 2; *Bader v Austria* App no 26633/95 (Commission decision, 15 May 1996) para 4; *Cumhuriyet Halk Partizi v Turkey* App no 48818/17 (ECtHR, 21 November 2017) para 33; *Moohan and Gillion v UK* App no. 22962/15 and 23345/15 (ECtHR, 13 June 2017) paras 40–41.

[16] *Moohan and Gillion v UK* App no. 22962/15 and 23345/15 (ECtHR, 13 June 2017) para 41.

[17] *Cumhuriyet Halk Partizi v Turkey* App no 48818/17 (ECtHR, 21 November 2017) para 33.

[18] *Cumhuriyet Halk Partizi v Turkey* App no 48818/17 (ECtHR, 21 November 2017) para 42.

[19] John Rawls, *A Theory of Justice* (Oxford University Press 1971) 239.

[20] Joseph Raz, *The Authority of Law: Essays on Law and Morality* (Ch 4, n 60) 217.

[21] Waldron, 'The Concept and the Rule of Law' (2008) 43 *Georgia Law Review* 1, 7; Jeremy Waldron, 'Rule-of-Law Rights and Populist Impatience' in Gerald L.

essential idea of procedure 'capture[s] a deep and important sense associated fundamentally with the idea of a legal system, that law is a mode of governing people that treats them with respect'.[22] In composing his list of procedural rights, Waldron lists all traditional fair trial guarantees as parts of the rule of law:[23]

(a)   A hearing by an impartial tribunal that is required to act on the basis of evidence and argument presented formally before it in relation to legal norms that govern the imposition of penalty, stigma, loss, and so forth.
(b)   A legally trained judicial officer, whose independence of other agencies of government is ensured.
(c)   A right to representation by counsel and to the time and opportunity required to prepare a case.
(d)   A right to be present at all critical stages of the proceeding.
(e)   A right to confront witnesses against the detainee.
(f)   A right to assurance that the evidence presented by the government has been gathered in a properly supervised way.
(g)   A right to present evidence in one's own behalf.
(h)   A right to make legal argument about the bearing of the evidence and about the bearing of the various legal norms relevant to the case.
(i)   A right to hear reasons from the tribunal when it reaches its decision that are responsive to the evidence and arguments presented before it; and
(j)   Some right to appeal to a higher tribunal of similar character.[24]

Lastly, the Revised Code of the Venice Commission is the most influential legal source on the selection of procedural guarantees, as the Code contains recommendations specifically for referendums. The Code prescribes requirements for institutional settings as well as for individual procedural rights. The Code emphasizes that an impartial body – preferably an independent central commission – must be entrusted with the organization and the supervision of referendums.[25] The Code also requires an effective system of appeal for referendum matters, with an impartial and independent appeal body 'endowed with the necessary powers of cognition and decision to afford an effective remedy, established by law, and bound to apply the law, with limited discre-

---

Neuman (ed), *Human Rights in a Time of Populism: Challenges and Responses* (New York: Cambridge University Press 2020) 44.
   [22]   Jeremy Waldron, 'The Rule of Law and the Importance of Procedure' (Ch 1, n 64) 347.
   [23]   See Rainey, Wicks, Ovey (n 14) 274–368; ECtHR Guide on Article 6 of the European Convention on Human Rights <https://www.echr.coe.int/documents/guide_art_6_eng.pdf>, accessed 15 March 2022.
   [24]   Waldron, 'The Rule of Law and the Importance of Procedure' (Ch 1, n 64) 347.
   [25]   Revised Code II.4.1.

tion. A final appeal to a court of law is the preferred option.'[26] Regarding the individual procedural rights, the Code states that all voters must be entitled to an appeal and the 'applicant's right to a hearing involving both parties must be protected'.[27]

Compared to the fair trial guarantees appearing in the ICCPR, the ECHR, or the rule-of-law literature, the Code does not contain any requirements about the presentation and rebuttal of evidence. The referendum authorization is a future-oriented, *a priori* dispute about the referendum proposal. Past events or other factual questions do not need to be proved in referendum authorization. Evidentiary procedures are not common in the practice either.[28] In states where referendum authorization procedures are carried out by political organs (parliaments, presidents) there are precedents for expert evidence, but these are exceptions.

The Code also omits any reference to the right to counsel, which can also be due to the special nature of referendum authorization procedures as opposed to civil or criminal trials. The subject of the referendum authorization is whether a referendum can take place and thus whether the right to vote can be exercised. A refusal decision does not entail sanctions or other detrimental legal consequences for the individual parties of the case. Thus, the assistance of a legal counsel is not so imperative as in criminal or even civil trials. Naturally, this does not mean that the participants of the referendum authorization procedure cannot rely on legal assistance to better their arguments, but it does not seem to be an essential requirement for these procedures.

The common set of procedural requirements comprises the impartiality and independence of the decision-maker, the right to an effective remedy, and the right to be heard. The Code does not mention the right to a reasoned decision, but this requirement is inseparable from the right to be heard. Without a reasoning, it is not clear what arguments were considered in reaching a certain decision. Thus, the reasoning is linked to participation rights: the reasoning of the decision is the output that shows the result of the oral or written inputs by the parties.[29] Consequently, these four procedural guarantees are regarded as minimum procedural guarantees in referendum authorization procedures. The next chapters analyze each procedural guarantee in the referendum practice, but also reflect on their necessity in referendum authorization procedures.

---

[26] Revised Code II.4.3.a.
[27] Revised Code II.4.3.f. and II.4.3.h.
[28] LIDD data dashboard > Explore data > By Instrument/Item > Theme: Formal/Substantive procedure on <http://lidd-project.org/data/>, accessed 15 March 2022.
[29] Jerry L. Mashaw, *Reasoned Administration and Democratic Legitimacy* (Cambridge University Press 2018) 50.

6. Impartiality and independence of the decision-maker

1. DEFINING IMPARTIALITY AND INDEPENDENCE

The procedural guarantees of impartiality and independence both ensure that the decision-maker acts in a neutral manner, treats the parties of the procedure equally, and reaches an unbiased decision.[1] The principles of independence and impartiality are traditional values of the judiciary. In most liberal democracies, judicial independence is ensured through an intricate system of legal guarantees that protect both the individual and the institutional independence of the judges.[2] The principle of judicial independence ensures that in the system of separation of powers the judiciary can function under the exclusive authority of law without the other two branches of government influencing the adjudication.[3] At the same time, the independence enables the judiciary to control the executive and the legislature in the system of checks and balances.[4] The independence of the judiciary also provides legal security for the individuals who want to resolve their legal disputes, and enhances the legitimacy and acceptance of the decisions.[5]

---

[1] M.E. Bayles, *Procedural Justice: Allocating to Individuals* (Dordrecht: Springer Netherlands 1990) 20; Joe McIntyre, *The Judicial Function: Fundamental Principles of Contemporary Judging* (Springer Singapore 2019) 168; Kohei Suzuki, Mehmet Akif Demircioglu, 'Is Impartiality Enough? Government Impartiality and Citizens' Perceptions of Public Service Quality' [2020] *Governance* 1–38, 3–4.

[2] Shimon Shetreet, 'Judicial Independence and Accountability' in H.P. Lee (ed), *Judiciaries in Comparative Perspective* (Cambridge University Press 2011) 20–21; Macdonald, Kong (Ch 4, n 102) 833.

[3] Tom S. Clark, *The Limits of Judicial Independence* (Oxford University Press 2012) 5.

[4] Shimon Shetreet, 'Judicial Independence and Accountability' (n 2) 10.

[5] Shimon Shetreet, 'Judicial Independence: New Conceptual Dimensions and Contemporary Challenges' in Shimon Shetreet, Jules Deschenes (eds), *Judicial Independence: The Contemporary Debate* (Martinus Nijhoff Publishers 1985) 594–595; Regina Kiener, *Richterliche Unabhängigkeit* (Stämpfli Verlag AG 2001) 6.

Impartiality generally requires the absence of bias or prejudice on the side of the decision-maker.[6] Independence makes it possible for the decision-maker to decide without improper outside influences from other state powers or from the parties.[7] In this sense, impartiality is a broader category that encompasses independence: the lack of improper outside influences is instrumental to achieving an unbiased decision.[8] In the following pages, the distinction between these two principles is based on two different threats to unbiased decision-making: dispute-specific threats and structural threats.[9] The principle of impartiality should ensure that dispute-specific threats do not distort the decision-making. *Dispute-specific threats* may derive from a personal interest in the outcome of the case or a personal bias unrelated to the merits of the matter.[10] It can be quite difficult to prove that a personal interest or bias actually influenced the decision, thus emphasis is also laid on the appearance of bias.[11] By prohibiting situations in which the decision-maker could be perceived as biased, the principle of impartiality also protects against the loss of confidence in the fairness of the decision-making process that could lead to demoralization and non-compliance.[12] Meanwhile, the principle of independence should counter structural threats to the decision-making process. *Structural threats* to unbiased decision-making may come from multiple sources: other state institutions, interest groups, political parties.[13] The independence of the decision-making organ is usually ensured through the separation of powers and other institutional guarantees such as the stability of the position, immunity, stable renumeration, or neutral appointment procedures.[14]

---

[6]   *Micallef v Malta* ECHR 2009-V 289 para 93. See also McIntyre (n 1) 170.

[7]   *Sramek v Austria* (1984) Series A no. 84 para 42; *Beaumartin v France* (1994) Series A no. 296-B para 38. See also Kiener, *Richterliche Unabhängigkeit* (n 5) 7; Hellen Keller, Severin Meier, 'Independence and Impartiality in *The Judicial Trilemma*' (2017) 111 *American Society of International Law* 344, 345.

[8]   Roland Hoffmann, *Verfahrensgerechtigkeit: Studien zu einer Theorie prozeduraler Gerechtigkeit* (Ferdinand Schöningh 1992)109; McIntyre (n 1) 169.

[9]   Hoffmann (n 8) 106; Peter Rädler, 'Independence and Impartiality of Judges' in David Weissbrodt, Rüdiger Wolfrum (eds), *The Right to a Fair Trial* (Springer 1998) 731; Richard Clayton, Hugh Tomlinson, *Fair Trial Rights* (Oxford University Press 2010) 171; McIntyre (n 1) 176.

[10]   Bayles (n 1) 21.

[11]   *Sramek v Austria* (1984) Series A no. 84 para 42. See also Bayles (n 1) 23; McIntyre (n 1) 183.

[12]   Bayles (n 1) 23–24.

[13]   Ibid 23–29.

[14]   *Kleyn and Others v The Netherlands* ECHR 2003-VI 63 para 190. See also McIntyre (n 1) 207; Diego M. Papayannis, 'Independence, Impartiality and Neutrality in Legal Adjudication' (2016) 28 *Revus – Journal for Constitutional Theory and Philosophy of Law* 33, 35.

2.   IMPARTIALITY AND INDEPENDENCE
IN REFERENDUM AUTHORIZATION
PROCEDURES

Independence and impartiality are core values for adjudication, when a neutral third party is needed to decide a dispute between private or public parties.[15] In the context of adjudication it seems unquestionable that the institution deciding about a legal dispute of parties shall be impartial and independent of undue influences. Not surprisingly, the independence of the judiciary is a requirement that often appears among the principles of rule of law,[16] while the right to a fair trial by an independent and impartial tribunal is integral to the international fair trial guarantees.[17] The Revised Code of the Venice Commission lays emphasis on the impartiality of the body organizing and supervising referendums, as well as on the impartiality and independence of the appeal body.[18]

The principles of independence and impartiality mostly attach to organs that primarily fulfill adjudicative functions, such as courts and tribunals,[19] and to a lesser extent administrative authorities.[20] Administrative authorities usually derive their legitimacy from the government or the parliament; they belong to the executive branch, thus requiring distance from the other branches of government is not feasible.[21] Even though administrative bodies are not independent and isolated from the other branches of government, the adjudicator usually has the autonomy in the individual case to reach a decision impartially, without outside interference.[22] However, for the state institutions that do not primarily adjudicate individual disputes (such as parliaments, governments, or presidents) independence and impartiality may seem alien concepts.

The referendum authorization procedure is adjudicatory in the sense that it is a dispute about the exercise of constitutionally protected rights: the right to initiate a referendum and the right to vote. Regardless of whether participation

---

[15]   Kiener, *Richterliche Unabhängigkeit* (n 5) 2–3; Shimon Shetreet, 'Creating a Culture of Judicial Independence: The Practical Challenge and the Conceptual and Constitutional Infrastructure' in Shimon Shetreet, Christopher Forsyth (eds), *The Culture of Judicial Independence: Conceptual Foundations and Practical Challenges* (Martinus Nijhoff Publishers 2012) 63.

[16]   Dicey (Ch 4, n 60) 110; Raz, *The Authority of Law: Essays on Law and Morality* (Ch 4, n 60) 216.

[17]   Art. 14 ICCPR, Art. 6 ECHR.

[18]   Revised Code II.4.1 and II.4.3.

[19]   McIntyre (n 1) 162.

[20]   Strauss (Ch 4, n 24) 312–317; Sir William Wade, Christopher Forsyth, *Administrative Law* (11th edn, Oxford: Oxford University Press 2014) 384.

[21]   Bayles (n 1) 20.

[22]   Kiener, *Richterliche Unabhängigkeit* (n 5) 24.

rights are ensured to the initiators and/or the voters, the authorization decision affects all of them: it prevents or allows the exercise of popular sovereignty. It is, therefore, important that the initiators and voters are treated equally, without bias or even the appearance of bias.

A further reason for the independence and the impartiality of the decision-maker lies in the legal nature of the authorization procedure. The state institution has to decide legal questions by applying the legal limits to the referendum proposal. It is therefore imperative that the evaluation of the legality or constitutionality of a referendum is carried out without the influence of political or other interests. The political, economic, or social ramifications of a referendum are naturally very important; however, these should only be taken into account in the authorization if they connect to a legal limit (e.g. limits on state finances), and only to the extent they are necessary to carry out the legal analysis.

Independence and impartiality in the referendum context is also important to ensure legal certainty and thus the rule of law. As the previous chapter showed, the review of most legal limits requires the exercise of discretion. If the decision-making process involves some form of bias or undue outside influence, then the discretionary powers can be used in an arbitrary way. Creating a consistent practice of the interpretation of legal limits is not an easy exercise even without other interests affecting the procedure. Consequently, it is important to minimize the risk that non-legal considerations penetrate the referendum authorization procedure.

In referendum authorization procedures, the choice of state institution can largely determine how the principles of impartiality and independence can be applied. For parliamentary, governmental, or presidential decision-making, independence is a non-applicable category because these bodies are necessarily political. However, the impartiality of these bodies can be evaluated to see whether there is a bias or prejudice that may influence the outcome of the referendum case. In the context of administrative procedures, independence usually plays a lesser role, while the impartiality of the decision-maker is still a guiding principle. In this regard, election commissions are atypical bodies: akin to administrative authorities, they adjudicate individual legal disputes, but they play an important role in protecting democracy, which also warrants a level of independence.[23] Thus, for referendum authorization procedures, both the impartiality and the independence of election commissions pose questions.

---

[23]   Mark Tushnet, *Advanced Introduction to Comparative Constitutional Law* (Edward Elgar 2018) 116; C.T. van Ham, Holly Ann Garnett, 'Building Impartial Electoral Management? Institutional Design, Independence and Electoral Integrity' (2019) 40(3) *International Political Science Review* 313–334.

The judicial bodies participating in the referendum authorization can also be required to be both impartial and independent.

3.   THE IMPARTIALITY OF PARLIAMENTS AND GOVERNMENTS AUTHORIZING REFERENDUMS

The impartiality of parliaments is a crucial question in referendum author-ization because parliamentary decision-making is one of the most popular institutional choices in the Council of Europe for substantive authorization procedures.[24] The impartiality of parliaments can be compromised by two potential issues.

On the one hand, these state institutions represent the people, and their composition is subject to periodical elections by the people. This dependency on voters is able to create a conflict for the members of parliament when they are also entrusted to uphold the legal limits on direct democracy against the electorate.[25] This is a *strategic conflict* in the sense that the elected representa-tives have to find the best solution to carry out their constitutional tasks and at the same time keep their electoral support.[26] This may influence their attitude toward referendum requests, depending on the perceived popularity of the ref-erendum. If the referendum request is perceived to be popular with the voters, they might take a more lenient approach to evaluating the limits. Meanwhile, if the referendum proposal seems to generate disapproval from the voters, then a more restrictive approach is possible.

On the other hand, parliaments are entrusted to decide the substantive poli-cies of the state. Parliaments make decisions on the most important economic, social, and political questions of the country by adopting legislation. The policy-making character of these organs can potentially create another con-flict with the voters. Voters initiate referendums on distinct policy issues and preempt the decisional competence of parliaments.[27] In contrast to the other conflict, this is an *ideology-based conflict* that may prompt the representative organs to follow a more stringent approach.

Both potential conflicts may compromise the impartiality of these insti-tutions in referendum authorizations. As Anna Christmann has pointed

---

[24]   See Chapter 2, section 4.1.
[25]   Kirchgässner (Ch 1, n 34) 84; Christmann, *Die Grenzen direkter Demokratie: Volkentscheide im Spannungsverhältnis von Demokratie und Rechtsstaat* (Ch 4, n 3) 155.
[26]   Christmann, *Die Grenzen direkter Demokratie: Volkentscheide im Spannungs-verhältnis von Demokratie und Rechtsstaat* (Ch 4, n 3) 181–182.
[27]   Frey, Stutzer, Neckermann (Ch 1, n 32) 108; Norton (Ch 4, n 102) 92.

out in her analysis of parliamentary referendum authorization procedures, parliamentarians tend to act either strategically or ideologically when voting about referendums.[28] Neither approach promotes the legal interpretation of the referendum proposal.

These potential conflicts may also be present for other state institutions that are elected by the voters and decide about economic, social, and political questions such as governments. However, governments and governmental bodies tend to decide only the technical authorization of referendums,[29] which mostly involves straightforward questions and does not necessitate the use of discretion. To date, the only actual challenge to the impartiality of any of these elected organs has been against the Government of Croatia. Otherwise, the impartiality of these state institutions has not been explicitly challenged in the referendum practice of the selected states.

3.1   Ideological Conflict of Interest

The ideological conflict of interest has been raised in a Croatian case, in which the impartiality of the government was challenged in relation to the technical authorization of a popular initiative.[30] The initiators of the 'Truth about the Istanbul Convention' referendum submitted over 370,000 signatures to the Parliament against the ratification of the Council of Europe Convention on preventing and combating violence against women and domestic violence (the Istanbul Convention).[31] The Parliament ordered the government to check the signatures, and the Ministry of Administration reached the decision that the number of valid signatures had not reached the 10 per cent threshold. The initiators challenged the decision at the Constitutional Court and argued that the government could not reach an unbiased decision on the correctness of the signatures. They claimed that because the government has previously supported the ratification of the Istanbul Convention and has spoken negatively about the objectives of the initiative in public, the executive is biased in the referendum procedure. According to the initiators, the bias is supported by the fact that the

---

[28]   Christmann, *Die Grenzen direkter Demokratie: Volkentscheide im Spannungs-verhältnis von Demokratie und Rechtsstaat* (Ch 4, n 3) 181–182.

[29]   See, for example, the Federal Chancellery in Switzerland checking the title of referendum, the official translations, and the signature list; or the government in Croatia counting the signatures.

[30]   Decision of the Constitutional Court of the Republic of Croatia No. U-VIIR-3260/2018 of 18 December 2018, Official Gazette. 8/2019, 183.

[31]   Podolnjak, 'Croatia' (Ch 3, n 10) 161.

Ministry of Administration has not allowed the representatives of the citizen group to be present during the signature verification process.[32]

The Constitutional Court found the application inadmissible, but still dealt with the claims made by the initiators. In the reasoning, the Court stated that the fact that the government has supported the ratification of the Convention does not in itself mean that the government is automatically unable or unwilling to implement the order of the Croatian Parliament to verify the correctness of collected signatures objectively and within its statutory powers.[33] Such an interpretation of bias would lead to the possibility of questioning almost any executive decision where the government does not agree with the parliamentary decision during its enactment and voting. Then the Court emphasized that the impartiality of the governmental decision is ensured in the system of separation of powers by the simultaneous oversight of Parliament and the Constitutional Court. It also highlighted that the government must always respect the fundamental rights and freedoms laid down by the Constitution. The Court declared that:

> these guarantees start from the presumption of trust in the institutions of state power established in the political system of constitutional democracy. This presumption is not absolute and does not mean that the executive cannot act arbitrarily or biased. However, it cannot be called into question solely on the basis of general allegations and personal assessments. The reasons for the bias and arbitrariness of the competent authorities must be factually concretized, clear, and convincing. Claims that the competent executive authorities are a priori incapable of acting lawfully and impartially only because they disagree with one's political interest, not only undermine citizens' minimum confidence in state institutions, but deny the ability of a democratic constitutional order to ensure respect for the rule of law through constitutional guarantees.[34]

The Croatian Constitutional Court rightly stresses that general allegations based on different views on policy questions do not necessarily lead to impartiality in a specific case and certainly do not mean that an institution is unfit for referendum authorization. Still, it is important to acknowledge that state institutions with policy-making functions may have a conflict of interest in referendum authorization procedures, which conflict is not present for other institutions, such as election commissions or courts. Referendums carve out issues from the decisional authority of the elected policy-makers and allow the

---

[32] Decision of the Constitutional Court of the Republic of Croatia No. U-VIIR -3260/2018 of 18 December 2018, Official Gazette. 8/2019, 183, para 8.3.

[33] Ibid, para 10.1.

[34] Decision of the Constitutional Court of the Republic of Croatia No. U-VIIR -3260/2018 of 18 December 2018, Official Gazette. 8/2019, 183, para 10.4 (DeepL Translator).

citizens to take over the task of decision-making.[35] In contrast to election commissions and judicial bodies, the core function of parliaments and governments is to decide about the most important political, economic, and social questions of the country. In this regard, referendums affect the decisional authority of parliaments and governments that are otherwise charged with reaching policy decisions in the representative system. Citizen-initiated referendums are specifically designed to challenge the policy preferences developed by the representative organs. The voters negate the decisions of the representative organs in successful rejective referendums, while in proactive referendums they are able to bring up issues that are disregarded by the policy-makers. Thus, citizens can voice their discontent with decisions or the lack of decisions through initiating referendums and can keep the elected representatives accountable.[36] This creates an inherent conflict between the citizens initiating a referendum and elected policy-makers: citizens not only take away decisional competences, but the initiation of referendums also signals their disagreement in policy questions.[37]

Successful referendums force elected bodies to implement certain policy choices. Moreover, most constitutional systems protect the decisions made through referendums with moratoriums. This way, the parliaments and governments are unable to override the will of the people within a given timeframe. Croatia imposes a one-year limit on the legislature to issue a legal act that would be contrary to the referendum decision.[38] In Hungary the limit is three years.[39] The moratorium is two years for constitutional referendums and one year for legislative ones in Slovenia.[40] No such limitations can be found in Switzerland and Liechtenstein. However, the lack of legal consequences for going against the will of the voters does not diminish the political consequences of disregarding the results of a popular vote. So, in the end, popular votes can lock down certain issues for longer periods, even years, and preempt parliamentary and governmental decision-making.

---

[35] Bruno S. Frey, Alois Stutzer, 'Direct Democracy: Designing a Living Constitution' in Stefan Voigt (ed), *Design of Constitutions* (Edward Elgar 2013) 492.

[36] Matsusaka, *Let the People Rule: How Direct Democracy Can Meet the Populist Challenge* (Ch 1, n 27) 155.

[37] Anna Christmann, 'Direct Democracy and the Rule of Law – Assessing a Tense Relationship' in Wilfried Marxer (ed), *Direct Democracy and Minorities* (Springer 2012) 59.

[38] Art. 8(2) Law on Referendum and Other Forms of Personal Participation in the Exercise of State Power and Local and Regional Self-Government.

[39] Art. 31(2) Act CCXXXVIII of 2013 on Initiating Referendums, the European Citizens' Initiative and Referendum Procedure.

[40] Art. 8 and Art. 25 Referendum and Popular Initiative Act.

The ideological conflict of interest of parliaments and governments would suggest that these institutions approach referendum authorization restrictively and would try to minimize possible clashes at the ballots. However, the practice shows that parliaments are one of the most lenient institutions when it comes to referendum authorization.[41] It must be acknowledged that a clear causal link between rejection rates and (im)partiality cannot be established based on this small number of cases. Still, the low rejection rates compared to other state institutions can signal that the ideological conflict with the voters does not affect the decision-making practice of parliaments. It might, however, be indicative of the strategic conflict of interest.

3.2   Strategic Conflict of Interest

Switzerland serves as an example for the frequent use of citizen-initiated referendums that helps the decision-making of representative organs to align with voter preferences. But it also serves as an example for parliamentary decision-making where the Federal Assembly only exceptionally invalidates citizen-initiated referendums: out of the more than 200 questions between 1990 and 2021, only two initiatives were stopped before the vote and one was partially invalidated.[42] The governmental recommendations also rarely suggest the invalidation of the initiative; instead, they mostly suggest that the parliament should recommend the rejection of the initiative at the polls. Similar trends can be seen in the parliamentary practices of Liechtenstein and Slovenia. In both states, the parliaments have declared only two proactive citizen-initiated referendums invalid since 1990,[43] although the Slovene National Assembly was more rigorous with referendums initiated by parliamentary minorities.[44] Meanwhile, the Croatian Parliament has not yet invalidated a referendum proposal.

The lenient approach may suggest that the strategic conflict of interest poses a challenge for representative organs when authorizing referendums.[45] This would mean that the members of parliament consider the risk of losing elec-

---

[41]   See Chapter 2, section 4.4.

[42]   LIDD Referendum events dashboard > Select Country > Vote trigger > Citizens (included) on <http://lidd-project.org/data2/>, accessed 15 March 2022. See also Keller, Lanter, Fischer (Ch 1, n 12) 126; Biaggini (Ch 1, n 12) 329–330; Moeckli, 'Switzerland' (Ch 2, n 14) 29–35.

[43]   Marxer, 'Liechtenstein' (Ch 2, n 14) 54.

[44]   Bruna Žuber, Igor Kaučič, 'Referendum Challenges in the Republic of Slovenia' (Ch 3, n 134) 144.

[45]   Christmann, *Die Grenzen direkter Demokratie: Volkentscheide im Spannungsverhältnis von Demokratie und Rechtsstaat* (Ch 4, n 3) 182.

toral support in the referendum authorization procedure. Parliaments embody the other limb of popular sovereignty, they represent the voters, meaning that voters may punish their elected representatives for going against the popular will.[46] This threat is more clearly present if the representative organs do not follow the policy preferences of the voters and disregard the results of the popular vote. However, the threat of losing votes can also be present if the representative organs prevent voters from voicing their policy preferences at the polls, especially if the initiative has already gathered support.

The dependence of the elected representatives on voters is also mentioned in the arguments of the Croatian Constitutional Court about the impartiality of the Croatian Government, although in support of balanced decision-making. The Court stated that the 'possibility of losing the citizens' trust through democratic elections deters arbitrary action'.[47] It may be true that the fear of retaliation at the elections reduces the chance that the elected representatives arbitrarily refuse the authorization of referendum proposals. However, this argument does not take into account that the lenient approach towards legal limits can lead to a situation in which the legal limits do not fulfill their functions, which also introduces uncertainty and arbitrariness to the referendum authorization system. The legal limits cannot fulfill their function of protecting individual rights, public interests, and the rule of law. For instance, the Swiss parliamentary practice regarding the application of the unity of substance requirement shows that virtually any topic can be bundled together with another, because there is always a level of abstraction at which they are connected. Energy tax can thus be connected to social security contributions,[48] inheritance tax to pension funds,[49] and immigration to foreign aid for birth control.[50] The principle of *in dubio pro populo* ensures that unless there is a clear violation of the legal limits, the referendum proposal must go forward.[51] The interpretation of legal limits such as the unity of substance requirement always involves some

---

[46]   Ibid 180–181.

[47]   Decision of the Constitutional Court of the Republic of Croatia No. U-VIIR -3260/2018 of 18 December 2018, Official Gazette. 8/2019, 183, para 10.3 (DeepL Translator).

[48]   Decision of the Federal Assembly on the citizens' initiative 'For a guaranteed old age-, widows- and orphans insurance – impose a tax on energy, not work!', Official Gazette, BBl 2001 2883.

[49]   Decision of the Federal Assembly on the citizens' initiative on the inheritance tax reform, Official Gazette, BBl 2014 9677.

[50]   Decision of the Federal Assembly on the citizens' initiative to 'Halt overpopulation – Preserve the natural environment' (Ecopop), Official Gazette, BBl 2014 5073. See also Moeckli, 'Die Teilungültigerklärung und Aufspaltung von Volksinitiativen' (Ch 4, n 87) 580.

[51]   Biaggini (Ch 1, n 12) 329–330.

level of discretion and the violation of this requirement is never completely clear, thus there is always a possibility to validate the proposal.

Regarding the strategic conflict of interest, the timing of the authorization procedure might also matter, because the more citizen support the referendum proposal gathers, the more reluctant the state institution might be to invalidate the proposal.[52] The Council of Europe member states all use pre-vote review procedures, while post-vote review is typical in the United States.[53] Reviewing the initiatives even before the initiators start collecting the signatures ensures that the initiators do not have to go through the signature collection campaign in vain. However, it can unnecessarily burden the state institutions if the initiators can register any number of questions without showing popular support.

If the authorization procedure follows the signature collection, then it can disrupt an already ongoing process of gathering citizen support and upset the expectations of the voters to be able to decide the given issue. This was the reasoning of the Government of Liechtenstein for changing the timing of the review: before changing the law, the substantive validity of the initiative was only determined after the signatures had been collected, which was often met with little understanding from the initiators in the event of an invalidation.[54] For this reason, in Liechtenstein, the initiatives are now checked for their conformity with the Constitution and international treaties before the signatures are collected.[55] In contrast, by only checking initiatives after the signature collection has been concluded, the reviewing state institutions can avoid checking initiatives with only marginal support, thus reducing the burden of deciding large number of requests. This reasoning appears in a Swiss parliamentary commission's report on the possible reform of the referendum authorization: 'it was not considered appropriate to carry out the time-consuming process of checking validity for popular initiatives which had not yet come into being and which were perhaps only supported by individuals'.[56]

In Slovenia, the timing of the authorization has been specifically challenged in the defense of marriage referendum case, as the National Assembly decided

---

[52]   Michael (Ch 1, n 103) 1233–1234.

[53]   James D. Gordon III, David B. Magleby, 'Pre-Election Judicial Review of Initiatives and Referendums' (1989) 64 *Notre Dame Law Review* 298, 305; Noyes (Ch 1, n 102) 99.

[54]   Government Proposal, BuA no. 2004/79 para 2.1.

[55]   Ibid.

[56]   Report of the Political Institutions Committee of the Council of States, Official Gazette, BBl 2015 7099, 7111 (DeepL Translator).

about the admissibility of the referendum while the signature collection was still in progress. In deciding the appeal, the Constitutional Court stated that:

> the reason for the possibility of the National Assembly deciding to reject a request to call a referendum already in the phase of collecting signatures follows from the fact that the laws regarding which a referendum is inadmissible in accordance with the second paragraph of Article 90 of the Constitution protect important constitutional values (i.e. the defense of the state, security, or the elimination of the consequences of natural disasters), ensure fundamental tax and financial bases, as well as sources for financing the state, enable the implementation of the state budget, or eliminate unconstitutionalities in the field of human rights and fundamental freedoms or any other unconstitutionalities. As regards the objectives pursued by these laws, it is necessary to enable any doubts regarding the constitutionality of decision-making in a referendum to be resolved as soon as possible, and hence to enable the legislative procedure in the broader sense to be completed as promptly as possible, which leads to the final decision whether a certain law that the National Assembly has already adopted should enter into force.[57]

According to the Court, allowing an admissibility decision even before the signature collection is also favorable for the voters, because:

> it is not reasonable to wait for the petition to also become a request formally (and hence to delay the entry into force of the law) if it is manifest already in that phase that subsequently it will not be admissible to put the question at issue to the same target population.[58]

The parliaments in Slovenia and Lichtenstein carry out the substantive authorization procedures before the initiative has gathered support, while in Switzerland and Croatia the signatures must be collected in advance of the authorization procedure. This latter practice may contribute to the reluctance for invalidating popular initiatives. Nonetheless, the difference in the rejection rates is not significant between states where authorization procedures precede signature collection *vis-à-vis* states where signature collection takes place first: each of the four parliaments has invalidated fewer than four referendum proposals.

3.3 State Practices Alleviating the Potential Bias

Overall, the impartiality of parliaments and governments is not frequently challenged in practice and there is no evidence to suggest partiality on the side

---

[57] Decision No. U-II-1/15 of 28 September 2015 of the Constitutional Court, Official Gazette Republic of Slovenia No. 80/15, para 38 (Official English translation).
[58] Ibid para 39 (Official English translation).

of these organs. Nonetheless, the principle of impartiality also requires that the decision-maker *appears* to be unbiased.[59] A claim can be made that there is a potential ideological and strategic conflict of interest in parliamentary and governmental referendum authorization that is not present for other state institutions. The lenient approach toward citizen-initiated referendums suggests that the strategic conflict is more often present, but it does not conclusively prove any partiality. Still, comparatively, these elected organs appear the least unbiased among the authorizing state institutions.

Arguably, the potential bias could be resolved through oversight by voters. If a parliament's actions are biased and it consistently blocks citizen-initiated referendums from reaching the polls, such actions can have political consequences at the next elections. Practice shows that parliaments indeed follow a lenient approach in referendum authorization and invalidate few citizen-initiated referendums. Thus, accountability to voters can promote the exercise of popular sovereignty but does not contribute to the enforcement of legal limits.

One solution for reaching a better balance between popular sovereignty and the rule of law is to involve experts in the decision-making process. The involvement of experts or even courts in the process not only can alleviate the appearance of bias, but also supplements the professional competencies of these bodies. Policy-makers such as parliaments are political bodies that may not have the necessary legal expertise to decide whether a citizen-initiated referendum is in violation of legal limits.[60] Just as courts may rely on experts to supplement their legal expertise, political bodies could also rely on legal experts when deciding referendum authorization cases.

One such example is Liechtenstein where, during the authorization of a popular initiative about pension reform, the government relied on an expert opinion to assess the constitutionality of the initiative.[61] The initiative proposed modifications to the government bill on the state's occupational pension plan. The government noted that it had commissioned experts to review the constitutionality of the government bill before its adoption. Likewise, it involved two experts to provide an opinion on the constitutionality of the initiative. The expert opinion was attached to the Government Proposal and made available to the public.[62] In analyzing the constitutionality of the initiative, the government relied exclusively on the expert opinion. The reasoning only repeated the con-

---

[59] Bayles (n 1) 23; McIntyre (n 1) 183.
[60] Keller, Lanter, Fischer (Ch 1, n 12) 123.
[61] Government Proposal, BuA no. 2013/85 para 2.3.
[62] Government Proposal, BuA no. 2013/85 'Grüner Teil'. See <https://bua.regierung.li/BuA/default.aspx?nr=85&year=2013&backurl=modus%3dnr%26filter1%3d2013>, accessed 15 March 2022.

clusions of the opinion that the proposed reduction of pensions granted before 2009 violated the vested rights and contradicted the principle of equality, while the cuts envisaged by the initiative were constitutionally questionable.[63] Based on this assessment, the government came to the conclusion that the initiative was not compatible with the Constitution and advised the Parliament to declare it null and void.[64] The Parliament took note of the Proposal and refused to authorize the initiative, but the decision was later overturned by the State Court.[65]

Slovakia and Croatia involve the constitutional courts as 'experts' in the authorization procedures. In both Slovakia and Croatia, the constitutional court review is an optional part of the first instance substantive authorization procedure, by the President or by the Parliament, respectively.[66] In these states, the President or the Parliament can initiate the judicial procedure before deciding about authorization. Thus, the constitutional courts act more as expert bodies than appellate courts. In the Slovak defense of marriage case, the President voiced concerns about the constitutionality of the popular initiative in its referral to the Constitutional Court.[67] The President argued that the questions may fall under the substantive limit on holding referendums regarding fundamental rights and freedoms, especially if this limitation is interpreted in light of the international law obligations of Slovakia.[68] The President also disputed the vagueness of some of the questions.[69] The Constitutional Court ruled that the first, the second and the fourth questions were in line with the Constitution,

---

[63]   Government Proposal, BuA no. 2013/85 para 2.3.
[64]   Government Proposal, BuA no. 2013/85 para 2.6.
[65]   Judgment 2013/183 of 28 February 2014 of the State Court.
[66]   Slovakia: Art. 95(2) Constitution; Croatia: Art. 95 Constitutional Law on the Constitutional Court of the Republic of Croatia.
[67]   Decision PL. ÚS 24/2014 of 28 October 2014 of the Constitutional Court, para 3. The questions were: (1) Do you agree that no cohabitation of persons other than a union between one man and one woman could be named marriage? (2) Do you agree that neither same-sex couples nor groups shall be allowed to adopt children and subsequently raise them? (3) Do you agree that no other cohabitation of persons than marriage should be granted special protection, rights and duties which are only granted to marriage and married couples by standards as of 1 March 2014 (especially acknowledgement or registration as a life partnership at a public authority, possibility to adopt a child by the second husband/ wife of a parent)? (4) Do you agree that schools should not require participation of children in classes dedicated to sexual behavior or euthanasia if their parents or the children themselves do not agree with the content of the lessons? See also Kamil Baraník, 'Slovakia' in Daniel Moeckli, Anna Forgács, Henri Ibi (eds), *The Legal Limits of Direct Democracy* (Edward Elgar Publishing 2021) 183.
[68]   Ibid.
[69]   Ibid para 7.

while the third question was in violation of it.[70] As a consequence, the President announced the referendum on three questions.[71] A striking difference in involving a constitutional court in the procedure as opposed to commissioning experts is that the decisions of constitutional courts have binding force. The primary decision-maker is not able to disregard them. Thus, the role of constitutional courts in these procedures is more akin to a co-decider than an organ providing expert evidence. This is even clearer in the case of Croatia, where the Constitutional Court expressly forbids the calling of the referendum if it finds it unconstitutional. Even though the Parliament reaches the final decision, it cannot disregard the decision of the Court. Regarding the initiative about minority language rights and the initiative on the prohibition of privatization, the Court explicitly stated that the Parliament 'is not allowed to call a referendum on the proposed referendum issue'.[72] This solution provides legal expertise for the political bodies and ensures that no bias can be attributed to the decision-making. However, it also pushes the responsibility for the decision onto the Constitutional Court.

4.   THE INDEPENDENCE OF ELECTION COMMISSIONS AUTHORIZING REFERENDUMS

Election commissions are election management bodies that oversee organizational and supervisory tasks during elections and referendums.[73] As part of their supervisory powers, election commissions must ensure the legality of different voting events. This may entail both the protection of individual rights and the protection of the legal order. They provide remedies for voters and other interested parties (e.g. political parties) at the different stages of the voting process. At the same time, election commissions ensure that the voting event and the establishment of the results are carried out in line with the legal provisions.[74]

Their decisional competences are most akin to administrative decision-making: they unilaterally decide individual legal disputes and their decisions

---

[70]   Ibid paras 110–114.

[71]   Decision of the President of the Slovak Republic of November 2014 on calling a referendum, Collection of Laws 320/2014.

[72]   Decision of the Constitutional Court of the Republic of Croatia No. U-VIIR-4640/2014 of 12 August 2014, Official Gazette 104/14 and Decision of the Constitutional Court of the Republic of Croatia No. U-VIIR-1159/2015 of 8 April 2015, Official Gazette 43/2015, 887 (Official Translation).

[73]   Wall et al. (Ch 2, n 19) 5–6.

[74]   M. Pal, 'Electoral Management Bodies as Fourth Branch of Government' (2016) 21(1) *Review of Constitutional Studies* 85–114, 86.

are binding on the parties.[75] They are almost never the final instance of decision-making, as – similarly to administrative decision-making – judicial remedies are provided against their decisions. Election commissions and other election management bodies may be part of the state administration, as most tasks they conduct are administrative in their nature. However, they usually entail more independence than most administrative authorities and are outside the hierarchical system of government agencies.[76] Some even argue that election commissions are independent institutions that constitute a separate branch of the government.[77]

Election commissions usually do operate with a high degree of independence from the other branches of government, as their core function is to protect the political process and democracy. However, these commissions often provide representation for the political parties. This ensures the participation of (some of) the interested parties in the decision-making but can undermine their political independence. As collegial bodies, their members are either delegated from political parties or elected by other state institutions. Their independence from politics is highly dependent on their composition and their position within the state organization.[78] Regarding the composition of election commissions, the Revised Code recommends that the commission should include at least one member of the judiciary or other independent legal expert.[79] The Code also highlights the independence of central election commissions.[80]

4.1 Composition of Election Commissions

In both Hungary and Latvia, referendum authorization is an exclusive competence of the central election commissions. These central election commissions are permanent entities, with members elected for at least one parliamentary term. In Latvia, the term of the Central Election Commissions lasts four years, and a new Commission must be set up after each parliamentary election.[81] In Hungary, the legal rules governing the National Election Commission since 2013 have increased the term of the Commission from four to nine years.[82]

---

[75] Strauss (Ch 4, n 24) 51; Craig, *Administrative Law* (Ch 4, n 24) 335; De Falco (Ch 4, n 24) 8.

[76] Wall et al. (Ch 2, n 19) 7.

[77] Denis Baranger, Christina Murray, 'Systems of Government' in Mark Tushnet et al. (eds), *Routledge Handbook of Constitutional Law* (Routledge 2013) 82; Pal (n 74) 85–114.

[78] Pal (n 74) 91.

[79] Revised Code, II.4.1.d.

[80] Ibid.

[81] Art. 1 Law on the Central Election Commission.

[82] Art. 20(1) Act XXXVI of 2013 on Electoral Procedure.

This could signal a greater independence, but the longer term is rather a sign that the current parliamentary majorities intend to determine the composition of the Commission for further elections. In both selected states, the parliaments elect the members of the election commissions. In Latvia, the chairperson along with seven out of the nine members of the Commission are elected by the Saeima. In addition, there is one judge member in the Commission elected by the Supreme Court. In Hungary, all the members are elected by the National Assembly on the proposal of the President. The selection of the candidates is left entirely to the discretion of these political institutions. The election of the members requires the votes of two-thirds of the members of the National Assembly present, thus in theory a wider political consensus is mandated.[83] This, however, is not a guarantee for non-partisan selection, as one party can possess the necessary majority.

The elected members of election commissions are often supplemented by delegated members who represent political parties. This ensures that the political parties can oversee the functioning of the election commissions in election matters and participate in the decision-making. The multiparty representation in election commissions also guarantees that the parties function as watchdogs over each other.[84] The Latvian Central Election Commission consists only of elected members,[85] while a mixed membership is a requirement in Hungary. The seven elected members of the National Election Commission are supplemented by delegated members representing all political parties that have a political group in the National Assembly.[86] Before the elections, the nominating organizations putting forward national candidate lists for general elections or European Parliament elections can also delegate members.[87] The balance between these two groups can determine whether the decision-making of the Commission is politically influenced. Hungary is an interesting example of unbalanced decision-making. For instance, 23 organizations put forward a national candidate list at the last general elections in 2018, which meant that 23 organizations gained the right to delegate a member to the National Election Commission. Nonetheless, this lack of balance lasts only for a couple of weeks before each election. It can also be argued that the partisan members – regardless of the numbers – are usually delegated by parties representing different political agendas, so they do not express a single political influence over the other members.

---

83   Art. 20(2) Act XXXVI of 2013 on Electoral Procedure.
84   Wall et al. (Ch 2, n 19) 110.
85   Art. 2 Law on the Central Election Commission.
86   Art. 27(1) Act XXXVI of 2013 on Electoral Procedure.
87   Art. 27(2)–(3) Act XXXVI of 2013 on Electoral Procedure.

4.2   Challenges to the Independence of Election Commissions

Even though it does not have any political delegates, the independence of the Latvian Central Election Commission was challenged in the authorization procedure of the Russian citizenship initiative. The initiative aimed to provide automatic Latvian citizenship to all 'non-citizens'.[88] The Central Election Commission refused to authorize the referendum, concluding that the proposal had not been fully elaborated and did not fit into the Latvian legal system.[89] The main argument of the Commission was that a new citizenship law would violate the principle of state continuity enshrined in the Latvian Constitution. The continuity of the state presupposes the continuity of citizenship that cannot be arbitrarily enlarged.[90] The Commission decision was challenged at the Supreme Court. According to the applicants, the Central Election Commission is not competent to assess the usefulness of the draft law or its compliance with the Constitution, as that would be contrary to the separation of powers principle under Article 1 of the Constitution. They argued that only the legislature has the authority to review a legislative initiative.[91]

The Supreme Court cited an earlier decision of the Constitutional Court which held that even though – at the time of that case – there had been no clear legal provisions establishing the referendum authorization competence of the Central Election Commission, it was a constitutional requirement that at least one public authority reviews the compliance of initiatives with the constitutional requirements.[92] Based on the earlier decision of the Constitutional Court, this competence belongs to the Commission, which has to assess whether the draft law is 'fully elaborated' in the meaning of Article 78 of the Constitution.[93] However, the extent of this competence, especially the Commission's authority to evaluate the constitutionality of an initiative, raised doubts in the Supreme Court, thus it turned again to the Constitutional Court. The Supreme Court argued that since eight out of the nine members of the Commission are elected by the Saeima, the legislature can indirectly influence decisions on citizens' initiatives. The allocation of such significant competence to the Central

---

[88]   Jarinovska (Ch 3, n 61) 155–157.

[89]   Decision No. 6 of 1 November 2012 of the Central Election Commission, Official publication No. 2012/175.7.

[90]   Ibid para 20. See also Ijabs (Ch 3, n 70) 305.

[91]   Judgment No. SA-1/2013 of 11 February 2013 of the Supreme Court paras 3.1–3.2.

[92]   Ibid para 24, citing Judgment No. 2012–03–01 of 19 December 2012 of the Constitutional Court, Official publication No. 2012/200.22, para 19.2.

[93]   Judgment No. 2012–03–01 of 19 December 2012 of the Constitutional Court, Official publication No. 2012/200.22, para 19.3.

Electoral Commission may have an inappropriate effect on the legislative role of voters as well as on the Saeima in the implementation of referendums.[94] The Supreme Court agreed with the applicants that the Saeima should review legislative initiatives. Consequently, it stayed the remedy procedure and initiated the legislative review procedure of the Constitutional Court over the competence of the Commission.

In its decision, the Constitutional Court noted that:

> pursuant to Section 1 of Law on the Central Election Commission, the CEC [Central Election Commission] is established following each Saeima election. The composition of the CEC reflects the range of political parties, which the majority of citizens with the right to vote had wished to see as their representatives. Moreover, the CEC in its activities must comply with the Satversme [Constitution] and other regulatory enactments. However, it must also be taken into consideration that the draft laws submitted by electors at the specific moment might not comply with the programs or political priorities of the political parties represented in the Saeima.[95]

Interestingly, this line of argumentation ended here, and the Court continued to elaborate on the importance of civic participation in the legislation without actually settling the question of independence. At the end of the reasoning, the Court circled back to the question of independence and suggested that the judicial review is important exactly for the reason that the Commission may not be neutral: 'since the CEC, possibly, is not politically totally neutral, it is only reasonable that its decision is examined by court, which examines all issues with utmost political neutrality'[96]. In the end, the Constitutional Court found that the composition of the election commission would not compromise its ability to fulfill its constitutional role.[97]

Although the rejection rates do not serve as conclusive proof of independence, the practice of the Latvian Central Election Commission shows a balance in the number of authorized and rejected citizen-initiated referendums: the data available on the website of the Commission shows that since 2012 only 13 initiatives have been rejected, while 20 have been authorized.[98]

The independence of the Hungarian National Election Commission has not been questioned in an individual case. The Office for Democratic Institutions and Human Rights (ODIHR) of the Organization for Security and

---

[94]   Judgment No. SA-1/2013 of 11 February 2013 of the Supreme Court para 29.
[95]   Judgment No. 2013–06–01 of 18 December 2013 of the Constitutional Court, Official publication No. 2013/250.67, para 14.1 (Official English translation).
[96]   Ibid para 15.4 (Official English translation).
[97]   Ibid para 15.4.
[98]   The decisions are available at <https://www.cvk.lv/lv/iniciativas/veletaju -iniciativas>, accessed 15 March 2022.

Co-operation in Europe (OSCE) published a report following the 2018 general elections, which indicated that the lack of consultation regarding the nomination and appointment of the members of the National Election Commission detracts from the overall trust in the election administration.[99] Nevertheless, the Report also acknowledged that the appointment procedure for the National Election Commission offers 'a reasonable basis for an independent and impartial election administration' and that the election commissions 'fulfilled their mandates and managed the elections in a professional and transparent manner at all levels'.[100]

The National Election Commission consistently rejects initiatives submitted by citizens, but this trend started in 2006–07, when the number of initiatives per year rose tenfold. While the average number of initiatives submitted during the 2002–06 parliamentary term was only 100 per term, between 2006 and 2010 this number reached 1022 per term and has been around 500 in the last two terms.[101] The influx of initiatives by citizens has resulted in a more searching review of the already existing legal limits, which continues in the present practice.[102] The National Election Commission is more rigorous than its predecessor, the State Election Commission, which fulfilled the functions of the central election commission until 2013. The National Election Commission has only validated 4 per cent of the initiatives submitted since 2014. In contrast, the State Election Commission had a 12 per cent acceptance rate between 2006 and 2010, and 7 per cent between 2010 and 2013. Both the former and the current central election commissions have had a mixed composition of elected and delegated members. The differences lie in the term of the office and the election process of the members. The exclusion of opposition parties from the election of the members taken together with the increasing rejection rates might signal a bias. However, the higher rejection rate can also be unrelated to the composition changes. As the practice has developed and started to expand the scope of the limits, it is almost inevitable that the rejection rates

---

[99] Hungary Parliamentary Elections 8 April 2018 – ODIHR Limited Election Observation Mission Final Report. Warsaw, 27 June 2018, p 7. Available at <https://www.osce.org/files/f/documents/0/9/385959.pdf>, accessed 15 March 2022.

[100] Ibid pp 7–8.

[101] The statistical data on the number of initiated referendums is available (in Hungarian) at <https://www.valasztas.hu/documents/20182/305738/Statisztik%C3%A1k+az+elb%C3%ADr%C3%A1lt+n%C3%A9pszavaz%C3%A1si+kezdem%C3%A9nyez%C3%A9sekr%C5%91l.pdf/a0655454-ecd7-412f-ab08-8a23dc419f5e>, accessed 15 March 2022. The statistical data has not been updated since 2020. On the reasons behind the increased numbers see Pállinger (Ch 3, n 29) 17.

[102] János Mécs, 'Az egyértelműség követelménye az országos népszavazási kérdések hitelesítése során' (Jogi Tanulmányok, ELTE Állam-és Jogtudományi Kar Állam-és Jogtudományi Doktori Iskola, 2018); Forgács (Ch 3, n 32) 212–213.

have become higher and higher. The same practice can also be interpreted conversely: the aim to block more and more initiatives from opposition parties and citizens has led to the expansion of the legal limits.

In general, election commissions can be subject to political capture as their composition is – to some extent – dependent on parliaments or other political actors.[103] This threat is usually alleviated by the legal remedies available against election commission decisions.[104] Election commissions are almost never the final instances for referendum authorization. In most states – including Latvia and Hungary – the decisions of the central election commissions can be challenged in regular courts.[105]

5.   THE INDEPENDENCE OF COURTS AUTHORIZING REFERENDUMS

In all the selected states – except for Switzerland – constitutional or regular courts play a role in the referendum authorization procedure. Courts participate in the referendum authorization procedure mostly as appellate bodies.[106] One exception is Italy, where the Court of Cassation carries out the technical authorization and the Constitutional Court decides about the formal and substantive authorization of the referendum request as first and single instance.[107] Meanwhile, in Slovakia and Croatia, the constitutional courts are involved as 'expert bodies' in the referendum authorization procedures.[108] The courts involved in the referendum authorization procedures are all the highest courts in these states: either constitutional courts or supreme courts. In regular courts, the independence of the judges is ensured through a variety of institutional features that protect the individual judge and the judiciary from undue outside pressures,[109] while procedural rules (e.g. recusal rules) protect impartiality.

---

[103]   Pal (n 74) 91.

[104]   The ECtHR case law also suggests that the subsequent control of a judicial body with full jurisdiction can compensate for the potential partiality of the first instance decision. See *Crompton v the United Kingdom* App no 42509/05 (ECtHR, 27 October 2009) para 79; *Denisov v Ukraine* App no 76639/11 (ECtHR, 25 September 2018) para 65.

[105]   See Chapter 2, section 4.2.

[106]   See Chapter 2, section 4.1.

[107]   Uleri, 'Institutions of Citizens' Political Participation in Italy: Crooked Forms, Hindered Institutionalization' (Ch 1, n 82) 76–77.

[108]   Slovakia: Art. 95(2) Constitution; Croatia: Art. 95 Constitutional Law on the Constitutional Court of the Republic of Croatia.

[109]   John Bell, *Judiciaries Within Europe: A Comparative Review* (Cambridge University Press, 2006) 27; Macdonald, Kong (Ch 4, n 102) 833; Daniel Smilov, 'The Judiciary: The Least Dangerous Branch?' in Michel Rosenfeld and András Sajó (eds),

Constitutional courts may be less insulated from the other branches of government. In most European states the judges of the constitutional courts are elected by political institutions for limited terms, thus they fall outside the career system for regular judges.[110] They are more endangered by political attacks and attempts of political capture than regular courts.[111] However, none of the referendum authorization cases mentioned explicit concerns about the independence of any of these high courts.

Nonetheless, the independence of the Hungarian Curia warrants a closer look, as the independence of the Hungarian judiciary has been brought into question by multiple forums in the recent years.[112] A recurring issue is the wide discretionary competences of the head of the judicial administration (President of the National Office for the Judiciary), especially in appointment procedures.[113] This is a crucial issue for the judiciary as a whole. However, the Curia is outside the competences of the National Office for the Judiciary, thus the unbalanced powers of the president of the judicial administration do not affect the appointment process of supreme court judges and judicial leaders. Nevertheless, special appointment rules have recently been introduced also for the Curia, allowing the judges of the Constitutional Court to request their appointment to the Curia without the ordinary application procedure or previous judicial experience.[114] As the European Commission's 2020 Rule of Law Report points out, this change 'de facto increased the role of parliament in

---

Oxford Handbook of Comparative Constitutional Law (Oxford University Press 2012) 859–860.

[110] Comella (Ch 2, n 20) 39; Alec Stone Sweet, 'Constitutional Courts' in Michel Rosenfeld and András Sajó (eds), *Oxford Handbook of Comparative Constitutional Law* (Oxford University Press 2012) 824; Giacomo Delledonne, 'Appointing and Electing Constitutional Judges: An Evolving Comparative Landscape' in Martin Belov (ed), *The Role of Courts in Contemporary Legal Orders* (Eleven International Publishing 2019) 161.

[111] Comella (Ch 2, n 20) 39.

[112] Commission Staff Working Document, 2020 Rule of Law Report Country Chapter on the rule of law situation in Hungary, SWD(2020) 316 final (2020 Rule of Law Report) and Commission Staff Working Document, 2021 Rule of Law Report Country Chapter on the rule of law situation in Hungary, SWD(2021) 714 final (2021 Rule of Law Report); European Parliament Resolution 2017/2131(INL) of 12 September 2018 on a proposal calling on the Council to determine, pursuant to Article 7(1) of the Treaty on European Union, the existence of a clear risk of a serious breach by Hungary of the values on which the Union is founded [2019] OJ C 433, 66–85.

[113] European Parliament Resolution 2017/2131(INL) of 12 September 2018 para 12; 2020 Rule of Law Report para 3; European Commission For Democracy Through Law (Venice Commission) Opinion on Act CLXII Of 2011 on the Legal Status and Remuneration of Judges and Act CLXI of 2011 on the Organization and Administration of Courts of Hungary, CDL-AD(2012)001-e, para 25.

[114] Art. 3(4a) Act CLXII of 2011 on the Legal Status and Remuneration of Judges.

judicial appointments to the Curia',[115] because the judges of the Constitutional Court are elected by the National Assembly with a two-thirds majority. The 15 current judges of the Constitutional Court were all elected after 2010, during which time the Fidesz Government has only lacked the two-thirds majority for a brief three-year period between 2015 and 2018.[116] In addition, the eligibility criteria for serving as the President of the Curia have also been amended to sidestep the requirement of prior judicial experience. This has enabled the appointment of the new President in 2021: a former prosecutor and judge of the Constitutional Court.[117] The effects of these composition changes on the independence of the Curia will only be seen in the future.

However, another point from the 2020 Rule of Law Report is worth mentioning. The Report highlights that the judges and lawyers are subject to negative media campaigns in the state-owned and pro-government media outlets regarding individual decisions.[118] The negative portrayal of judges and lawyers has intensified in early 2020, although it is not entirely new. After the 2018 general elections, Prime Minister Viktor Orbán publicly criticized the election decision of the Curia that had invalidated votes arriving in irregular envelopes. He also 'publicly shamed the head of the electoral commission after it fined him for campaigning in kindergartens'.[119] This former head of the National Election Commission is now the Vice President of Curia and the head of one of the judicial panels deciding about referendum authorization procedures.[120]

Naturally, it is almost impossible to prove the effects of such informal pressures on single decisions. However, it is interesting to compare the authorization decision of the government-initiated migrant quota referendum with the practice of the National Election Commission and the Curia with regard to citizen-initiated referendums. The available statistical information shows that since 2014, the election commission has validated only 4 per cent of the initi-

---

[115]   2020 Rule of Law Report para 6.

[116]   Four of the 15 Constitutional Court judges were elected in 2016 and thus needed the support of the opposition. <http://hunconcourt.hu/current-members>, accessed 15 March 2022.

[117]   Viktor Z. Kazai, Ágnes Kovács, 'The Last Days of the Independent Supreme Court of Hungary?' (Verfassungsblog, 13 October 2020) <https://verfassungsblog .de/the-last-days-of-the-independent-supreme-court-of-hungary/>, accessed 15 March 2022.

[118]   2020 Rule of Law Report paras 5–6.

[119]   These instances are mentioned in the 2019 Freedom House report on Hungary: <https://freedomhouse.org/country/hungary/freedom-world/2019>, accessed 15 March 2022.

[120]   See the internal rules for the distribution of cases (in Hungarian) at <https://kuria -kozadatok.birosag.hu/sites/default/files/field_attachment/ugyelosztasi_rend_2022_01 _01_am_vegleges_0.pdf>, accessed 15 March 2022.

atives (17 out of 422), and the Curia has upheld the decisions of the election commission in 78 per cent of the cases.[121] Most of the initiatives are submitted by private individuals or political parties, with the exception of the 2016 quota referendum,[122] which was initiated by the government.

In the 2016 migrant quota referendum, the government proposed the question 'Do you want the European Union to be able to mandate the obligatory resettlement of non-Hungarian citizens into Hungary even without the approval of the National Assembly?' for a popular vote. The National Election Commission authorized the initiative, simply stating that it complies with the legal requirements laid down in the Fundamental Law and the Referendum Act.[123] Multiple voters challenged the decision. One argument of the parties challenging the quota decision was that the question did not even belong to the competences of the National Assembly. The government is allowed to take part in the EU decision-making procedures, and the National Assembly has no influence on EU decisions reached in the Council. The Curia laconically refused these arguments by stating that the legislative competences of the National Assembly are open toward any social relation and that the National Assembly can regulate any issue.[124]

In 2018, in a referendum case about joining the European Public Prosecutor's Office, the Curia emphasized that the decision to participate in the Council Regulation on the establishment of the European Public Prosecutor's Office[125] is left to the government as the main actor of the Council and is outside the scope of functions of the National Assembly.[126] A similarly restrictive interpretation of the positive scope of referendums had been adopted by the court in cases prior to the government-initiated referendum. In 2012, the Curia reviewed the question 'Do you agree that no football stadium should be built by 31 December 2014 in Felcsút using public funds?' The Curia held that

---

[121] The statistical data is available (in Hungarian) at <https://www.valasztas.hu/documents/20182/305738/Statisztik%C3%A1k+az+elb%C3%ADr%C3%A1lt+n%C3%A9pszavaz%C3%A1si+kezdem%C3%A9nyez%C3%A9sekr%C5%91l.pdf/a0655454-ecd7–412f-ab08–8a23dc419f5e>, accessed 15 March 2022.

[122] Andrew MacDowall, 'Voters back Viktor Orbán's rejection of EU migrant quotas' (Politico 2 October 2016) <https://www.politico.eu/article/hungary-referendum-eu-migration-viktor-orban/>, accessed 15 March 2022.

[123] Decision 14/2016 of the National Election Commission.

[124] Decision Knk.IV.37.222/2016/9 of the Curia para 38. The decision quoted Decision Knk.IV.37.807/2012/2 of the Curia which reached significantly different conclusions about legislative and executive power, see Chapter 7, section 4.

[125] Council Regulation 2017/1939 of 12 October 2017 on implementing enhanced cooperation on the establishment of the European Public Prosecutor's Office ('the EPPO') [2017] OJ L 283.

[126] Decision Knk.VII.37.942/2018/2 of the Curia.

the question falls within the powers of the executive and is thus outside the positive scope of referendums. According to the court, if this competence is understood to be a legislative competence, then any question can be interpreted as such, making this positive condition meaningless.[127] This line of argument is completely reversed in the migrant quota decision but then picked up again in the decision about the referendum on joining the European Public Prosecutor's Office. The deviation from previous practice does not conclusively prove the lack of independence of the Curia in deciding referendum cases. Nonetheless, it is telling about the subtle and informal pressures that a consistently restrictive practice completely breaks down for the government-initiated referendum.

This tendency to apply a more lenient approach to referendums initiated by the government as opposed to citizen-initiated referendums has continued recently when the Hungarian Government submitted five referendum questions about 'protecting children from the LGBTQ propaganda'.[128] The National Election Commission authorized all five questions, which were then challenged by citizens and opposition parties at the Curia. The Curia decided all questions separately, in different judicial panels. One question was rejected,[129] while in the four other cases the authorization decisions of the election commission were upheld.[130] The one rejection decision found that the referendum about prohibiting gender reassignment surgeries for minors would violate the right to human dignity, but the decision was later annulled by the Constitutional Court.[131] The other four decisions did not find any violation of the formal or substantive limits. One of the decisions – penned by the new President of the Curia – even emphasized that the referendum requests submitted by the government should not be assessed according to the same standards as citizen-initiated referendums.[132] The argument for the differentiation was that if the initiators of citizen-initiated referendums collect the necessary number of signatures, then the National Assembly is obliged to call the referendum. Meanwhile, in cases where the referendum is initiated by the

---

[127] Decision Knk.37.807/2012/2 of the Curia para III.5. See also Decisions Knk. VII.37.647/2018/2 and Knk.IV.38.258/2018/2 of the Curia.

[128] Gergely Szakacs, Anita Komuves, 'Hungarian election panel clears questions of LGBT referendum' (Reuters 30 July 2021) <https://www.reuters.com/world/europe/hungarian-election-panel-clears-questions-lgbt-referendum-2021-07-30/>, accessed 15 March 2022.

[129] Decision Knk.II.40.646/2021/9 of the Curia. The decision was later annulled by the Constitutional Court in Decision 33/2021. (XII. 22.) of the Constitutional Court, Official Gazette of the Constitutional Court 1/2022, 39.

[130] Decisions Knk.IV.40.645/2021/19, Knk.III.40.647/2021/18, Knk.III.40.644/2021/15, and Knk.IV.40.648/2021/23 of the Curia.

[131] Decision Knk.II.40.646/2021/9 of the Curia para 65.

[132] Decision Knk.IV.40.645/2021/19 of the Curia paras 30–31.

government (or the President), then the National Assembly can still veto the calling of the referendum (facultative referendum).[133] According to the Curia, this means that the court only has to reject government-initiated referendums that 'clearly and directly' violate the Constitution, otherwise it can leave the decision up to the National Assembly.[134] This interpretation completely disregards that the legal rules impose the same substantive and formal limits on all types of referendums and clearly place the competence to review the limits to the Curia. In addition, this solution also places the responsibility of deciding a legal dispute to a political organ, where the majority is aligned with the government requesting the referendum.

6.   CONCLUSIONS FROM THE STATE PRACTICE

The impartiality and independence of the decision-maker are principles that should guide the referendum authorization. State institutions that are constructed with guarantees that insulate them from politics are best to act and appear unbiased. Regular courts are best protected from undue outside influences, while governments and parliaments are the least well protected. These institutions usually consider a number of legal and non-legal reasons when adopting a policy decision.[135] Thus, the exclusion of political and other non-legal interests from decision-making seems more difficult to achieve in comparison to decisions made by courts or election commissions. In most European states, the independence of regular courts is ensured through a variety of institutional features that protect the individual judge and the judiciary from undue outside pressures. Election commissions stand in the middle. Even though they do not have competences in policy-making that could create a bias, their insulation from politics is highly dependent on the rules of their composition. In all selected states – and generally in Europe – the members of the election commissions are elected by political institutions, and it is conceivable that they are captured by these institutions. Constitutional courts can also be subject to political capture;[136] however, their lack of independence or impartiality has not been questioned in the referendum context.

A differentiation must be made between state institutions where political elements are necessary parts of the decision-making, such as parliaments or governments, and situations when state institutions that should be independ-

---

[133] Art. 8 Fundamental Law.

[134] Decision Knk.IV.40.645/2021/19 of the Curia para 33.

[135] Christmann, *Die Grenzen direkter Demokratie: Volkentscheide im Spannungsverhältnis von Demokratie und Rechtsstaat* (Ch 4, n 3) 156.

[136] Kim Lane Scheppele, 'Autocratic Legalism' (2018) 85(2) *The University of Chicago Law Review* 545, 550.

ent from political influences are compromised. In the latter case, the undue outside influence is a malfunction of the state institution, while in the former, the political considerations are not undue influences but belong to the normal functioning of the institution. Thus, the independence and impartiality of a decision-maker can be affected by factors that are inherently coded into the normal functioning of the state institution as well as by the malfunctioning of the institution. Here the analysis of independence and impartiality can only go so far to make a claim about how these principles apply in the normal function-ing of the state institution. The main argument is that in the normal functioning of state institutions, the independence and impartiality of the decision-making can be better ensured in courts and election commissions than in parliaments or governments. The concerns about the independence of the Hungarian Curia are mentioned only to provide a complete picture about the current challenges. However, the possible solutions to that situation require an entirely different analysis.

Based on the examples from the current practice, it seems that concerns about impartiality and independence are not prevalent in the referendum practice. Only two cases have raised such questions explicitly. Both the Croatian and the Latvian challenges to the competences of, respectively, the government and the Central Election Commission have raised structural issues. The Latvian appeal challenged the independence of the Commission based on its composition. The Croatian challenge was more dispute-specific, as it questioned the impartiality of the government based on its previously expressed support for the Istanbul Convention. Nevertheless, it is still connected to the structural question that referendums take away decisional competences from the governments and parliaments. In both challenges the normal functioning of these institutions was deemed biased by the initiators. One common feature of the Croatian and Latvian judgments is that both courts emphasize the importance of separation of powers and the oversight by other state institutions in relation to impartiality and independence. Even though the Croatian Constitutional Court refused to accept that a general disagreement in policy choices can result in a biased decision-making, it still laid emphasis on the importance of oversight by Parliament and the Constitutional Court.[137] Its Latvian counterpart also highlighted that the potential bias of the election commission can be countered if its decision is examined by a court.[138]

---

[137] Decision of the Constitutional Court of the Republic of Croatia No. U-VIIR -3260/2018 of 18 December 2018, Official Gazette. 8/2019, 183, para 10.4.

[138] Judgment No. 2013–06–01 of 18 December 2013 of the Constitutional Court, Official publication No. 2013/250.67, para 15.4.

Providing remedies against referendum authorization decisions is one common way to reduce the possibility of bias. A remedy ensures that a further state institution – in most cases an impartial and independent court – reviews the decisions that may have been influenced by non-legal interests. The mere existence of remedies can keep decision-makers from arbitrary decision-making. In addition, the availability of a remedy also increases the appearance of impartiality for the interested parties. In referendum authorization procedures, the decisions of governments and election commissions can be challenged in regular courts in almost every state.[139] In contrast, judicial remedies are less common against parliamentary or presidential decision-making.

Almost all selected states have devised a system for referendum authorization procedures that ensures the impartiality and independence of the decision-maker through institutional choices, the provision of remedies and/ or expert involvement. Italy distributes the referendum authorization competences between two judicial bodies, which possess high levels of independence in the constitutional system.[140] Hungary and Latvia entrust election commissions with elected experts (and, in the case of Hungary, delegated multiparty representatives) with decision-making. In addition, they also provide judicial remedies against these decisions. Within the realms of the normal functioning of these institutions, impartiality and independence do not pose a challenge. These state institutions are not dependent on the voters, and the referendums do not carve out issues from their competences. Parliaments, presidents, and governments are the most vulnerable to biased decision-making. In Slovenia and Liechtenstein, the threat of bias is alleviated by remedy rights against the parliamentary decisions. In Slovakia and Croatia, the involvement of the constitutional courts as co-deciding expert bodies provides a partial solution, because their participation depends on the decision of the Parliament, or the President. Meanwhile, Switzerland is the only state that has not devised any procedure for reducing the potential bias or appearance of bias of the Federal Assembly.

---

[139] See also in Chapter 2, section 4.2, and LIDD data dashboard > Explore data > By Instrument/Item > Theme: Substantive/Formal procedure on http://lidd-project.org/data/, accessed 15 March 2022.

[140] Gabriella Mangione, 'Presentation at the Conference: Brief Remarks on Referendums in Italy' (2018) 4(1) International Comparative Jurisprudence 7–16.

7.   Right to a reasoned decision

1.   DEFINING THE RIGHT TO A REASONED DECISION

By the provision of reasoning, the decision-maker articulates the thought process behind the decision and justifies the choice between alternative outcomes. The reasoning shows that the decision-maker decided rationally, basing the decision on reason and evidence.[1] In *legal* reasoning this means that 'the premises are matters of fact, law, and interpretation, and the conclusion is the proposition describing the decision in the case'.[2] Legal reasoning can be the subject of research from multiple angles. It is a prominent topic of legal theory and goes back to the core of our understanding of law and its functions.[3]

The present inquiry focuses on reasoning as a procedural guarantee for the participants and for the wider public. In legal adjudication, the reasoning proves the 'substantive reasonableness' of the decision, so that the decision-maker has considered all relevant facts and arguments, has not committed an error in legal interpretation, and has not abused its discretion.[4] The reasoning promotes the accountability of the decision-maker both toward the parties and toward the wider public.[5] The reasoning shows the parties that they have been heard and promotes the general acceptance of the decision.[6] The reasoning provides

---

[1]   T.R.S. Allan, 'Requiring Reasons for Reasons of Fairness and Reasonableness' (1994) 53(2) *The Cambridge Law Journal* 207–210; Mashaw (Ch 5, n 29) 54.

[2]   Michael S. Moore, 'The Plain Truth about Legal Truth' (2003) 26 *Harvard Journal of Law and Policy* 23, 25.

[3]   Ronald Dworkin, *Law's Empire* (Harvard University Press 1986); Joseph Raz, 'On the Autonomy of Legal Reasoning' (1993) 6 *Ratio Juris* 1; H.L.A. Hart, *The Concept of Law* (Oxford: Clarendon Press 1994); Neil MacCormick, *Legal Reasoning and Legal Theory* (Oxford University Press 1994); Robert Alexy, *A Theory of Legal Argumentation: The Theory of Rational Discourse as Theory of Legal Justification* (Oxford University Press 2010).

[4]   Allan (n 1) 207–210; Mashaw (Ch 5, n 29) 54.

[5]   Sophie Boyron, Wendy Lacey, 'Procedural fairness generally' in Mark Tushnet, Thomas Fleiner, Cheryl Saunders (eds), *Routledge Handbook of Constitutional Law* (Routledge 2013) 265; Mashaw (Ch 5, n 29) 41.

[6]   *Taxquet v Belgium* ECHR 2010-VI 145 para 91; *Magnin v France* App no 26219/08 (ECtHR, 10 April 2012) para 29.

transparency to the decision-making process and creates a reference for future practice. The right to a reasoned decision is in an instrumental relationship with other procedural guarantees: it provides the basis for appeals and other remedies.[7]

In this procedural understanding, the right to a reasoned decision requires that the decision-maker provides an account of the relevant facts, the procedural actions taken (e.g., a hearing), the applicable law, and the legal arguments for authorizing or refusing a referendum proposal. In order to fulfill its above-mentioned functions, the reasoning has to be detailed enough so that it can attest that the decision-maker has not misused its powers.

2.   RIGHT TO A REASONED DECISION IN REFERENDUM AUTHORIZATION PROCEDURES

Although the Revised Code of the Venice Commission is silent about the right to a reasoned decision, the provision of reasoning is an integral element of the right to a fair trial.[8] In referendum authorization procedures, the provision of reasons is necessary for two major reasons. On the one hand, reasoning is indispensable for the exercise of other procedural rights. On the other hand, the provision of reasons shows how the decision-maker exercised its discretion and limits the chance of arbitrary decision-making.

The initiators (and the voters) have a legal interest in the outcome of the procedure, thus giving them an account of the arguments behind the decision not only allows them to exercise their procedural rights but also pays respect to them. The reasoning proves that parties 'are treated respectfully, if formalistically, but, above all, they are listened to by a tribunal that ... is bound in some manner to attend to the evidence presented and to respond to the submissions that are made in the reasons it eventually gives for its decision'.[9] In this way the reasoning pays respect to the parties by taking them along the thought-process of the decision-maker and by reflecting on their arguments.

The reasoning is instrumental to the other procedural rights of the participants: the reasoning of the decision is the output that shows the result of the

---

[7]   Glaser (Ch 1, n 81) 529; Mashaw (Ch 5, n 29) 50.

[8]   *Taxquet v Belgium* ECHR 2010-VI 145 para 91; *Magnin v France* App no 26219/08 (ECtHR, 10 April 2012) para 29.

[9]   Allan (n 1) 207; Mark Elliott, 'Has the Common Law Duty to Give Reasons Come of Age Yet?' [2011] *Public Law* 56, 63; Waldron, 'The Rule of Law and the Importance of Procedure' (Ch 1, n 64) 347.

oral or written inputs by the parties.[10] The reasoning stands as proof that the arguments of the parties were considered and explains why the given decision was reached.[11] The reasoning thus shows the parties that the decision is rational, legitimate, and to be accepted.[12]

A reasoned decision is also indispensable for the exercise of remedy rights.[13] If the referendum proposal is invalidated, then the reasoning provides the basis for legal challenges. The parties can only successfully challenge the decision on its merits if the arguments for the decision are not kept secret. Without reasoning, the decision-maker provides only a declaration about the rights of the initiators and voters. Such a declaration could not be challenged in a remedy procedure because it would give nothing substantial to argue against.

Lastly, a right to a reasoned decision is also an integral part of impartial decision-making. It shows to the parties that all presented arguments were considered equally.[14] For the state institutions that face problems with the appearance of impartiality, such as parliaments, providing a reasoning for referendum authorization decisions is one way to improve transparency and to prove that legal considerations guided the decision instead of political ones.

Providing reasons is also crucial for showing that the exercise of discretionary powers was not arbitrary. The confinement of discretionary powers appears in the Revised Code. According to the Code, the appeal body must exercise its legally defined competence with 'limited discretion'.[15] As shown in the previous chapter, the review of most legal limits allows the state institution to exercise discretion in defining the scope of the limits. The reasoning provides the justification for choosing between the different legitimate options that the legal interpretation of the limits offers. This way, even if participation rights are not provided and referendum authorization is regarded as an abstract review, providing reasons for the authorization decision should be a compulsory part of the procedure.

---

[10]   René Wiederkehr, *Fairness als Verfassungsgrundsatz* (Bern: Stämpfli Verlag AG 2006) 21; Boyron, Lacey (n 5) 267.

[11]   *Taxquet v Belgium* ECHR 2010-VI 145 para 91; *Magnin v France* App no 26219/08 (ECtHR, 10 April 2012) para 29. See also Michael Fordham, 'Reasons: The Third Dimension' (1998) 3(3) *Judicial Review* 158–164; Giacinto della Cananea, *Due Process of Law Beyond the State: Requirements of Administrative Procedure* (Oxford University Press 2016) 63.

[12]   Le Sueur, 'Legal Duties to Give Reasons' (1999) 52 *Current Legal Problems* 150, 154–155; Elliott (n 9) 61.

[13]   *Hirvizaari v Finland* App no 49684/99 (ECtHR 27 September 2001) para 30. See also Clayton, Tomlinson (Ch 6, n 9) 162; P.D. Marshall, 'A comparative analysis of the right to appeal' (2011) 22(1) *Duke Journal of Comparative & International Law* 1, 41.

[14]   della Cananea (n 11) 62.

[15]   Revised Code II.4.3.a.

The reasoning in the individual cases also works as a reference for the future practice, regardless of whether the state has a legal system building on *stare decisis* or not. The availability of a reasoning promotes legal certainty through the creation of a consistent and stable interpretation of the legal limits.[16] The decisions published with detailed justifications guide the lower-level decision-making bodies as well as inform the wider public about the practice of the decision-maker, which aids citizens in planning and formulating initiatives. Generally, it increases the transparency of the referendum authorization procedure, which is a clear value in a democratic decision-making process,[17] especially if it concerns the exercise of popular sovereignty.

3. THE AVAILABILITY OF REASONING

The practice of the selected states shows that there are considerable differences in providing reasoning for referendum authorization decisions. There are distinctions between the different state institutions: courts and election commissions usually provide a more detailed reasoning for their referendum authorization decisions, while parliaments and presidents rarely provide a justification for their decisions. This difference might be due to multiple factors. One can be the difference between the availability of remedies: parliamentary and presidential decisions are, in most states, final. Thus, the understanding of the deliberation process is not vital for submitting an appeal and reviewing the first instance decision. An additional factor can be the difference in the core functions of the state institutions: the decision-making process of parliaments and presidents is not designed to adopt decisions with extensive reasoning, as opposed to election commissions and courts that produce reasoned decisions in the course of legal adjudication.

3.1   Parliamentary and Presidential Procedures

When referendum authorization procedures are entrusted to parliaments or presidents, then a legal obligation to provide a reasoning for the decision is not common. Accordingly, the justification for the validation or invalidation of the referendum proposal is rarely available to the public.

In Switzerland, the Federal Assembly does not provide any coherent reasoning for its decisions. Regardless of whether the decision is an authorization or a rejection, the parliamentary decisions only state whether the initiative is valid

---

[16]   Shetreet, 'Judicial Independence and Accountability' (Ch 6, n 2) 7.
[17]   Hoffmann (Ch 6, n 8) 121.

or not.[18] The Federal Council prepares a recommendation that reviews the compatibility of the citizen-initiated referendum proposal with the legal limits and provides the governmental position on the initiative.[19] Some of the reasons for the decision can be found in either the recommendation provided by the Federal Council or in the minutes of the parliamentary debate, but neither of these sources can reflect why the majority of parliamentarians voted to authorize or reject an initiative. The actual deliberation process of the Federal Assembly can only be deciphered from the minutes of the parliamentary debate.

One example is the so-called 'Ecopop' initiative, which aimed to limit immigration to Switzerland to no more than 0.2 per cent of the permanent resident population and at the same time provide international aid for birth control and family planning in developing countries. The initiative presented a challenge to the unity of substance requirement, which came up multiple times in the parliamentary debate. The minutes of the debate clearly illustrate the possible arguments for and against regarding the unity of substance requirement.[20] One standpoint was that the initiative had an inner logic, an inner consistency, and a single goal to have fewer people in the world, which – regardless of the rationality of the measures – bound the two proposals together and fulfilled the requirement of unity of substance.[21] According to the opposing views, the initiative created the impression that restricting immigration would have a positive ecological effect and would help counter the galloping global consumption of resources. The connection between the restriction of immigration and family planning was arbitrary, and absurd. If this was sufficient for the unity of substance, then – according to the opposers of validation – any two issues could fulfill the requirement.[22] Thus, the arguments centered around

---

[18] See e.g. Decision of the Federal Assembly on the citizens' initiative to 'Halt overpopulation – Preserve the natural environment' (Ecopop), Official Gazette, BBl 2014 5073, or Decision of the Federal Assembly on the citizens' initiative 'for a reasonable asylum policy', Official Gazette, BBl 1996 I 1355.

[19] See e.g. Recommendation about the citizens' initiative 'Halt overpopulation – Preserve the natural environment' (Ecopop) Official Gazette, BBl 2013 8693; Recommendation about the citizens' initiatives 'for a reasonable asylum policy' and 'against illegal immigration, Official Gazette, BBl 1994 III 1486. See also Biaggini (Ch 1, n 12) 329.

[20] National Council debate 2014 summer 6th session 10.06.14, Official Bulletin 2014, 951–962. The minutes of the parliamentary debate are available also at <https://www.parlament.ch/de/ratsbetrieb/suche-curia-vista/geschaeft?AffairId=20130086>, accessed 15 March 2022.

[21] National Council debate 2014 summer 6th session 10.06.14, MEP Andreas Gross, Official Bulletin 2014, 951.

[22] National Council debate 2014 summer 6th session 10.06.14, MEP Gerhard Pfister, MEP Marianne Streiff-Feller, MEP Silvia Schenker, Official Bulletin 2014, 952–962.

the question whether a distant connection between multiple topics was sufficient for the unity of substance requirement to be fulfilled.[23] However, these arguments are only visible if one reads the minutes of the sessions of both the National Council and the Council of States. The final parliamentary decision on the authorization of the referendum is very brief. It cites the text of the initiative, and states that following the recommendation of the Federal Council it is declared valid and that the Federal Assembly recommends the voters to reject the proposal.[24]

The lack of reasoning is even more striking in the rare cases when the Federal Assembly rejects the authorization of a citizen-initiated referendum. In 1996 the parliament rejected the authorization of a citizen-initiated referendum that aimed to introduce the automatic expulsion of asylum-seekers who had entered Switzerland illegally.[25] The parliamentary decision is structured similarly to decisions authorizing referendums: it contains the text of the referendum proposal and states that following the recommendation of the Federal Council the initiative is declared invalid and will not be voted on by the people. Thus, the parliamentary decision refers to the recommendation as reasoning, which indeed contains an analysis about the legality of the referendum proposal.[26] The Federal Council has proposed the invalidation of the initiative because it violated the mandatory provisions of international law by disregarding the *non-refoulement* principle.

The recommendation of the Federal Council is, however, not able to substitute for the reasoning of the final decision. The recommendation is a non-binding preparatory document. If the parliamentary decision follows the recommendation, it can be considered as a guidance document for the reasoning. However, it is not a proper substitute for the reasoning of the final decision, as it does not contain any considerations from the actual deliberation process, from the parliamentary debate. In addition, if parliament were to disregard the governmental recommendation, then the recommendation could not stand as reasoning and no coherent explanation would be provided either for the final decision or for the deviation from the recommendation. Similarly, the minutes of the parliamentary debate are not able to provide unified reasons for the decision, as they just reflect the various opinions of the members of

---

[23] See on this issue Chapter 4, section 3.2.

[24] Decision of the Federal Assembly on the citizens' initiative to 'Halt overpopulation – Preserve the natural environment' (Ecopop), Official Gazette, BBl 2014 5073.

[25] Decision of the Federal Assembly on the citizens' initiative 'for a reasonable asylum policy', Official Gazette, BBl 1996 I 1355. See also Keller, Lanter, Fischer (Ch 1, n 12) 126; Biaggini (Ch 1, n 12) 329–330.

[26] Recommendation about the citizens' initiatives 'for a reasonable asylum policy' and 'against illegal immigration', Official Gazette, BBl 1994 III 1486.

parliament. In addition, the legal arguments appear in fragments as part of the political debate but do not form a coherent justification for the decision.

Similarly in Croatia, the parliamentary decisions are not supported by reasons, or at least have not been in the past practice. However, the Parliament has not rejected a referendum proposal since the introduction of popular initiatives in 2000.[27] So far, the Parliament has either called the referendum or asked the Constitutional Court to evaluate the constitutionality of the referendum. In some cases, it has preempted the referendum request by adopting the proposal of the citizens.[28] In the case of the defense of marriage referendum, the Parliament first debated the initiative in its committees. The Committee on the Constitution, Standing Orders and Political System published a proposal,[29] which recommended that the referendum should be understood as the first step in the process of amending the Constitution without compromising the competence of the Parliament to decide about the adoption of constitutional amendments.[30] As an uninitiated response, the Constitutional Court issued a document titled 'Warning'[31] which details how referendums can only be interpreted as means of making final decisions about constitutional change. Pursuant to the Warning, the Parliament adopted a decision to call the referendum.[32] The decision to call the referendum does not contain any reasons, it only cites the question proposed for the referendum, the legal consequences of the vote, and the date of the vote.

In the case of the Vukovar initiative about minority language rights, which aimed to increase the threshold for the official use of the languages of national minorities,[33] the parliamentary deliberation is only traceable in the committee opinions and the minutes of the debate.[34] The Vukovar initiative was debated in the Committee on Human Rights and the Rights of National Minorities before the plenary debate. The Committee published a draft decision recom-

---

[27]   Čepo, Čakar (Ch 1, n 90) 27–48; Podolnjak, 'Croatia' (Ch 3, n 10) 161–162.

[28]   Podolnjak, 'Croatia' (Ch 3, n 10) 161–162.

[29]   Proposal of Decision 014-01/13-01/04 of 24 October 2013 of Committee on the Constitution, Standing Orders and Political System. Available at <https://www.sabor .hr/hr/radna-tijela/odbori-i-povjerenstva/prijedlog-odluke-odbora-za-ustav-poslovnik-i -politicki-sustav-8>, accessed 15 March 2022. See also Podolnjak, 'Croatia' (Ch 3, n 10) 159–160.

[30]   Ibid.

[31]   Warning of the Constitutional Court of the Republic of Croatia No. U-VIIR-5292/2013 of 28 October 2013, Official Gazette 131/2013, 2869.

[32]   Decision 014-01/13-01/03 of the Parliament on Calling a State Referendum, Official Gazette no. 134 of 9 November 2013.

[33]   Dudás (Ch 3, n 16) 126; Čepo, Čakar (Ch 1, n 90) 34.

[34]   Available at <https://www.sabor.hr/hr/prijedlog-odluke-u-povodu-zahtjeva-za -raspizivanje-drzavnog-referenduma-gradanske-inicijative>, accessed 15 March 2022.

mending the submission of the initiative to the Constitutional Court before the Parliament reached a final decision.[35] The Committee highlighted that a successful referendum restricting minority language rights would violate Croatia's commitment in the EU accession process to strengthen the protection of minorities, and 'numerous international documents'. The referendum proposal was then referred to the Constitutional Court, which decided that calling the referendum would violate the Constitution.[36] The Parliament did not prepare a separate reasoning for the rejection. As mentioned in relation to Swiss practice, the preparatory documents in the decision-making process along with the minutes of the debate may provide some guidance about the arguments but do not substitute for a coherent and final reasoning.

There is, however, one exception to parliaments reaching unreasoned referendum authorization decisions. The Slovene National Assembly is legally obliged to adopt a resolution about rejecting a referendum proposal and state the reasons for not calling the referendum.[37] For example, the parliamentary decision to reject the referendum on the Act Amending the Marriage and Family Relations Act (ZZZDR) is a decision with a detailed, 16-page-long reasoning.[38] This Slovenian defense of marriage referendum decision has a clear operative part, declaring the referendum inadmissible, then a short description of the factual basis, followed by the reasoning. In the reasoning, the National Assembly went into procedural issues such as the timing of the review. It cited a previous Constitutional Court decision which held that the parliament already has the competence to review the constitutionality of a referendum question during the collection of signatures.[39] On the substance of the initiative, the National Assembly relied on the legal standards established by the Constitutional Court for reviewing the legal limit on fundamental rights. The National Assembly reasoned that the legal act cannot be abrogated by a referendum, because it eliminates the discrimination against same-sex partners pursuant to the decisions of the Constitutional Court. According to

---

[35] See Proposal of Decision on the request for announcement of the state referendum of the citizens' initiative 'Headquarters for the defense of Vukovar' by the Committee on the Constitution, Rules of Procedure and the Political System. A press release is available at <https://www.sabor.hr/radna-tijela/odbori-i-povjerenstva/izvjesce-odbora-za-ljudska-prava-i-prava-nacionalnih-manjina-206>, accessed 15 March 2022.

[36] Decision of the Constitutional Court of the Republic of Croatia No. U-VIIR-4640/2014 of 12 August 2014, Official Gazette 104/14.

[37] Art. 21 (1) Referendum and Popular Initiative Act.

[38] Decision No. 005-02/15-1/27EPA 412 – VII of 26 March 2015 of the National Assembly on refusing to call a legislative referendum on the Act Amending the Marriage and Family Relations Act, Official Gazette of the Republic of Slovenia, No. 20/2015.

[39] Ibid.

the parliament, the legal act goes further than what the decisions of the Court necessitated and eliminates the discrimination based on sexual orientation in other fields as well (e.g. health care and health insurance, criminal procedure, etc.). The National Assembly underlined the need for such measures by giving an account of how discrimination based on sexual orientation has evolved since 1991. Finally, the National Assembly listed all the laws affected by the ZZZDR and described how discrimination against same-sex couples is eliminated in the different fields.[40]

Thus, the Slovene National Assembly adopted a judgment-like resolution containing legal arguments about the rejection of a referendum proposal. The legal reasons for rejecting the referendum request are somewhat blended into the reasons for adopting the legal act in the first place, but at least they are clearly mentioned. It must, however, be emphasized that in Slovenia the referendum authorization decision of the parliament can be challenged at the Constitutional Court, thus the reasoning is necessary to provide a basis for the appeal and the judicial decision. In contrast, in both Switzerland and Croatia the parliaments are the final instances of referendum authorization.

Presidential decision-making is even less reasoned and less transparent. In Slovakia, the work of the president is supported by a bureaucratic organization.[41] The preparatory work carried out by the Office of the President is not accessible to the public. The actual decision-making process of the president is also not transparent to anyone. The final decisions are published in the official journal and are made available to the public, but they do not reveal the deliberation.[42] The Slovak referendum authorization practice is comparable to that of Croatia in that the president can also refer the referendum proposal to the Constitutional Court for an opinion on its constitutionality. So far, the president has either approved the referendum request or referred it to the Constitutional Court, which makes it possible that the president has never had to adopt a rejection decision. The reasonings of the approval decisions only cite the referendum questions, state the ordering of the referendum, and set the date for the vote.[43]

---

[40]   Ibid.
[41]   Act on the Office of the President of the Slovak Republic, Collection of Laws no. 16/1993.
[42]   For example, Decision of the President of the Slovak Republic of November 2014 on calling a referendum, Collection of Laws 320/2014 (defense of marriage referendum), or Decision of the President of the Slovak Republic of 13 March 1997 on calling a referendum, Collection of Laws, 76/1997 (direct election of the president).
[43]   Available at <https://www.slov-lex.sk/vyhladavanie-pravnych-predpisov?text= referenda>, accessed 15 March 2022.

3.2   Election Commission and Judicial Procedures

Election commissions and courts communicate their decisions in individual cases by formulating resolutions and judgments. These decisions always contain an operative part, and reasoning that gives an account of the facts and the legal interpretation of the applicable legal provisions. The referendum authorization procedure is no exception: in all the selected states with these state institutions authorizing referendums, the decisions contain reasoning. There may be some variation in how approval decisions are reasoned, but the rejection decisions are always accompanied by a detailed legal justification.

In Hungary, the National Election Commission reaches the first instance decision in the form of an administrative act with an operative part and a reasoning. The Commission uses a clear structure for the reasoning. It first analyzes the fulfillment of the technical requirements regarding the submission of the question, then the compliance with substantive limits, and finally reviews the clarity of the question. In the rare cases when the Commission authorizes a referendum, it does not provide detailed reasoning but only states that the proposal is in line with the constitutional requirements.[44] In contrast, the Commission often bases its refusal decisions on multiple legal grounds. For example, the Commission refused to authorize the question 'Do you agree that someone who was elected prime minister two times shall not be allowed to be nominated again?' based on the violation of a substantive limit and the clarity requirement. The Commission held that a successful referendum would lead to the amendment of the Fundamental Law which belongs to the exclusive competence of the National Assembly. In the reasoning, it relied on a previous decision of the Curia which held that the introduction of a restriction on the reelection of the prime minister would intrude into the decision-making sovereignty of the parliament and would therefore require the amendment of the Constitution.[45] Regarding the clarity requirement, the Commission held that it is not clear whether the limitation would only apply to two consecutive governmental cycles or to two cycles in general.[46] At this stage of the referendum process, the Commission has to decide about the authorization of the referendum question without a claim limiting the scope of its review, so it is justified that the decision provides a reasoning for all grounds of inadmissibility.

In the case about term limits, the initiator of the referendum submitted an appeal to the Curia, but the court upheld the first instance decision.[47] The

---

[44]   E.g. Decision 14/2016 of the National Election Commission.
[45]   Decision 50/2017 of the National Election Commission para 11.
[46]   Ibid para 17.
[47]   Decision Knk.IV.37.393/2017/3 of the Curia.

reasoning of the Curia follows the classic tripartite structure of operative part, facts, and legal reasoning. In the operative part, the court first declared that the first instance decision of the election commission was upheld, then went on to describe the factual background of the case. In this part of the reasoning, the court cited the reasoning of the first instance decision and detailed the appeal of the initiator.[48] In the legal reasoning, the court first established that the initiator has legal standing to appeal the first instance decision. Then the Curia refuted the arguments of the initiator about the substantive limit on constitutional amendments by citing the previous practice of the Curia and elaborating on the constitutional position of the prime minister.[49] The court held that a successful referendum would distort the balance of the current parliamentary system and introduce a new requirement more common in presidential and semi-presidential systems.[50] According to the court, this new limit on the prime minister's term would require constitutional regulation, thus cannot be decided in a referendum.[51] As the court did not find a reason to overturn this part, it did not review the clarity question.[52]

Latvia provides a very similar picture. The Central Election Commission only provides reasons for rejection decisions. In decisions about registering referendum proposals, the Commission does not even present the text of the initiative and merely states that after getting acquainted with the draft law, the Commission establishes that it has been fully developed in terms of form and content.[53] The reason for the lack of reasoning can be traced back to the lack of remedies against approval decisions. Meanwhile, the rejection decisions of the Commission usually follow the form of an administrative act with an operative part and detailed reasoning.[54] Where the first instance rejection decisions can be appealed, the Senate of the Supreme Court decides in judgments with comprehensive legal reasoning.[55]

The Italian Constitutional Court also decides referendum authorization requests in reasoned decisions. The judgments are divided into a factual background, a legal reasoning, and an operative part.[56] Dissenting or concurring

---

48   Ibid paras 2–15.
49   Ibid paras 17–24.
50   Ibid para 21.
51   Ibid para 25.
52   Ibid para 32.
53   See for instance Decision No. 6 of 1 November 2012 of the Central Election Commission, Official Publication No. 2012/175.7.
54   Decision No. 1 of 3 January of 2020 of the Central Election Commission, Official Publication No. 2020/6.21.
55   Judgment No. SA-1/2013 of 11 February 2013 of the Supreme Court.
56   E.g. Judgment no. 49 of 2005 of the Constitutional Court, Official Gazette, 1st Special Series no. 5 of 2 February 2005.

opinions are generally not allowed to be published by the Court,[57] thus there is a single reasoning provided for the decision. Due to the strict deadlines in the Italian referendum process, the Court can decide in a single decision about all submitted referendum requests, but it provides separate rulings and reasonings for each request.[58] In 2012 the Constitutional Court decided about two citizen-initiated referendum requests that aimed to abrogate different elements of the election laws.[59] In the decision, the Court first listed the paragraphs that are the subject of the request, then elaborated on the facts of the case. The Court made reference to the procedural steps taken before and during its procedure, such as the results of the technical authorization at the Central Office of the Court of Cassation, the results of the signature collection, and the hearing held at the Constitutional Court with the representatives of the referendum committee. As part of the factual basis, the reasoning describes the submissions and the presentations of the parties.[60] The second part of the decision is the Court's legal reasoning. First, the Court stated that since both referendum requests relate to the same law, it is reasonable to bring the cases together and decide in a single judgment. Then, the Court went on to describe its judicial practice in relation to referendums initiated on election laws and stated that such referendum requests have to fulfill a double requirement: the questions submitted to voters have to be 'homogeneous and traceable to a rationally unitary matrix', and there must remain 'a coherent residual legislation, immediately applicable' in order to guarantee the functioning and continuity of the constitutional system.[61] Finally, the Court applied these legal standards and held that the referendum request about abolishing the whole legal act central to the election of the parliament violates the second requirement, while the referendum request abrogating only certain parts of the same legal act violates the clarity requirement. The Court also emphasized that neither solution would lead to the automatic revival of the previous election system as the initiators intended.[62] The reasoning ends with a separate operative part declaring the referendum requests invalid.

---

[57]   Katalin Kelemen, 'Dissenting Opinions in Constitutional Courts' (2013) 14(8) *German Law Journal* 1345–1371, 1345.

[58]   Ibi (Ch 3, n 41) 83.

[59]   Judgment no. 13 of 2012 of the Constitutional Court, Official Gazette, 1st Special Series no. 4 of 25 January 2012.

[60]   Ibid, Factual part, para 3.

[61]   Ibid, Legal reasoning, para 4 (DeepL translator).

[62]   Ibid, Legal reasoning, paras 5–6.

The formulation of the reasoning is similar in the practice of the constitutional courts in Liechtenstein, Croatia, and Slovakia.[63] In Slovakia and Croatia the judges opposing the majority decision can also elaborate their legal arguments in dissenting opinions,[64] which is a useful tool to learn about the arguments that have arisen during the decision-making process and to get a more well-rounded and balanced reasoning.

4.   THE SUFFICIENCY OF REASONING

Since I focus on the procedural aspects of referendum authorization, the content of the reasoning in individual cases – that is, the arguments and specific legal standards used by the state institution to authorize or reject a referendum proposal – is outside the scope of the analysis. Nonetheless, from a procedural standpoint a reasoned decision should be able to attest that the decision-maker has not abused its discretion. Thus, one question about the content of the reasoning warrants a closer look: whether sufficient reasons are provided when the state institution exercises discretionary powers.

Legal interpretation is not an exact science, thus a broader or narrower interpretation of legal limits is not problematic per se. It is also difficult to assess whether the decision-maker exercised its discretion within the permissible scope of the limits or whether it expanded the legal limits in an arbitrary way. However, in referendum authorization two instances can be identified where the exercise of discretionary powers should be accompanied by very thorough reasoning. The first is when the decision-maker deviates from the previous practice and interprets the legal limit differently. The second arises if the decision-maker deducts further, implicit legal limits from other constitutional principles or provisions. In all the selected states, the constitutions and referendum acts explicitly list those cases where the referendum is prohibited on formal or substantive grounds.[65] The consistent interpretation of these limits can cause challenges, and deviation from previous interpretations might raise concerns about legal certainty and the rule of law. An additional uncertainty

---

[63]   Liechtenstein: Decision 2013/183 of the State Court; Croatia: Decision of the Constitutional Court of the Republic of Croatia No. U-VIIR-1159/2015 of 8 April 2015, Official Gazette 43/2015, 887; Slovakia: Decision PL. ÚS 24/2014 of 28 October 2014 the Constitutional Court.

[64]   Slovakia: Art. 179 Act no. 314/2018 Coll. Act on the Constitutional Court of the Slovak Republic. See for example Decision PL. ÚS 24/2014 of 28 October 2014 the Constitutional Court. Croatia: Art. 27 (4) Constitutional Law on the Constitutional Court of the Republic of Croatia.

[65]   See Chapter 3, section 1.

can be introduced to the decision-making if the decision-maker prohibits referendums based on limits not explicitly listed.

In these instances, it is crucial that the decision-maker provides sufficient reasoning for the deviation from previous practice or for the introduction of implicit limits. In this part, I show some examples from the selected states both of deviation from the previous practice and of the introduction of implicit limits. Hungary will serve as an example of the deviation from previous practice, Italy and Slovakia of the introduction of implicit limits. Latvia could also serve as an example of this latter practice, because the Constitutional Court has interpreted the requirement to fully elaborate the referendum proposal to contain a number of substantive and formal limits.[66] However, Latvia is not analyzed here, because the Constitutional Court introduced the implicit limits in decisions about reviewing the referendum act and not as part of a referendum authorization procedure.

The question of whether sufficient reasons were provided is also a question of interpretation: it is not easy to assess what constitutes sufficient reasoning. Examining the following examples, I try to determine whether significant questions about the exercise of discretion have been left open in the reasoning.

4.1   Deviation from Previous Practice

The Hungarian example of the deviation from previous practice has already been mentioned in relation to the independence of courts. The Curia has deviated from its previous interpretation of legal limits in authorizing the government-initiated migrant quota referendum in 2016. In the authorization procedure one of the main questions was whether the issue belongs to the competence of the National Assembly.

The provision of the Hungarian Fundamental Law that requires referendums to be held about matters falling within the functions and powers of the National Assembly has been interpreted by the Constitutional Court as well as the Curia. Before the authorization competence was transferred to the Curia, the Constitutional Court had developed a consistent and lenient practice about this limit. According to the Constitutional Court, any national issue can be the subject of a referendum, as the powers of the National Assembly are complete and open.[67] The authorization competence was delegated to the Curia by the

---

[66]   Judgment No. 2012-03-01 of 19 December 2012 of the Constitutional Court, Official publication No. 2012/200.22, and Judgment No. 2013-06-01 of 18 December 2013 of the Constitutional Court, Official publication No. 2013/250.67.

[67]   Decision 53/2001 (XI. 29.) of the Constitutional Court, Official Gazette of the Constitutional Court 134/2001, 9425, and later Decision 46/2006 (X. 5.) of the Constitutional Court, Official Gazette of the Constitutional Court 10/2006, 754,

new constitution in 2011, and the court had already deviated from the practice of the Constitutional Court by 2012.[68] The election commission rejected the authorization of the question 'Do you agree that no football stadium should be built by 31 December 2014 in Felcsút using public funds?'[69] The question was submitted by opposition parties and it had symbolic importance, because it not only went against governmental plans to build new football stadiums all over the country, but it also targeted the stadium in Felcsút, which is the hometown of the Prime Minister. The Curia upheld the rejection decision of the election commission. The reasoning stated that the question belongs to the competence of the Government. According to the court, if all issues that belong to the competence of the Government were be interpreted as also belonging to the competence of the National Assembly, then the constitutional provision limiting referendums to issues falling within the functions of the National Assembly would become meaningless.[70] The Curia referenced the previous decisions of the Constitutional Court and emphasized that the previous practice is applicable, even after the adoption of the new Fundamental Law.[71] However, the Curia did not then provide any reasons for distinguishing the case from its predecessors, thus it has not established why the deviation from the previous practice is necessary. In addition, the Curia hinted that due to the nature of parliamentary democracy, the Fundamental Law does not clearly separate the competences of the Government and the National Assembly, thus the question of competence can only be decided on a case-by-case basis.[72] This way, the court has deviated from the previous practice without providing any meaningful reasons, and introduced a further element of uncertainty by failing to establish a legal standard for deciding future cases.

The Curia had to analyze the limit again in the decision about the government-initiated migrant quota referendum. The citizens who challenged the approval decision of the National Election Commission argued that the referendum aims to influence decision-making at the level of the European Union. The National Assembly has no competence to take part or approve the decision-making processes of the EU institutions, thus it is not clear what kind of legislative obligation would arise from a successful referendum.[73] The Curia rejected these arguments and held that the legislative competence of the

---

Decision 90/2008 (VI. 19.) of the Constitutional Court, Official Gazette of the Constitutional Court 6/2008, 893.

[68]   Decision Knk.37.807/2012/2 of the Curia.
[69]   Decision 93/2012. (XI. 16.) of the State Election Commission.
[70]   Decision Knk.37.807/2012/2 of the Curia para III.5.
[71]   Ibid para III.3.
[72]   Ibid para III.6.
[73]   Decision Knk.IV.37.222/2016/9 of the Curia paras 6, 13, and 16.

National Assembly must be considered open to any social relationship.[74] In the reasoning, the court emphasized that the parliament can decide to regulate any issue, even if the Government also has regulatory competences. The reasoning referred to the previous practice of the Constitutional Court. It also referenced the Felcsút stadium case but only to confirm that the Curia must decide on a case-by-case basis whether a given matter falls within the competence of the National Assembly.[75] The Curia did not provide any reasoning for why it abandoned its interpretation that the limit on the legislative competence would become meaningless if the parliament can freely decide to regulate any issue. Consequently, the court reverted back to the original practice, but again without providing sufficient reasoning.

The Hungarian practice shows that the lack of reasoning can contribute to the arbitrariness of the decision. The Curia does not provide any meaningful reasons for the deviation from the established practice or for the return to it. Stating that the limit must be evaluated on a case-by-case basis even acknowledges that the court does not even attempt to develop a legal standard and a consistent practice. It can be argued that the decision to authorize the government-initiated referendum was arbitrary, which is the reason why no proper reasoning could be given. The court wanted to serve the Government's interests and disregarded its prior practice, which could not be reasoned by legal arguments, only political ones.

4.2 Introduction of Implicit Limits

The Italian referendum authorization practice is an example of implicit limits playing a large role in the authorization procedure. Although the Constitution lists only three substantive limits, the Constitutional Court has relied on both additional substantive limits and implicit formal limits in authorizing referendums. The Constitutional Court established the implicit limits for abrogative referendums as early as in 1978.[76] In this judgment, the Court decided about the authorization of eight separate referendum requests regarding laws on the military penal code and the military judicial system; on party financing; on the treaty between the Holy See and Italy; on asylum; on the protection of public order; on prosecution; and on the criminal code.

The Court found that it would be too restrictive if its sole task was to verify whether a referendum request concerns matters that Article 75(2) of the

---

[74]   Ibid para 38.
[75]   Ibid.
[76]   Judgment no. 16 of 1978 of the Constitutional Court, Official Gazette, 1st Special Series no. 39 of 8 February 1978.

Constitution excludes from popular votes: tax and budget laws, amnesty and pardon, or laws ratifying international treaties.[77] The Court noted that its competence – according to the provisions of Constitutional Law no. 1 of 1953 and Ordinary Law no. 352 of 1970 – is to review the compatibility of the referendum request with Article 75(2) of the Constitution. However, according to its interpretation, this does not mean that this provision must be isolated, ignoring its links to the other components of the regulatory framework of abrogative referendums. The interpretative process must instead move in the opposite direction and the Court must establish whether other constitutionally relevant instances exist when an abrogative referendum must be ruled out.[78] The Court based the expansion of the limits on the need to protect other constitutional values beyond the list of prohibited subjects and listed four additional cases of inadmissibility.[79]

One implicit formal limit is that the referendum request must not contain such a plurality of heterogeneous questions lacking a rationally unitary matrix that would hinder the genuine manifestation of popular sovereignty.[80] The second implicit limit is that the referendum request must concern legislative acts having the force of ordinary laws and cannot aim to repeal the Constitution or constitutional laws.[81] The third limit prohibits the abrogation of 'ordinary legislative provisions with constitutionally binding content, the core of which cannot be altered or rendered ineffective without the corresponding provisions of the Constitution (or other constitutional laws) being affected'.[82] Lastly, when applying the explicit substantive limits of the Constitution, the Court must also exclude laws from the referendum that are closely linked to the expressly prohibited subjects.[83]

The Court referred only to the need of protecting other constitutional values in the referendum procedure, but otherwise no reasoning was provided for any of the four implicit limits. Thus, the decision does not make it clear whether these are the only implicit limits that can be deduced from the Constitution. It was also not explained why these four limits had been chosen to apply for referendum authorization. In this way the reasoning is not able to persuasively show that the choice of implicit limits has not been arbitrary.

The later practice of the Constitutional Court has relied extensively on these implicit limits, which has clarified both the scope and the aim of the limits. For

---

[77]   Ibid para 2.
[78]   Ibid.
[79]   Ibid para 3.
[80]   Ibid.
[81]   Ibid.
[82]   Ibid (DeepL Translator).
[83]   Ibid.

instance, the limit on changing the constitutionally binding content of legal acts appears in several referendum cases on election laws.[84] By abrogating only words, certain sentences, or smaller parts of the legal act, the partial abrogation can become akin to a proactive referendum.[85] After the abrogated parts disappear from the legal act, the remaining parts may have a completely different meaning than before. According to the later practice of the Court, the implicit substantive limit on abrogating the constitutionally binding content of the legal acts ensures that no regulatory vacuum occurs and it is always possible to hold elections.[86] Without this implicit limit, the elimination of election laws would affect fundamental constitutional principles and the functioning of fundamental state organs.[87] The gradual clarification of these principles through practice can reduce the chance of arbitrary decision-making, but only over time.

Lastly, the practice of the Slovak Constitutional Court serves as a further example for the introduction of implicit limits. The Court has a less extensive referendum practice than the Hungarian Curia or the Italian Constitutional Court: it only decided its second case of *ex ante* referendum review in 2021.[88] In this case, the Slovak Constitutional Court applied an implicit legal limit to block a citizen-initiated referendum. The Constitution only lists basic rights and freedoms, and taxes, levies, and the state budget as prohibited subjects of a referendum.[89] However, in the case of the early elections initiative, the Court invoked the *material core of the Constitution* as a limit on direct democracy.

In May 2021, petitioners initiated a referendum on ending the term of the current National Council and calling for early elections. The initiative was a response to the alleged failures of tackling the pandemic in Slovakia and gathered the support of more than 500,000 citizens.[90] The President received the petition and initiated the procedure of the Constitutional Court to review the constitutionality of the initiative. The Court held that the initiative as in

---

[84]   Judgment no. 47 of 1991 of the Constitutional Court, Official Gazette, 1st Special Series no. 6 of 2 June 1991, Judgment no. 5 of 1995 of the Constitutional Court, Official Gazette, 1st Special Series no. 3 of 18 January 1995, and Judgment no. 26 of 1997 of the Constitutional Court, Official Gazette, 1st Special Series no. 7 of 12 February 1997.

[85]   Pier Vincenzo Uleri, 'On Referendum Voting in Italy: YES, NO or Non-Vote? How Italian Parties Learned to Control Referendums' (Ch 3, n 35) 868.

[86]   Ibi (Ch 3, n 41) 76–77.

[87]   Judgment no. 16 of 1978 of the Constitutional Court, Official Gazette, 1st Special Series no. 39 of 8 February 1978. See also Ibi (Ch 3, n 41) 76–77.

[88]   The first one was the defense of marriage referendum in 2014 (Decision PL. ÚS 24/2014 of 28 October 2014 the Constitutional Court). See also Drugda (Ch 3, n 115).

[89]   Art. 93(3) Constitution.

[90]   Drugda (Ch 3, n 115).

violation of the Constitution.[91] The reasoning stated that when people exercise their power directly, they act as lawmakers and are bound by the same constitutional restrictions as the legislature. In this regard, the Court highlighted that the material core of the Constitution cannot be amended by either the representative government or the people. According to the Court, the early election initiative violates the principles of both rule of law and separation of powers as part of the material core of the Constitution. The Court stated that the generality of laws as an integral part of the rule of law is violated if a referendum is allowed on a specific event such as ending the term of the current parliament.[92] The referendum would also violate the separation of powers as the recall of the parliament belongs to other branches of the government under the current constitutional order.[93]

The Court then went on to provide reasons why the violation of the material core of the Constitution should be applied as a legal limit. The Court first pointed out that its practice has developed in interpreting the legal force and the binding nature of referendums. In a decision in 1997, the Court had stated that citizens cannot change the Constitution directly in a referendum.[94] The decision was adopted at a time when the Court did not yet have the competence to exercise *ex ante* control over the constitutionality of referendums. Then, the first – and only other – case decided using the *ex ante* competence in 2014 established that it is possible to adopt generally binding legal norms in a referendum, even with the force of a constitutional law.[95] The Constitutional Court noted the contradiction in its case law, but argued that the interpretation from 1997 must be understood in the context of the case. In effect, it introduced a limit on constitutional changes that could violate the principles of democracy and rule of law. In the current case, the Court highlighted that citizens exercise state and legislative power directly in a referendum, in a manner equivalent to the National Council. This includes the power to amend the Constitution, but it also means that citizens cannot act without any restrictions and are subject to the Constitution adopted by them.[96]

The Court then went on to discuss the doctrine of the material core of the Constitution, as a restriction on legislative power. When the previous referen-

---

[91] Judgement PL. ÚS 7/2021 of 7 July 2021 of the Constitutional Court, Collection of Laws 280/2021.

[92] Ibid para 126.

[93] Ibid para 154.

[94] Decision II. ÚS 31/97 of 21 May 1997 of the Constitutional Court, ECLI: SK: USSR: 2016: 2.US.31.1997.1.

[95] Decision PL. ÚS 24/2014 of 28 October 2014 the Constitutional Court, para 24.

[96] Judgment PL. ÚS 7/2021 of 7 July 2021 of the Constitutional Court, Collection of Laws 280/2021, para 102–103.

dum decision about the defense of marriage case was decided in 2014, the Court did not rely on the doctrine. Nonetheless, the Court reasoned that the defense of marriage case already revolved around the immutable provisions of the Constitution. In the defense of marriage case, the Court established that citizens do not have the right to decrease the standard of protection of fundamental rights and freedoms enshrined in the Constitution.[97] Then, in 2019, the doctrine of the material core of the Constitution was developed further in the practice of the Court.[98] In a landmark case, the Court held that the material core of the Constitution includes the values on which the very essence of the Constitution is based, such as the principle of the rule of law with all its components, or the principle of a democratic state.[99]

Considering these developments, the Court then interpreted its own competence to review referendums. The Constitution states that the role of the Constitutional Court is to examine the compliance of the subject of the referendum with the 'Constitution or with constitutional law'.[100] The Court reasoned that it follows from this competence rule that the Constitution itself does not limit the review competence to the explicit limits.[101]

The Slovak early election referendum case is an example of providing sufficient reasons for applying implicit limits in referendum authorization. The Court acknowledges that its practice contains contradictions, but it also shows how its jurisprudence has developed over the years both regarding referendums and the doctrine of the material core. This way, the Court is able to establish that the application of the implicit limit is part of an organic development of the case law.

5.   CONCLUSIONS FROM THE STATE PRACTICE

The state practice shows that providing a reasoning is exceptional in the referendum authorization practice of parliaments and presidents, while common in case of election commissions and courts. This difference can derive from the fact that referendum authorization procedures as legal disputes are more akin to the other constitutional functions of election commissions and courts than to the other constitutional functions of legislatures and presidents.

The traditional constitutional functions of election commissions and of regular and constitutional courts include different adjudicatory competences

---

[97]   Ibid para 109.

[98]   Judgment PL. ÚS 7/2021 of 7 July 2021 of the Constitutional Court, Collection of Laws 280/2021, para 111.

[99]   Ibid.

[100]   Ibid para 113, referring to Art 125b(1) Constitution.

[101]   Ibid.

and entail formulating decisions with detailed legal reasoning, such as deciding voter complaints, civil law disputes or constitutional challenges against
legislation. Consequently, referendum authorization procedures do not require
any changes in their regular practices. The generally used formulation of
resolutions and judgments can be easily applied for referendum authorization
cases.

In contrast, the provision of detailed legal reasoning is not common for
parliamentary or presidential decision-making.[102] These state institutions do
not regularly decide legal disputes which would warrant a legal reasoning.
However, as the example of the Slovene Parliament shows, it would not be
impossible to incorporate a reasoning in their decision-making. The parliamentary procedure could easily accommodate draft reasoned decisions, where
the reasoning of the referendum authorization decision would also become
part of the debate. Similar to draft legislative acts, draft referendum authorization decisions could also be discussed in committee and plenary sessions,
be subject to amendments, and then adopted by a vote. In Switzerland or
Liechtenstein, this would not even require a major accommodation of the
current practice since the preparatory documents of the governments could
be the basis for draft referendum authorization decisions. Consequently, the
differences in the traditional constitutional functions of the state institutions
authorizing referendums cannot justify the lack of reasoning.

The state practice suggests that when introducing a reasoning requirement,
most states regard the question from the perspective of individual procedural
rights: legal reasoning is likely to be provided if remedies are available.
Some of the states provide a reasoning only for rejection decisions, while
the approval decision just confirms that the referendum proposal complies
with the legal requirements.[103] Naturally, if the referendum proposal is legally
sound, then it does not require lengthy reasoning. However, if remedies are
provided against the decision and not only the initiators but voters in general
are able to challenge the authorization, then approval decisions may also be
disputed. In these cases, the state institution should also give an account of the
deliberation process that resulted in validating the proposal.

Focusing on the connection between reasoning and other procedural rights
such as remedy rights is naturally important. As mentioned in the introduction
to the chapter, the reasoning serves as a basis for the parties to challenge
the referendum authorization decision and for the appeal body to review the

---

[102] Mashaw (Ch 5, n 29) 3.
[103] Slovakia: Decision of the President of the Slovak Republic of November 2014 on
calling a referendum, Collection of Laws 320/2014; Hungary: Decision 14/2016 of the
National Election Commission.

decision. In addition, if participation rights are provided in the procedure, it is important that the decision reflects the arguments of the parties and shows that they were taken into account during the deliberation.

However, the right to a reasoned decision should be generally available in referendum authorization procedures, even in cases where the initiators or the voters do not have procedural rights. Without a reasoned decision neither the initiators nor the wider public can understand how the state institution has exercised its discretion in reviewing the legal limits. Due to the wide discretionary powers the state institutions possess, both the approval and rejection decisions on referendum authorization should contain legal reasons to show that the decision is not arbitrary. The rejection of the referendum proposal can arbitrarily limit the exercise of popular sovereignty, while approval can arbitrarily allow referendums that violate individual rights, public interests, or the rule of law. The provision of reasons can be especially important in situations when the decision-maker deviates from its previous practice or relies on implicit legal limits. Without sufficient reasoning, both exercises of discretionary powers can bring arbitrariness to the referendum authorization practice. They can make the procedures unpredictable and inconsistent from the standpoint of the initiators and voters. In such situations, a detailed reasoning can largely contribute to the acceptance of the decision.

Overall, the practice of giving reasons for all referendum authorization decisions could best contribute to creating transparency and preventing arbitrariness. Nonetheless, the right to a reasoned decision should apply to rejection decisions as a minimum requirement. As the state practice shows, this would be feasible in all selected states regardless of the type of authorizing state institution.

8. Right to be heard and other participation rights

1. DEFINING THE RIGHT TO BE HEARD

The right to be heard ensures that the parties to the dispute are not objects of the procedure but equally respected subjects, who can actively participate in the decision-making.[1] The right to be heard contains a number of specific rights: the right to present arguments, the right to access the case files and the evidence, and the right to submit and comment on the evidence.[2] The right to be heard necessarily evokes the right to an oral hearing, but based on the specific nature of the procedure, other forms of participation might fulfil the objectives of hearing rights. Consequently, in this chapter, the different forms of participation rights will be investigated under the umbrella of the right to be heard.

Participation rights ensure that the parties are informed about the decision-making and can contribute to the deliberation. Participation rights serve information-gathering purposes, because they ensure that the decision-maker hears all the relevant information for deciding the case.[3] Participation rights help the decision-maker reach a balanced decision by allowing a chance to present and counter arguments. In addition, participation rights also build trust in the decision-making process by allowing the interested parties to closely follow and shape the procedure. By providing a chance for the parties to be part of the procedure, participation rights ensure that the parties are treated with respect and as 'capable agents of their fate'.[4] The right to be heard ensures that the decisions are not reached in secrecy.[5] The involvement of the parties increases the transparency of the procedure and serves as a check on the decision-maker to conduct an impartial and well-rounded procedure.[6]

---

[1] Hoffmann (Ch 6, n 8) 113; Wiederkehr (Ch 7, n 10) 20.
[2] Wiederkehr (Ch 7, n 10) 20.
[3] Bayles (Ch 6, n 1) 47; Hoffmann (Ch 6, n 8) 112; Wiederkehr (Ch 7, n 10) 22.
[4] Bayles (Ch 6, n 1) 42; Wiederkehr (Ch 7, n 10) 2; Waldron, 'The Rule of Law and the Importance of Procedure' (Ch 1, n 64) 347; Boyron, Lacey (Ch 7, n 5) 265.
[5] *Malhous v The Czech Republic* App no 3307/96 (ECtHR, 12 July 2001) para 55.
[6] Clayton, Tomlinson (Ch 6, n 9) 174; della Cananea (Ch 7, n 11) 110–111.

Participation rights open the procedure up towards the interested parties, so the transparency can reduce the chance of arbitrary decision-making.[7]

2. PARTICIPATION RIGHTS IN REFERENDUM AUTHORIZATION PROCEDURES

The right to be heard as an element of fair trial stems from criminal procedures, where – due to the potentially severe detrimental consequences of the verdict – it is crucial that the accused persons are able to properly defend themselves and have a chance to present their defense in person.[8] In referendum authorization procedures, neither the initiators nor the voters are likely to find their physical liberty or financial stability affected by a decision that refuses to authorize a referendum. A refusal does not impose a burden on the parties or change their legal status, while an authorization decision is beneficial, as it provides a 'permit' to continue the referendum process. Still, the state institution determines in the referendum authorization procedure whether the initiators and the voters can exercise their right to vote. This element warrants some form of participation rights for the holders of this political right.

The Revised Code of the Venice Commission mentions the right to be heard in relation to the effective system of appeal.[9] The Code aims to protect the applicants' right to a hearing but also refers to a hearing 'involving both parties', thus to an adversarial procedure. Looking into the functions of participation rights in referendum authorization, I argue that the subjects and the scope of participation rights may vary, but still fulfill the functions of this procedural guarantee.

In referendum authorization procedures, participation rights can fulfill three core functions: they can serve information-gathering purposes, they can have a control function on the work of the decision-maker, and they can fulfill a more symbolic, dignitarian purpose of paying respect to the views of the initiators and voters.[10] Depending on which function is emphasized in the regulatory framework of referendums, the scope of the participation rights can vary. However, ideally all three functions should be acknowledged when providing participation rights in referendum authorization.

The *information-gathering function* ensures that the decision-maker possesses all the necessary information to reach a balanced and well-grounded decision.[11] This function plays a more limited role in referendum authorization

---

[7]   Bayles (Ch 6, n 1) 42; Hoffmann (Ch 6, n 8) 119.
[8]   Bayles (Ch 6, n 1) 39; Boyron, Lacey (Ch 7, n 5) 266.
[9]   Revised Code II.4.3.f.
[10] Bayles (Ch 6, n 1) 42.
[11] Bayles (Ch 6, n 1) 47; Hoffmann (Ch 6, n 8) 112; Wiederkehr (Ch 7, n 10) 22.

procedures than in other public law disputes. Referendum authorization is an *a priori* decision about the legality of the referendum proposal, thus the proposal has not yet caused any changes in the legal situation of people. There is no factual background to be uncovered for the authorization, just as evidentiary procedures are not common in referendum authorization. In referendum authorization procedures, the information-gathering means that the state institution understands all the possible consequences of a successful referendum and has all the relevant legal arguments to decide whether the referendum request conforms to the legal limits. The statements of the initiators, the voters, and the civil society can contribute to clarifying the arguments about the legality of the referendum proposal.

The *control function* of participation rights can play a key role in referendum authorization procedures. By allowing the interested parties to follow the fate of their proposal, they can attest that the decision is not arbitrary, and the decision-maker has acted impartially. Conversely, the presence and participation of the interested parties can keep a check on the decision-maker.[12] Participation rights can positively influence the decision-maker to conduct a thorough and impartial procedure and reach a well-balanced decision. In this way, participation rights increase the transparency of the procedure and thus reduce the chance of arbitrary action. This is an advantage of participation rights that is present for any public law dispute, and referendum authorization procedures are no exception.

Lastly, the *symbolic function* of participation rights is also crucial in referendum authorization procedures. The opportunity to take part in the procedure shows that the parties are equally respected and that their contributions matter in the decision-making process, which builds trust in the procedure and helps the acceptance of the decision.[13] In referendum authorization procedures this element is important, because the procedure determines the exercise of popular sovereignty and affects the rights of all voters. Thus, the perception of fairness through participation is necessary to build trust in the procedure.

The information-gathering goal can be achieved even without an oral hearing, through written submissions. This is also supported by the case law of the ECtHR, which acknowledges that the hearing might be dispensed with if the facts of the case are not contested or if the case involves only questions of law.[14] The control and the symbolic functions can be best served by providing an oral hearing to the interested parties. A hearing allows the parties

---

[12] Clayton, Tomlinson (Ch 6, n 9) 174; della Cananea (Ch 7, n 11) 110–111.
[13] Klaming, Giesen (Ch 1, n 66) 525.
[14] *Miller v Sweden* App no 55853/00 (ECtHR, 8 February 2005) para 30; *Mirovni Institut v Slovenia* App no 32303/13 (ECtHR, 13 March 2018) para 65.

to be present, observe, and shape the procedure. For all three purposes it is vital that the parties can react to the developments of the procedure. So, if the decision-maker commissions opinions from experts or relies on other evidence, then the parties should be presented with the submissions and given an opportunity to comment.

3.   THE SUBJECTS OF THE PARTICIPATION RIGHTS

In this section, I investigate who is afforded participation rights in referendum authorization procedures. Based on the state practice, three models are established: (1) no participation rights are provided in the procedure; (2) the participation rights of the initiators are ensured; (3) participation rights are available for all voters and/or civil society organizations. This chapter looks into the participation rights in both the first instance and remedy procedures to provide a more complete picture of who is able to influence the procedure and to what extent. The next chapter, on the right to an effective remedy, analyzes the questions of the legal standing to challenge the decision.

Looking at whose rights are acknowledged in referendum authorization procedures, it can be seen that the majority of the selected states either regard referendum authorization as an abstract review where neither the initiators nor the wider public are afforded participation rights or only allow the participation of the initiators. As Table 8.1 on p. 166 shows, the voters or civil society organizations can participate only exceptionally. A procedure without participation rights is common for parliamentary and presidential decision-making, but not unprecedented for constitutional courts either. Election commissions and regular courts are more accommodating towards participation rights.

3.1   No Participation Rights

In the practice of the selected states none of the parliamentary referendum authorization procedures accommodate the participation rights of either the initiators or the wider public. The same is true for the presidential decision-making in Slovakia. In the states where no remedies are granted for the initiators or voters, the whole referendum authorization procedure is carried out without their involvement, thus none of the purposes of participation rights – the information-gathering, control, or dignitarian functions – are fulfilled. This is clearly the case in Switzerland, where the Federal Assembly decides as the single instance.

In Croatia, too, the initiators or the wider public cannot participate in the decision-making of either the Parliament or the Constitutional Court. Only the

Table 8.1   Subjects of participation rights

	No one	Initiators	Voters and civil society
Croatia – Parliament	X		
Croatia – Constitutional Court	X		
Italy – Constitutional Court			X
Hungary – Election Commission			X
Hungary – Regular court			X
Latvia – Election Commission	X		
Latvia – Regular court		X	
Liechtenstein – Parliament	X		
Liechtenstein – Constitutional Court		X	
Slovakia – President	X		
Slovakia – Constitutional Court		X	
Slovenia – Parliament	X		
Slovenia – Constitutional Court		X	
Switzerland – Parliament	X		

Parliament can initiate the procedure of the Constitutional Court,[15] but even if the Court reviews the referendum proposal, the initiators cannot actively participate in its procedure.[16]

Similarly in the Slovak legal system, only the President can refer the referendum request to the Constitutional Court.[17] The initiators and the voters are allowed neither to participate in the presidential referendum authorization procedure nor to appeal its outcome. In case the President involves the Constitutional Court as an 'expert body' in the authorization procedure, the Court provides participation rights for the initiators of the referendum.[18] In the defense of marriage referendum, the President referred the questions to the Constitutional Court, and therefore the initiators were able to submit their opinion on the President's proposal.[19] Thus, the initiators have enforceable

---

[15]   Art. 95 Constitutional Law on the Constitutional Court of the Republic of Croatia.

[16]   Decision of the Constitutional Court of the Republic of Croatia No. U-VIIR-4640/2014 of 12 August 2014, Official Gazette 104/14, para 18 (Official English translation).

[17]   Art. 95(2) and Art. 125b Constitution.

[18]   Art. 58(1)(c) Act no. 314/2018 on the Constitutional Court of Slovak Republic.

[19]   Decision PL. ÚS 24/2014 of 28 October 2014 of the Constitutional Court, para 9.

rights to participate in the judicial procedures, but these are conditional on the decision of the President.

3.2   Participation of the Initiators

Most selected states allow the initiators to participate in some way in the referendum authorization procedure. This approach acknowledges that the initiators have a legal interest in the outcome of the referendum authorization procedure, and that they should be involved in the procedure in some way.

In Liechtenstein and Slovenia, the parliamentary decision can be appealed by the initiators and the judicial procedures offer participation rights.[20] The same applies for the referendum authorization procedure in Latvia: the initiators are not able to participate in the procedure of the election commission but have extensive participation rights in the judicial appeal.[21] In Italy, the initiators also have extensive participation rights in the decision-making in the Constitutional Court.[22] In Hungary, they have limited participation rights in the procedure both of the election commissions and of the Curia.[23]

3.3   Participation of Voters or Civil Society Organizations

The participation of the voters or civil society organizations is rare in referendum authorization procedures. Theoretically, the involvement of voters or civil society can be based on either an *individual legal interest* in the referendum authorization (i.e., every voter's right to vote is affected by the referendum decision) or on *public interest* (i.e., everyone has an interest in upholding the legality of the referendum procedure).[24] Participation rights based on public interest reflect the difference between public and private law disputes, as public law disputes are never only about providing remedy against individual harms, but always contain an element of restoring legality and constitutional order.[25] Providing participation rights to protect public interests does not

---

[20]   Liechtenstein: Art. 70 and Art. 70b People's Rights Act; Slovenia: Art. 35 Constitutional Court Act; Art. 47(3) and Art. 51 Rules of Procedure of the Constitutional Court.

[21]   Art. 145 Administrative Procedure Law.

[22]   Art. 33 Law no. 352 of 1970.

[23]   Art. 43 and Art. 229 Act XXXVI of 2013 on Electoral Procedure.

[24]   See more on this in Chapter 9, section 3.

[25]   Joanna Miles, 'Standing under the Human Rights Act 1998: Theories of Rights Enforcement & the Nature of Public Law Adjudication' (2000) 59(1) *Cambridge Law Journal* 133–167, 150; Jan Darpö, 'Pulling the Trigger: ENGO Standing Rights and the Enforcement of Environmental Obligations in EU Law' in Sanja Bogojević, Rosemary Rayfuse (eds), *Environmental Rights in Europe and Beyond* (Hart Publishing 2018)

necessarily mean that anyone can be the subject of the procedure and that no standing rules apply, only that it is possible to participate in a procedure even without an individual legal interest in the outcome. In this case, the emphasis is shifted from the possible individual legal consequences of a successful referendum to the general protection of the rule of law. In referendum cases, this solution can offer participation for civil society organizations representing the social groups potentially affected by the referendum or protecting other public interests.

Hungary is the only state that gives party status to every voter. The party status is based on their individual affectedness but – as the next chapter details – it is in fact a public interest standing.[26] In Hungary, the first instance referendum authorization decision can be challenged by any voter, which means that the appellant voter can express their arguments about the referendum proposal in the appeal procedure.[27]

Meanwhile, Italy is the only state that allows civil society organizations to participate in the referendum authorization. The initiators have the right to participate in the procedure of the Constitutional Court, but the Court can also allow associations and non-governmental organizations to intervene in the procedure. In 2005, the Constitutional Court decided a series of referendum requests about reproductive rights.[28] The Court allowed a number of civil society organizations to file memorandums to the case, but it emphasized that this does not translate into the same position as the initiators of the referendum.[29] The civil society organizations intervening in the procedure may submit written arguments and, exceptionally, the Court may allow them to present oral arguments. However, in contrast to the initiators of the referendum, they do not have the right to be heard. The initiators can be present and communicate their arguments in the chamber sessions of the Court, while the public interest interveners can submit written arguments and present oral arguments at the discretion of the Court.[30] The Court highlighted that the submissions from the civil society organizations contribute to the decision-making with additional

---

253–281, 264; Krisztina F. Rozsnyai, 'Current Tendencies of Judicial Review as Reflected in the New Hungarian Code of Administrative Court Procedure' (2018) 17(1) *Central European Public Administration Review* 7–23, 11.

[26]　Decision Knk.IV.37.222/2016/9 of the Curia, para 25. See Chapter 9, section 3.

[27]　Art. 222 and Art. 229 Act XXXVI of 2013 on Electoral Procedure.

[28]　Judgment No. 49 of 2005 of the Constitutional Court, Official Gazette, 1st Special Series no. 5 of 2 February 2005; Judgment No. 47 of 2005, Official Gazette, 1st Special Series no. 5 of 2 February 2005; Judgment No. 46 of 2005, Official Gazette, 1st Special Series no. 5 of 2 February 2005.

[29]　Judgment No. 46 of 2005, Official Gazette, 1st Special Series no. 5 of 2 February 2005, Legal considerations, para 2.

[30]　Ibid.

arguments, which might otherwise not be available.[31] This example shows that civil society organizations and other public interest groups can be involved in the referendum authorization procedure in a way that offers them a channel to express their arguments but also signals that their interest in the outcome of the case is not as direct as the initiators'.

It must also be noted that the willingness of the wider public to participate presupposes that the referendum request has already gathered public attention. This is possible in states where the referendum authorization procedure follows the signature collection, thus the signature collection has already drawn attention to the proposal. Half the selected states require the signatures to be collected before the authorization, so the involvement of the wider public would be possible in Croatia, Latvia, Slovakia, and Switzerland.[32] Nevertheless, only Italy allows submissions from civil society. In states like Hungary, Slovenia, and Liechtenstein, where the first step of the referendum process is the authorization procedure, only the initiators have knowledge about the proposal. In this case, the involvement of voters or civil society organizations would require the decision-maker to publish a notice about the upcoming cases and allow enough time for the public to get involved.

4. THE SCOPE OF THE PARTICIPATION RIGHTS

Based on the practice of the selected states, the following participation rights are provided to the parties of the referendum authorization procedure: (1) the right to be present in the decision-making process; (2) the right to submit written arguments; (3) the right to be heard. The different forms of participation rights offer different levels of transparency and opportunity to present arguments. An additional element of participation rights is the opportunity to follow and comment on the developments of the case. So, this part of the inquiry will also explore how the participants are able to react to the evidence and to the arguments of others.

The scope of participation rights is limited in referendum authorization procedures. A hearing, where the initiators and the voters can simultaneously present their arguments, is exceptional. As Table 8.2 shows, in most states only written submissions are allowed. Based on the extent of participation rights, the selected states may be grouped into five categories: (1) some states do not allow any kind of participation; (2) some allow the parties to be present during the decision-making; (3) some allow written submissions in the procedure; (4) some leave it to the discretion of the decision-making body whether a hearing is held; while in others (5) a hearing is mandatory.

---

[31] Ibid.
[32] See Chapter 3, section 1.

Table 8.2   *Scope of participation rights*

	No participation	Presence	Written submission	Optional hearing	Mandatory hearing
Croatia (parliament)	X				
Croatia (constitutional court)	X				
Italy (constitutional court)				X	X
Hungary (election commission)		X		X	
Hungary (regular court)			X		
Latvia (election commission)				X	
Latvia (regular court)					X
Liechtenstein (parliament.)	X				
Liechtenstein (constitutional court)				X	
Slovakia (president)					
Slovakia (constitutional court)					X
Slovenia (parliament)	X				
Slovenia (constitutional court)				X	
Switzerland (parliament)	X				

Parliamentary and presidential decision-making is the least accommodating for participation rights. Election commissions allow some restricted forms of participation, while courts are the most open to participation in their procedures. This difference between the practices of the state institutions – similar to the differences in providing reasoning – can be traced back to their core functions and their traditional decision-making procedures.

4.1   Parliamentary and Presidential Procedures

Many of the selected states regard referendum authorization procedures as completely abstract reviews where neither the initiators nor the voters are allowed to take part in the procedure. Parliamentary and presidential decision-making especially lacks participation rights. None of the parliaments in Croatia, Liechtenstein, or Slovenia involve the initiators or the voters in the deliberation. Meanwhile, in Switzerland only the technical corrections of the initiative can be observed by the initiators.[33] The Slovak President does not allow participation in the procedure either.

The parliamentary and presidential procedures are not particularly designed to accommodate 'outside' participants. However, it would be entirely possible to invite written submissions or to allow oral presentations at the commission or plenary sessions, but this does not seem to be part of the practice in the selected states. Informal channels may exist for the members of parliament or the political parties to discuss the referendum proposals with the initiators,[34] but official and enforceable avenues of participation do not exist.

4.2   Election Commission Procedures

The procedures of election commissions in Latvia and Hungary are slightly more accommodating for participation rights. In Hungary, the sessions of the National Election Commission are open to the public,[35] which means that both the initiators and the interested voters can be present at the discussion of the referendum request. However, it is left completely to the discretion of the Commission whether it allows active participation in the sessions. The Commission can decide freely what evidence it deems necessary for the case. By request it may allow the initiators to present oral statements, but this is not mandatory. If the initiators present oral arguments, then the opposing parties shall also be entitled to make a statement.[36] The minutes of the sessions of the National Election Commission show that typically only the members of the Commission are present at the sessions,[37] thus the optional hearing rights do not influence the referendum authorization practice.

The Latvian rules for the procedure of the Central Election Commission are similar to the Hungarian rules: it is at the discretion of the Commission as to what kind of evidence it uses to reach the decision and who it invites to partic-ipate in the procedure. The rules do not explicitly refer to the involvement of the initiators but emphasize the freedom of the Commission to request the nec-essary information from various sources. The Commission 'may request the

---

[33]   Art. 99(2) Federal Act on the Federal Assembly.
[34]   Marxer, 'Liechtenstein' (Ch 2, n 14) 60.
[35]   Art. 40 Act XXXVI of 2013 on Electoral Procedure.
[36]   Ibid.
[37]   The minutes are available here in Hungarian at <https://www.valasztas.hu/nvb -ules-jegyzokonyvek>, accessed 15 March 2022.

data, explanations, and opinions necessary for resolving such issue from State and local government institutions, as well as invite experts'.[38] The minutes of the sessions are not available, but the final decisions of the Commission can indicate how it exercises its discretion in gathering evidence. As mentioned previously, the Latvian Central Election Commission invited a number of experts to participate in the decision-making procedure about the citizenship referendum. The Commission decision, however, does not mention that the initiators of the referendum participated in the decision-making in any way.[39] Based on the facts of the decision, they were not offered an opportunity to express their arguments or to react to the statements of the experts. In the end, the Central Election Commission, relying largely on the expert opinions, refused to authorize the referendum, concluding that it had not been fully elaborated and did not fit into the Latvian legal system.[40] The invitation of experts to submit arguments clearly contributes to reaching a well-rounded decision. However, in this case, the initiators are not offered active participation, they cannot react to the procedural developments of the case and are only able to challenge the final decision of the Commission.

4.3   Regular Court Procedures

Regular courts usually operate under extensive procedural rules and fulfill adjudicatory procedures that center around a trial that provides an opportunity to present oral arguments and counterarguments.[41] This would suggest that the participation rights in referendum authorization procedures are the most extensive if general courts are involved in the decision-making.

The Latvian remedy procedure of the Senate of the Supreme Court Department of Administrative Law can best display a full-fledged spectrum of participation rights in referendum authorization cases. If the authorization of the referendum request is refused by the Central Election Commission, the initiative group can appeal the refusal decision at the Supreme Court.[42] The Administrative Procedure Law regulates the procedure of the Court.[43] The

---

[38]   Art. 23(6) Law on National Referendum, Legislative Initiative and European Citizens' Initiative.

[39]   Decision No. 6 of 1 November 2012 of the Central Election Commission, Official publication No. 2012/175.7.

[40]   Ibid.

[41]   Latvia: Administrative Procedure Law; Hungary: Act I of 2017 on the Code of Administrative Court Procedure.

[42]   Art. 23(1 prim) Law on National Referendum, Legislative Initiative and European Citizens' Initiative.

[43]   Art. 13 Law on the Central Election Commission.

Administrative Procedure Law is the general Act about administrative procedures and administrative law trials. It contains an extensive catalogue of participation rights. According to the Act, the applicant and the defendant – in the case of referendum authorization, the initiators and the Central Election Commission – have the right to access the case materials, to participate in a court hearing, to submit evidence, and to provide oral and written explanations to the Court.[44] The provisions on administrative trials even highlight that the participants have the right to reply to each other and actively debate the presented arguments and evidence.[45] The initiators of the citizenship referendum appealed the decision of the Central Election Commission refusing to authorize the referendum.[46] The initiators presented their arguments about the lack of competence of the election commission to determine the constitutionality of the referendum request, as well as their arguments on why the draft law is in conformity with the Latvian legal system. The Commission disputed the application in writing. Then a hearing was held where both the applicants and the defendant maintained their statements and added new arguments based on the recent decision of the Constitutional Court on the competence of the election commission to authorize referendums.[47] This way – in contrast to the procedure of the election commission – the judicial remedy offers a procedure where all the parties are able to present their arguments, react to each other, and comment on the developments of the case.

In contrast to the Latvian practice, the Hungarian Curia does not allow an open hearing for the parties. Similarly to the Latvian solution, the Administrative Department of the Curia handles referendum authorization cases in three-judge panels acting as a first instance court. However, the referendum cases are considerably different from other administrative law trials. The referendum Act determines a 90-day deadline for reaching a decision (30 days if the first instance resolution was not on the merits of the question). The decision is reached in a 'non-trial procedure' which means that the three-judge panel decides in chambers based on written submission.[48] A trial or an open hearing cannot be held in referendum cases, thus the parties do not have the right to be heard. Written submissions are possible in the procedure, but the Curia does not commission any statements from the parties. Thus, in most cases, the decision is based exclusively on the first instance decision and the appeal. This can lead to a situation where the initiators of the referendum are

---

[44] Art. 145 Administrative Procedure Law.
[45] Art. 242 Administrative Procedure Law.
[46] Decision No. 6 of 1 November 2012 of the Central Election Commission, Official publication No. 2012/175.7.
[47] Judgment No. SA-1/2013 of 11 February 2013 of the Supreme Court, para 6.
[48] Art 229 Act XXXVI of 2013 on Electoral Procedure.

not even part of the judicial procedure. In Hungary, the referendum author-ization decisions of the National Election Commission can be challenged by any voter,[49] which means that the decisions authorizing the referendum proposal can also be appealed. This was the case in 2017, when the National Election Commission approved a question submitted by a citizen that aimed to increase the statutory limitation times for corruption crimes.[50] Another citizen challenged the validation decision and argued that the *ratione temporis* of the question was not clear, which violated the principles of rule of law and *nulla poena sine lege*, as the longer statutory limitations would apply for crimes that had already been committed. The Curia reviewed the first instance decision solely based on the arguments of the appeal without providing an opportunity for the initiator to express their opinion about the appeal. The Curia upheld the decision of the National Election Commission, thus the appeal was not successful, and the rights of the initiator were not affected by this particular decision.[51] Nevertheless, the initiator was completely left out of the judicial process.

The only exceptions to this practice have been the cases of the government-initiated referendums on the migrant quota[52] and more recently on the protection of children from LGBTQ propaganda.[53] In these procedures the questions were validated by the National Election Commission and were then challenged by voters at the Curia. The government intervened in the judicial procedures and submitted written arguments. The court did not actively initiate the intervention by sending out a notice about the appeals, but it accepted the intervention and considered the submitted arguments in its decision.[54]

In other administrative law cases, the Curia has to notify everyone whose rights or legal interests are directly affected by the disputed administrative action about the submission of an appeal and offer the chance for these parties to intervene in the judicial procedure.[55] In the adjudication of election and referendum cases, the court actively involves parties only if the decision may detrimentally affect the rights and legal interests of third parties not yet participating in the procedure.[56] This usually occurs in cases about campaign

---

[49]   See Chapter 9, section 3.

[50]   Decision 42/2017 of the National Election Commission.

[51]   Decision Knk.VII.37.424/2017/2 of the Curia.

[52]   Decision Knk.VII.37.222/2016/9 of the Curia.

[53]   Decisions Knk.II.40.646/2021/9, Knk.IV.40.645/2021/19, Knk.III.40.647/2021/18, Knk.III.40.644/2021/15, and Knk.IV.40.648/2021/23 of the Curia.

[54]   Decision Knk.VII.37.222/2016/9 of the Curia, paras 18–21.

[55]   Art. 20 Act I of 2017 on the Code of Administrative Court Procedure.

[56]   See the Summary Report of 14 March 2018 of the Curia on the jurisprudence analysis of election and referendum proceedings. Available (in Hungarian) at https://

complaints if the legal dispute started between a voter and a political party, but the court has to oblige a third party (e.g., a media outlet) to refrain from further violations of the law, or the court has to impose a fine on such a third party. In referendum authorization cases, the question of actively involving parties – including the initiators – has not yet been raised. As the examples of the government-initiated referendums show, the Curia is open to such intervention, but the initiators must closely follow the case and initiate the interventions themselves.

4.4   Constitutional Court Procedures

The procedural rules for the constitutional courts are mostly contained in the organizational acts and rules of procedures of the courts. However, these do not normally include extensive rules on referendum authorization procedures.[57] Generally, the organizational acts and the rules of procedures only regulate some procedural questions, while the constitutional courts may apply other procedural regimes if no special rules are to be found.[58]

The Constitutional Court of Slovakia is the only court with a legal obligation to hold a hearing in its procedure. However, the initiation of this procedure is dependent on the decision of the president, so if he or she does not start the procedure, then no participation rights are offered to the applicants. The Act on the Constitutional Court clearly states that an oral hearing shall be held in proceedings of the Court on the conformity of the subject of the referendum, according to Art. 125b of the Constitution.[59] The 'participants in the proceedings, the person concerned, and their representatives shall have the right to be present at the oral hearing'.[60] The hearing can only be waived if the participants of the proceeding consent to the waiver.[61] Interestingly, the

---

kuria-birosag.hu/sites/default/files/joggyak/valasztasi_nepszavazasi_joggyak.pdf, accessed 15 March 2022.

[57]   For instance, in Slovakia, Act no. 314/2018 on the Constitutional Court contains seven articles on referendum authorization (Art. 102–109), while the Constitutional Act on the Constitutional Court in Croatia has nine articles on both election and referendum disputes (Art. 87–96). The Constitutional Court Act in Slovenia does not even contain special rules.

[58]   In Liechtenstein, Art. 38 (1) of the Act on the State Court references the administrative and the civil procedure laws. In Slovenia, Art. 6 of the Constitutional Court Act leaves it up to the Court to choose the procedural rules based on the legal nature of the case.

[59]   Article 58(1)c of Act no. 314/2018 on the Constitutional Court.

[60]   Article 58(2) of Act no. 314/2018 on the Constitutional Court (Official English translation).

[61]   Article 58(3) of Act no. 314/2018 on the Constitutional Court.

decision on the defense of marriage referendum is completely silent about a hearing. There is no indication in the decision that the Court held a hearing, but there is also no reference to the participants waiving their rights to an oral hearing. The decision only reveals written communications with the Court, stating that the 'Constitutional Court by letter of 23 September 2014 asked the representative of the Committee on Petitions to comment on the President's proposal'.[62] The initiators submitted their detailed written opinion, which is cited in the reasoning of the decision. Similarly, the more recent judgment of the Constitutional Court on the early elections initiative does not contain any reference to a hearing.[63] The decision shows that the initiators and the National Council provided written submissions. In both cases the initiators had access to the submissions of the other parties and were able to submit their arguments about the constitutionality of the referendum proposal, but without a hearing.

The initiators have limited involvement in the referendum authorization procedure in Croatia. In 2014, the Croatian Parliament initiated the procedure of the Constitutional Court to review the constitutionality of the Vukovar minority rights initiative that aimed to increase the threshold for the official use of the minority language. The initiative tapped into the extremely sensitive topic of minority rights in Croatia and aimed to restrict the use of the minority language and script in municipalities where the members of a specific national minority do not comprise at least one half of the population.[64] The Court found the initiative to be unconstitutional and prohibited the referendum. The Court did not rely on any arguments from either the Parliament or the initiators, or at least the reasoning of the decision does not reference any submission from the parties. However, after concluding the arguments for the unconstitutionality of the initiative, the Court turned to 'other questions considered in the proceeding' and among these to the reasons the initiators attached to the referendum request. The Court noted that 'the current legislation does not contain rules on the obligation to explain the request to call a referendum, but that an explanation of the request is relevant for decision-making by the Croatian Parliament ... and also for decision-making by the Constitutional Court'.[65] The Court went on to declare that

---

[62] Decision PL. ÚS 24/2014 of 28 October 2014 of the Constitutional Court, para 9 (DeepL Translator).

[63] Judgment PL. ÚS 7/2021 of 7 July 2021 of the Constitutional Court, Collection of Laws 280/2021.

[64] Dudás (Ch 3, n 16) 126; Čepo, Čakar (Ch 1, n 90) 34.

[65] Decision of the Constitutional Court of the Republic of Croatia No. U-VIIR -4640/2014 of 12 August 2014, Official Gazette 104/14, para 18 (Official English translation).

each future request to call a referendum submitted to the Croatian Parliament pursuant to Article 87.3 of the Constitution must contain a detailed presentation of the facts and circumstances which were the reason for setting the referendum question in the proposed content, and a sufficient and relevant statement of reasons for the request to call a referendum. Any new submissions which organizing committees … may prepare and send to the Constitutional Court after the Croatian Parliament has requested the Court to proceed pursuant to Article 95 of the Constitutional Act cannot be deemed to be a part of their request since they have not been previously sent to the Croatian Parliament. The Constitutional Court will not consider such submissions. This rule does not exclude the authority of the Constitutional Court to request additional information from the organizing committees or documents to clarify the request itself submitted to the Croatian Parliament.[66]

The Court repeated this obligation also in the operative part of the decision, thus creating a new procedural obligation to provide reasoning for popular initiatives. At the same time, it has prohibited any further written submissions that include new arguments during the judicial procedure. The Court then continued to cite various parts of the reasoning provided by the initiators and provided counterarguments.[67] Interestingly, this part of the reasoning is completely separate from the first part on finding the initiative unconstitutional; it is more about meticulously rebutting all the arguments and concerns of the initiators. It seems that the function of this part is to openly demonstrate that the arguments of the initiators have been considered in the deliberation process. The emphasis is not on how the submissions contribute to the decision-making but on acknowledging the initiators as participants of the procedure and paying respect to their arguments by providing reasons against them.

Similarly to the previous examples, the State Court of Liechtenstein also usually decides without holding a hearing in referendum authorization cases. According to the legal provisions governing the State Court, the Court holds a public oral hearing unless the chairman – after hearing the rapporteur of the case –considers an oral hearing unnecessary.[68] This way even though an oral hearing is the rule for the procedure, it is at the discretion of the chairman to decide whether the arguments of the participants will be heard. In the appeal procedure about the initiative on the pension reform, the initiators requested a public oral hearing. The initiators argued that their arguments had never been heard in the procedure. The parliamentary procedure does not provide for participation, thus the remedy procedure at the State Court is not preceded by a judicial or an administrative procedure where the right to be heard and

---

[66]   Ibid (Official English translation).
[67]   Ibid paras 22–22.1.
[68]   Art. 47 Act on the State Court.

the right to ask questions would be allowed.[69] The Government, in preparing the decision of the Parliament, commissioned an expert opinion that the initiators could not react to and could not challenge its validity due to the lack of participation. The State Court decided to dispense with a public hearing.[70] The reasoning states that the Court 'is aware that it is the first and only court instance in the present proceedings'.[71] However, based on the written pleas submitted by the parties as well as the entire content of the file, the Court was of the opinion that the facts of the case and the legal situation had been sufficiently clarified and no further clarification could be expected from an oral discussion.[72] Based on the reasoning, the written arguments of the initiators were taken into account in the deliberation. However, by rejecting the request for a hearing the Court clearly laid more emphasis on the information-gathering purpose of participation rights than on the more symbolic purpose of empowering the parties or providing control over the procedure.

In Slovenia, the Act on the Constitutional Court also leaves it up to the Court whether it decides its cases in a closed session or in a public hearing.[73] In the Slovene defense of marriage referendum case, the Court only relied on written submissions by the parties – the initiators and the National Assembly – to reverse the decision of the parliament and allow the referendum to take place. Most of the arguments of the initiators were submitted in the appeal against the parliamentary decision. The parliament was offered a chance to defend its decision, while the Court also commissioned the initiators to react to the arguments of the parliament.[74] Thus, even without a hearing there was a chance for discourse between the parties.

The most extensive participation rights can be found in the procedure of the Italian Constitutional Court, even though the legal provisions on the Court only regulate the right of the initiators to submit written arguments.[75] The Court has developed a practice that allows the initiators of the referendum and the government to take part in the closed chamber sessions of the Court and present their arguments there.[76] In the judgments about the referendum requests on reproduction rights, the Court referred to a hearing in the rea-

---

[69] Decision 2013/183 of the State Court, Facts, para 6.3.
[70] Ibid, Facts para 8.
[71] Ibid, Reasoning para 1.3 (DeepL Translator).
[72] Ibid.
[73] Art. 29 and Art. 49 Constitutional Court Act.
[74] Decision No. U-II-1/15 of 28 September 2015 of the Constitutional Court, Official Gazette Republic of Slovenia No. 80/15.
[75] Art. 33 Law no. 352 of 1970.
[76] Judgment no. 46 of 2005, Official Gazette, 1st Special Series no. 5 of 2 February 2005, Legal considerations para 2; Judgment no. 16 of 2008 of the Constitutional Court, Official Gazette, 1st Special Series no. 6 of 2 May 2008, Legal considerations para 2.

soning. The reasoning does not provide an account of the content of the hearing but provides a detailed account of the initiators' written arguments.[77] In this setting, the hearing may give an opportunity for the initiators and the government to simultaneously reflect on each other's arguments and the previous written submissions, which would ensure that the interests of the initiators and of the government are both represented in a balanced way. In the reproduction cases, the initiators intended to broaden the scope of the laws on medically assisted procreation, which restricted the access to medically assisted procreation techniques to married heterosexual couples affected by sterility or infertility.[78] The Attorney General, on behalf of the government, raised arguments for not allowing the abrogative referendum. Based on the written submissions, he relied on the constitutional protection of the rights of children, the violation of international obligations such as the Oviedo Convention on the protection of human rights in biomedicine,[79] the heterogeneity of the question, and lastly on the internal inconsistencies of the legal Act resulting from the abrogation of certain sentences.[80] The initiators countered these arguments by emphasizing the fundamental rights of women to health, the rule of consent for health interventions based on the Oviedo Convention, and the unreasonableness of the legislation. The heterogeneity of the question was rebutted by the 'existence of a rationally unitary matrix, identifiable in the desire to abrogate some prescriptions aimed at limiting ... access to medically assisted procreation'.[81] In this way the arguments from the two sides laid out the key issues for the judicial reasoning, thus the procedure not only served the information-gathering purpose of participation rights but also offered control and respect to the initiators.

5. CONCLUSIONS FROM THE STATE PRACTICE

The practice of the selected states shows that the right to be heard and other participation rights are generally not available in referendum authorization

---

[77] Judgment no. 46 of 2005, Official Gazette, 1st Special Series no. 5 of 2 February 2005, Heading and Factual considerations para 4.

[78] Andrea Boggio, 'Italy Enacts New Law on Medically Assisted Reproduction' (2005) 20(5) *Human Reproduction* 1153–1157; Irene Riezzo, Margherita Neri, Stefania Bello, Cristoforo Pomara, Emanuela Turillazzi, 'Italian Law on Medically Assisted Reproduction: Do Women's Autonomy and Health Matter?' (2016) 16 *BMC Womens Health* 44.

[79] Convention on Human Rights and Biomedicine, ETS No 164, Oviedo 4 April 1997.

[80] Judgment no. 47 of 2005, Official Gazette, 1st Special Series no. 5 of 2 February 2005, Factual considerations para 4.

[81] Ibid para 5 (DeepL Translator).

procedures. Hearing is rarely provided even for the initiators. Written submissions are the most common form of participation rights, but these are also
not always available. A number of states do not afford any participation rights
to either the initiators or the voters. The involvement of the wider public is
especially rare in referendum authorization procedures. A common feature of
the procedures is that the participation rights are regulated in a rather ad hoc
manner, and rarely extensively. In comparison to administrative procedures –
as the prototype for extensively regulated public law procedures – referendum
authorization procedures are underregulated and offer only few clear participation rights for the interested parties.

Parliaments and presidents are the least accommodating for participation
rights in referendum authorization procedures. The referendum authorization
is an ancillary function for the parliaments and presidents, and otherwise they
do not carry out adjudicatory functions. Their procedures (e.g. parliamentary
procedures for adopting legislative Acts) are not designed to provide individual participation rights to parties having a legal interest in the decision-making.
In contrast, election commissions as well as regular and constitutional courts
provide more extensive participation rights, although the practice shows that
the extent of these rights varies: the initiators or other parties are generally able
to submit written arguments, but an oral hearing or even an active involvement
in the developments of the case is not common. These state institutions usually
rely on more detailed procedural regulations. However, in some states the
participants of the referendum authorization procedures are not afforded the
same procedural guarantees as the parties of other public law debates. As the
Hungarian example shows, it is possible that even though an administrative
court adjudicates the referendum authorization disputes, the same procedural
guarantees as in other administrative law cases do not apply.

When the authorizing state institutions carry out their other constitutional
functions, the oral presentation of arguments is usually part of the procedure.
The only exception is presidential decision-making. Parliamentary debate and
judicial decision-making both center around the oral presentation of arguments. A hearing is an integral – although not compulsory – part of administrative procedures. Thus, the state institutions authorizing referendums would
have the ability to accommodate the hearing of the parties.

The provision of participation rights might not be necessary for
information-gathering purposes, but more for their symbolic purpose of
paying respect to citizens exercising popular sovereignty and for providing the
initiators an opportunity to oversee the procedure and attest to its non-arbitrari-
ness. The state practice shows that an oral hearing that could fulfill all these
functions is only available in Italy – without legal basis – and is a written
rule in Slovakia – without practice. In many states the decision-maker can
freely decide whether to provide an opportunity for a hearing or not, which

derogates the effectiveness of the participation rights fulfilling their functions – especially the control and symbolic functions. The election commissions in Hungary and Latvia, the State Court of Liechtenstein, and the Constitutional Court of Slovenia all have the discretion to block the exercise of participation rights. As the Liechtenstein example shows, the state institutions may focus more on the information-gathering purpose of participation rights and not allow participation for other reasons.

It can be argued that procedural actions not strictly necessary for the decision do not serve the efficiency and the timeliness of the procedures. In this case, other procedural guarantees should ensure the control and dignitarian functions of participation rights. Even when there is no oral hearing, the adversarial nature of the dispute can be upheld if the interested parties are made aware of the developments of the case (e.g. expert opinions, arguments submitted by other parties) and can react to these developments. It is a minimum requirement of participation rights that the parties can follow the case, but it is surprisingly not common in referendum authorization procedures. The Croatian Constitutional Court explicitly forbids the submission of new arguments by the initiators. The Hungarian Curia can leave the initiators out of the whole appeal procedure if a voter appeals the authorization decision. The Latvian Central Election Commission does not provide an opportunity for the initiators to comment on expert opinions. And these are just examples from states where participation rights are actually provided by the legal acts regulating referendums.

The Italian practice is exemplary in providing participation rights both to initiators and to the civil society. Involving civil society organizations can be beneficial for both the information-gathering function and the control function of participation rights. As the Italian Constitutional Court highlighted in the reproduction referendum cases, civil society organizations may provide arguments otherwise not available to the decision-maker.[82] The involvement of civil society organizations may not make sense in all referendum authorization cases, but it can be useful in cases touching on fundamental rights and freedoms in order to dispel the threat of the tyranny of the majority. The Italian example of the reproduction rights cases proves this point: reproduction rights is a sensitive and controversial issue that raises questions about the right to human dignity, the right to privacy, and the right to health. The civil society organizations could present valuable arguments and balance the arguments of the state. Similarly, the involvement of civil society could have been useful in the defense of marriage referendum cases in Croatia, Slovenia, and Slovakia,

---

[82] Judgment no. 45 of 2005, Official Gazette, 1st Special Series no. 5 of 2 February 2005, Legal considerations para 2.

where the later campaigns for and against the referendum were driven by LGBTQ and religious organizations.[83]

Beyond Italy, the practice of the Latvian Supreme Court is also exemplary, where all the procedural guarantees of an administrative procedure apply for referendum authorization. The practice of the Slovene Constitutional Court also ensures that the written submissions are circulated between the initiators and the National Assembly and that each party can react to the new submissions. In general, even if an oral hearing is not provided for the parties, the right of the initiators to actively follow the case and submit written arguments should be ensured to reduce the chance of arbitrary decision-making and pay respect to the initiators.

---

[83]   Kużelewska (Ch 1, n 10) 19–22.

9. Right to an effective remedy

1. DEFINING THE RIGHT TO AN EFFECTIVE REMEDY

The right to an effective remedy is a crucial element of the procedural under-standing of the rule of law. The right to an effective remedy traditionally ensures that a person suffering an injury to their personal liberty, security, or property has an avenue available to dispute the injury and seek restoration.[1] The core function of the right to a remedy is to correct the inevitable errors of legal decision-making and protect against the miscarriage of justice.[2] It ensures that the party losing in a legal dispute has a chance to argue against the decision and point out potential errors in fact-finding or legal interpretation.[3] Remedies also ensure that the lower-level decision-makers are held accountable for their decisions, which can contribute to building trust and public confidence in the decision-making.[4] The mere existence of remedies – even if not exercised in the concrete case – can prevent the abuse of power and strengthen the legiti-macy of the decision.[5]

Building on the interpretation of Article 13 of the ECHR by the ECtHR, the right to an effective remedy guarantees that the injured party can seek relief from a competent authority, which is usually a judicial body, but depending on its powers and the procedural guarantees it affords, can also be a non-judicial

---

[1] William Blackstone, *Commentaries on the Laws of England in Four Books.* Notes selected from the editions of Archibold, Christian, Coleridge, Chitty, Stewart, Kerr, and others, Barron Field's Analysis, and Additional Notes, and a Life of the Author by George Sharswood. In Two Volumes. (Philadelphia: J.B. Lippincott Co. 1893) 124–129; Thomas R. Phillips, 'The Constitutional Right to a Remedy' (2003) 78 *New York University Law Review* 1309, 1320–1322.

[2] Harlon Leigh Dalton, 'Taking the Right to Appeal (More or Less) Seriously' (1985) 95(1) *The Yale Law Journal* 62–107, 67; Hoffmann (Ch 6, n 8) 123; Richard Nobles, David Schiff, 'The Right to Appeal and Workable Systems of Justice' (2003) 65(5) *The Modern Law Review* 676–701; Marshall (Ch 7, n 13) 67.

[3] Dalton (n 2) 67.

[4] Marshall (Ch 7, n 13) 3–4.

[5] Dalton (n 2) 101.

body.[6] The effectiveness of the remedy entails that the remedy must be both accessible to the injured party and capable of remedying the situation.[7] The remedy is accessible if the injured party can directly challenge the detrimental decision at a reasonable cost, with legal aid available for those in need.[8] Reasonable deadlines should apply for the remedy procedure.[9] The right to a remedy is an opportunity right, thus it establishes an avenue to challenge the decision, but does not guarantee a certain outcome.[10] The effectiveness of the remedy requires only that the review covers the merits of the case and offers appropriate redress.[11]

In the following parts, the right to an effective remedy will be understood as the right of the affected parties to dispute the legal interpretation of the legal limits by the state institution authorizing referendums. The effectiveness of the remedy covers that the remedy is accessible to affected parties and ensures that the decision-maker can ultimately decide whether the popular vote takes place.

2.   RIGHT TO AN EFFECTIVE REMEDY IN REFERENDUM AUTHORIZATION PROCEDURES

The remedies within the referendum authorization procedure provide an opportunity for the interested parties to challenge the interpretation of the formal and substantive legal limits. The Revised Code of the Venice Commission does not contain a reference to the right to an effective remedy but highlights the importance of an effective system of appeal. The Code foresees an appeal body that is competent to deal with the substantive and formal authorization of the referendum proposal before the vote.[12]

The Code highlights a number of requirements regarding the procedure of the appeal body that evoke the requirements of the right to an effective

---

[6]   *Klass and Others v Germany* (1978) Series A no 28, 30, para 67; *Leander v Sweden* (1987) Series A no 116, para 77.

[7]   Marshall (Ch 7, n 13) 18–19.

[8]   *Sargin and Yagci v. Turkey* (1989) 61 DR 250, *Petkov and Others v Bulgaria* App nos 77568/01, 178/02, 505/02 (ECtHR 11 June 2009) para 82.

[9]   *Pine Valley Developments Ltd. and others v Ireland* (1991) Series A no 222, 25, para 47. See also Shetreet, 'Judicial Independence and Accountability' (Ch 6, n 2) 6.

[10]   *Kudła v. Poland* ECHR 2000-XI 197 para 157; *Swedish Engine Drivers' Union v. Sweden*, (1976) Series A no 20 para 50. See also Marshall (Ch 7, n 13) 43.

[11]   UN Human Rights Committee CCPR General Comment No. 32 [2007] UCCPR/C/GC/32 para 48. ECtHR: *Smith and Grady v UK* ECHR 1999-VI para138; *Kudła v. Poland* ECHR 2000-XI 197 para 158; *Glas Nadejda EOOD and Anatoli Elenkov v Bulgaria* ECHR 2007-XI para 69.

[12]   Revised Code II.4.3.d.

remedy. The appeal body must be impartial and independent in order to be able to afford an effective remedy.[13] The Code emphasizes that a final appeal to a court of law is preferred. The procedure of the appeal body and particularly the admissibility of the appeals must be simple and devoid of formalism.[14] The time-limits for the procedure must be short.[15] The appeal body must have the authority to annul the referendum and *ex officio* to rectify or set aside the decisions of lower election commissions.[16] The Code also makes recommendations for legal standing and participation in the appeal procedure by stating that 'all voters are entitled to an appeal'[17] and that the 'applicant's right to a hearing involving both parties must be protected'.[18]

However, it must be emphasized that the Code makes recommendations for all the possible appeal procedures in the referendum process, including appeals about the electoral registers, about campaign financing, or about the results of the vote. In the referendum process, which starts with the formulation of the referendum proposal and ends after the popular vote with the implementation of the direct-democratic decision, a number of different remedies may be available to the initiators and the voters. The initiators and voters may challenge the results of the signature collection, the different events of the referendum campaign, or the referendum results. The Code contains common provisions for all of these remedies, hence the procedural guarantees listed in the Code are not specifically tailored for referendum authorization procedures.

In referendum authorization procedures, two aspects of the right to remedy must be highlighted: its correctional function and its control function. The *correctional function* contributes to reaching the substantively 'right' decision by double-checking the legal interpretation of limits.[19] The initiators (or the voters) can dispute the legal interpretation by the first instance referendum authorization body, which is in most of the cases not a judicial body. A judicial forum or other competent authority has the final word on the legality of the referendum proposal. Meanwhile, the *control function* works in two ways: the parties to the procedure are able to keep the decision-maker in check; and the mere availability of a remedy incentivizes the decision-maker to reach an unbiased and well-rounded decision.[20] Both functions are crucial in referendum authorization procedures, especially if the legal limits are reviewed by state

---

[13]   Ibid II.4.3.a.
[14]   Ibid II.4.3.b.
[15]   Ibid II.4.3.g.
[16]   Ibid II.4.3.e., II.4.3.i.
[17]   Ibid II.4.3.f.
[18]   Ibid II.4.3.h.
[19]   Dalton (n 2) 67.
[20]   Ibid 101.

institutions with potential bias or the appearance of bias. It is, therefore, not surprising that in the few cases where the impartiality and the independence of the authorizing state institutions have been questioned, the availability of judicial remedies has always been highlighted.[21]

The correctional function of remedies is important due to the legal nature of referendum authorization procedures and the complexity of the legal limits. The availability of a judicial remedy to review the interpretation of the limits is crucial at least in cases when the initial authorization decision is not reached by courts but by parliaments, presidents, governmental bodies, or election commissions. Theoretically, it is also possible that a non-judicial but independent and impartial authority with legal expertise provides oversight over the first instance referendum authorization, but none of the Council of Europe member states have opted for non-judicial remedies. The judicial remedy can ensure that the interpretation of the legal limits is not arbitrary, and that the discretionary powers have been exercised within their bounds.

The right to an effective remedy – similarly to the right to be heard – also enables the parties to the referendum authorization procedure to have some control over the procedure. The parties have a chance to dispute the result of the first instance decision and present reasons for (or against) the referendum proposal. As the previous chapter shows, the initiators (and the wider public) have limited opportunities to participate in the referendum authorization procedure, thus voicing their concerns about the decision might be the only chance to actively participate in the referendum authorization.

In addition, the control function of the right to an effective remedy also works without the parties actually challenging the decision. The availability of a judicial remedy against the first instance decision can already enhance the quality of the decision. The chance that the parties may challenge the decision can force the decision-maker to conduct an unbiased procedure, to deliberate more carefully, and to provide a more detailed justification on why the referendum proposal violates the legal limits or not. It also juridifies the referendum authorization procedure: it can ensure that referendum authorization is regarded as a legal procedure and that political (or other non-legal) considerations are left out of the evaluation of the proposal.

---

[21]   See Chapter 6, section 3. In both Latvia and Croatia, the constitutional courts emphasized the importance of the availability of remedies, when the impartiality of the referendum authorization had been challenged.

3. LEGAL STANDING

Similarly to participation rights, one of the questions about the right to an effective remedy is the question of legal standing: who has the right to challenge a referendum authorization decision. Legal standing, or *locus standi*, is a term used to describe the capacity to bring a claim to a court.[22] It sums up the legal requirements the applicants have to fulfill in order for their claim to be considered. Traditionally, at least three different solutions exist for providing party status in public law disputes. The most restrictive standing regimes build on a close connection between the rights of the applicant and the contested issue.[23] This is the case in classic adjudicatory procedures where the aim of the procedure is to decide 'claims of right and accusations of guilt'.[24] An individualized affectedness is required for *locus standi* in a number of public law disputes. In the US the applicants have to show an 'injury' that is traceable to the unlawful government action,[25] in the jurisprudence of the ECtHR the applicant has to be the 'victim' of an unlawful act,[26] while in EU law the challenged act has to be a 'direct and individual concern' of the applicant.[27] Alternatively, it is possible to provide legal standing based on the protection of public interests – just as certain participation rights can be provided on this basis.[28] Lastly, in some cases no legal rules restrict standing at courts, leading to an *actio popularis*, where everyone is entitled to petition the court. The reasons behind allowing anyone to challenge public law decisions is the claim that the preservation of constitutionality is not an individual interest, but the interest of everyone.[29]

In referendum authorization procedures, it could be argued that both the initiators and the voters have a right to challenge the first instance decision based on individual legal interests. The procedure is decisive for a submission of the

---

[22] M. Eliantonio, Ch.W. Backes, C.H. van Rhee, T. Spronken, A. Berlee, *Standing up for Your Right(s) in Europe: A Comparative Study on Legal Standing (Locus Standi) before the EU and Member States' Courts* (Cambridge: Intersentia 2013) 11.

[23] Miles (Ch 8, n 25) 148.

[24] Lon L. Fuller, 'Forms and Limits of Adjudication' (1978) 92 *Harvard Law Review* 353, 369.

[25] *Allen v Wright* 468 U.S. 737 (1984) See also Strauss (Ch 4, n 24) 1218.

[26] Article 34 ECHR. See also Miles (Ch 8, n 25) 137.

[27] Article 263 Treaty on the Functioning of the European Union OJ C 326 (TFEU). See also Paul Craig, 'Standing, Rights, and the Structure of Legal Argument' (2003) 9(4) *European Public Law* 493–508, 494.

[28] See Chapter 8, section 3.

[29] Sadurski (Ch 1, n 104) 6; Fruzsina Gárdos-Orosz, 'The Hungarian Constitutional Court in Transition – from Actio Popularis to Constitutional Complaint' (2012) 53(4) *Acta Juridica Hungarica* 302–315, 304.

initiators. At the same time, it determines whether the voters are able to go to the ballots or not. In addition, the content of the referendum proposal could affect certain societal groups more than others, which may also warrant standing in the procedure.[30] Thus, the authorization procedure affects the initiators' right to initiate a referendum, the voters' right to participate in the vote, and potentially the rights or legal interests of certain groups or individuals affected by the content of the referendum. The first question is, then, how directly the given right is affected by the authorization procedure and whether the affectedness is close enough to provide standing in the procedure. If standing based on individual affectedness does not seem viable, then the question is whether party status might be provided based on public interest.

All the selected states that provide legal remedies in referendum authorization procedures base the right to remedy on individual affectedness. However, only the courts of Liechtenstein and Hungary have dealt with the question of legal standing in their practice.

The practice of the Liechtenstein State Court makes a clear distinction between the rights of the initiators and those of the voters. In 2002, the State Court reviewed a voter's complaint against the Prince's initiative to amend the Constitution.[31] The voter claimed – among others things – that the Prince has no right to initiate a referendum and therefore the initiative should be declared void. The complaint was rejected on its merits first by the government[32] and then by the administrative court.[33] The State Court held that the complaint was premature and that the voters do not have standing at this stage of the procedure. The Court stated that initiators, signatories, and voters have to be differentiated based on their different interests at the different stages of the procedure. According to the Court, a referendum process has three distinct stages: the first is the formal and substantive preliminary examination of the initiative by the government and the Parliament; the second is the collection of signatures; while the third is the ordering of and the preparation for the referendum:

> In the first stage of the procedure, only the initiators are involved in terms of interests. Since it is the declared aim of the initiators to make their initiative a success, it is largely in their interest that the state organs correctly perform the duties incumbent on them in this procedural stage. The situation is similar with those people who, in the second stage of the procedure, are among those who have supported the initiative with their signature. With them, too, the main interest is that the control measures within the meaning of Article 71 of the People's Rights Act are correctly

---

30 Glaser (Ch 1, n 81) 524.
31 Decision 2002/73 of 3 February 2003 of the State Court.
32 Government Proposal, BuA no 2002/88.
33 Decision 2002/96 of 12 November 2002 of the Administrative Court.

carried out by the competent state bodies. As far as the third stage of the procedure is concerned, it should be noted that the entire active citizenship (all voters) has an interest in the legal and correct implementation of the referendum.[34]

These different interests determine the standing in the different stages of the procedure: only the initiators have a right to remedy if the initiative is declared null and void by the Parliament, while voters only have standing in the third stage. In this case, the Court held that the voter submitted the complaint prematurely, because before the referendum is ordered, voters' legal sphere is not affected.[35]

This interpretation means that only the initiators can take part in the referendum authorization procedure, while the voters can enforce their rights during the campaign and the voting, but are unable to contest the authorization of the referendum issue. According to this position, the initiators have a direct legal interest in the outcome of the referendum authorization, while voters are not directly affected by the selection of the referendum issues but only by the legality of the voting event.

In contrast, the Curia of Hungary consistently holds that in the case of a national referendum request all voters have standing. The Act on Electoral Procedure regulates standing based on the individual interest of the applicant, stating that 'natural and legal persons and associations without a legal personality affected by the case may request the judicial review'.[36] However, the Curia has interpreted the affectedness of the applicant widely. In 2016, multiple applicants challenged the first instance approval of the government-initiated migration quota referendum. One of them was an individual who claimed that they had standing because they are Hungarian residents.[37] The government, as the initiator, requested that the application be rejected by the court, claiming that Hungarian residency alone does not establish a link between the legal status of the applicant and the case. The government argued that affectedness only exists if the claimed legal violation directly affects the rights or obligations of the applicant.[38] The Curia refused this line of argument. Since the same standing rules apply, the Court drew a comparison between election disputes and referendum authorization procedures. The Court stated that election disputes are multilevel procedures where the judicial remedy follows a first

---

[34]   Decision 2002/73 of 3 February 2003 of the State Court para 3.1 (DeepL Translator).

[35]   Ibid.

[36]   Art. 222 (1) Act XXXVI of 2013 on Electoral Procedure (Official English translation).

[37]   Decision Knk.IV.37.222/2016/9 of the Curia, para 4.

[38]   Ibid para 19.

instance procedure, which enables a narrower interpretation of affectedness. However, the nature of referendum cases is different from election disputes because they often relate to fundamental rights without extensive procedural prelude. In referendum cases, standing depends on the nature of the proposed referendum question and can be decided based on analyzing the content of the question. The question about the migration quota referendum affects all voters and all Hungarian residents, thus the applicant has standing before the Court.[39]

Comparing the voters' access to remedy in these referendum cases, it is interesting to note that both Liechtenstein and Hungary build on the individual legitimation of standing. The core question in both cases is whether the legal interests of voters are affected by the decision. The Hungarian argument about the distinction between election and referendum disputes is not convincing enough to differentiate between the standing rules. Referendum disputes – similarly to election disputes – are multilevel procedures where the judicial remedy follows the decision of the election commission. Referendum disputes can relate to fundamental rights, but this is equally true for election disputes that ensure the right to vote. However, the argument that standing has to be linked to the scope and nature of the referendum question has its merits. It acknowledges that a national referendum affects all voters, thus the voters have a legal interest in the selection of the subject of the referendum, which warrants participation already at the authorization stage.

Based on these cases, it seems uncontestable that the initiators of the referendum have a legal interest in the authorization procedure and should have remedy rights. In all selected states, the right to initiate a referendum and the right to vote are enshrined in the constitutions as political rights of the citizens. The decision rejecting a referendum proposal causes an 'injury' to the initiators who are prevented from promoting the referendum and exercising their right to vote. The initiators formulate the initiative and support it throughout the referendum process, thus they are directly affected by the referendum authorization decision.

The standing of voters is more controversial. Voters can either support or oppose the referendum proposal and can claim different legal interests accordingly. Voters *in support of* the referendum can rely on similar claims for standing as the initiators. They are also affected by the decision rejecting the referendum proposal, as the rejection decision prevents them from exercising their political rights to participate in the legislative process. However, this legal interest is already represented in the case by the initiators who are more directly affected. Providing standing for voters in support of the referendum based on the same reasons as for the initiators might be redundant for practical

---

reasons. If the initiators choose to give up on the referendum (e.g. they do not appeal the rejection, withdraw the proposal, or do not collect the signatures), then the referendum might fail regardless of voter support. Alternatively, the provision of standing creates an additional lifeline for the referendum: even if the initiators do not challenge the rejection decision, the voters supporting the referendum can step in. This can happen particularly if the authorization procedure follows the signature collection, and the referendum proposal has gathered support from voters.

Voters *opposing* the referendum proposal can make a claim for standing based on the content of the referendum: a successful vote on the referendum issue would affect them. This approach was the basis in the Hungarian case on the legal standing of voters. The affectedness based on the issue can have two variations. Voters have to establish either that the legal change adopted in the referendum would be detrimental to them individually or that their legal interest lies in not having unlawful referendums and thus in upholding the rule of law.

In the first case, it is claimed that the legal change adopted in the referendum would violate the rights of the individuals and social groups, which warrant a remedy for them. This would, in fact, be a restriction on the remedy rights of voters because it would require the court to assess the potential injuries that the successful referendum would cause to the applicant. It cannot be contested that some referendums can severely and negatively affect the rights of individuals or groups. In fact, sometimes that is the aim of the referendum. The marriage referendums in Eastern Europe directly aimed to restrict the legal status of same-sex couples.[40] The Swiss initiative on the expulsion of asylum seekers who had entered the country illegally would have severely affected people who were to be expelled to their home countries.[41] Similarly, referendums about spatial planning (for instance the construction of highways or nuclear power plants) can affect individuals located in the area.[42] It is, however, questionable whether the referendum authorization procedure is the procedural stage where a remedy should be provided against such injuries. The affectedness of individuals and groups at this stage is distant and provisory. The injury to their rights that can occur is conditional on the referendum being supported at the polls, and on the implementation measures the state takes. Even if the referendum is successful and the legal changes enter into force, the affected individuals and groups might have other legal opportunities to challenge either the decision that directly affects their rights or the legal norm itself. Thus, the

---

[40] Kużelewska (Ch 1, n 10) 13–27.
[41] Baumann (Ch 4, n 52) 196.
[42] Glaser (Ch 1, n 81) 524.

potential individual injury of the individuals and groups affected by the content of the referendum does not seem direct enough to be the basis of standing.

The other option – which eventually the Hungarian Curia took – is that the legal standing of the voters is based on their individual interest in the legality of the referendum. As voters they are automatically affected by any issue put to a national vote and they have an interest in not having an unlawful vote that could either not be implemented or whose implementation would violate rights. Even though the Curia framed the standing of voters in terms of individual affectedness, it is impossible to differentiate this type of standing from standing based on public interest or from *actio popularis*. In this case, the voters can challenge the referendum authorization decision on the basis that everyone has an interest in upholding constitutionality and the rule of law, and everyone would be affected by an unlawful referendum.

In the Council of Europe and in the selected states, a remedy is usually provided only against rejection decisions and only to the initiators. From the 13 states that provide a remedy in the referendum authorization procedure, only three allow anyone to challenge the authorization decision (Bulgaria, Hungary, Russia).[43] Limiting the remedy rights to the initiators emphasizes that the injury occurs primarily to the initiators and not to the wider public. It promotes the standpoint that a decision authorizing a referendum should be considered favorable for voters as they are able to exercise their right to vote. It disregards the possibility that voters might have a legal interest in preventing unlawful referendum proposals from reaching the polls.

4.   THE AVAILABILITY AND ACCESSIBILITY OF REMEDIES

The availability of remedies against the first instance referendum authorization decision is not prevalent in the eight selected states. Only half of them allow the first instance decision to be challenged. The selected states represent the general trend among Council of Europe member states: remedies are almost always available against election commission decisions, while parliamentary and presidential decisions are often final.[44] If a remedy is provided, then it is generally accessible in most of the selected states. The conditions of initiating

---

[43]   See Chapter 2, section 4.3, and LIDD data dashboard > Explore data > By Instrument/Item > Theme: Formal/Substantive procedure on <http://lidd-project.org/data/> accessed 15 March 2022.

[44]   See Chapter 2, section 4.2, and LIDD data dashboard > Explore data > By Instrument/Item > Theme: Formal/Substantive procedure on http://lidd-project.org/data/, statistics correct as at 15 March 2022.

the remedy do not seem to be so burdensome as to hinder the effectiveness of the remedy.

4.1   No Remedies

The parliamentary decisions in Croatia and Switzerland as well as the presidential decisions in Slovakia are final. As mentioned before, the Croatian Parliament and the Slovak President can initiate the review of the constitutional courts.[45] In these two states the judicial review process is not a judicial remedy, since the judicial decision is integrated in the first instance decision-making and the constitutional courts function as expert co-deciding bodies. The procedure is not linked to the appeal of the parties. In this way, the judicial review does not offer a remedy for the injuries of the initiators or voters. Nonetheless, the judicial review still contributes to building trust in the referendum authorization procedure and reaching the substantively correct decision, because the courts are able to provide the necessary constitutional expertise that is lacking on the side of the Parliament or the President. The Slovak President has relied on the Constitutional Court in the most recent popular initiatives: both the defense of marriage initiative and the early election initiative have been referred to the Constitutional Court.[46] Similarly, the Croatian Parliament often involves the Constitutional Court in the decision-making: in recent years the judicial review has been initiated with regard to the Vukovar minority rights initiative as well as the initiative on the prohibition of the outsourcing of auxiliary services in the public sector, and the proposed ban on the monetization of highways.[47] The Constitutional Court was not petitioned in the Croatian defense of marriage case, but the Court issued legal opinions *ex officio*.[48]

Similarly, Switzerland does not provide a remedy for the initiators or the voters in the formal or substantive authorization procedure.[49] Several scholars

---

[45]   Croatia: Art. 125 Constitution; Slovakia: Art. 95(2) and Art. 125b Constitution.

[46]   The defense of marriage initiative was decided in Decision PL. ÚS 24/2014 of 28 October 2014 of the Constitutional Court while the early election initiative in Judgement PL. ÚS 7/2021 of 7 July 2021 of the Constitutional Court, Collection of Laws 280/2021. See also Drugda (Ch 3, n 115).

[47]   Decision of the Constitutional Court of the Republic of Croatia No. U-VIIR -4640/2014 of 12 August 2014, Official Gazette 104/14, and Decision of the Constitutional Court of the Republic of Croatia No. U-VIIR-1159/2015 of 8 April 2015, Official Gazette 43/2015, 887. See also Gardašević (Ch 3, n 14) 1; Podolnjak, 'Croatia' (Ch 3, n 10) 161.

[48]   Communication of the Constitutional Court on the Citizens' Constitutional Referendum on the Definition of Marriage, SuS-1/2013, 14 November 2013.

[49]   A remedy is only available with regard to the technical authorization of the Federal Chancellery. See Art. 80(3) Federal Act on Political Rights.

have suggested that the Federal Assembly is incapable of carrying out a legal review of referendum proposals.[50] However, all reform attempts have failed so far.[51] The lack of judicial remedies can lead to situations where new constitutional norms are approved in referendums that are not in conformity with the other provisions of the Constitution or international law. In recent years some popular initiatives have been adopted by the Swiss people that arguably violate international law, especially the provisions of the ECHR.[52] The Swiss people have approved a ban on building minarets, the automatic expulsion of foreign criminals and the life-long incarceration of extremely dangerous sexual or violent offenders.[53]

In 2012 the Swiss Federal Supreme Court decided a case about a Macedonian complainant who was expelled from Switzerland following a conditionally enforceable prison sentence for drug trafficking.[54] In the decision, the Court reflected on the new constitutional provisions about the automatic expulsion of foreign criminals that had entered into force in 2010. The Court emphasized that in the historical development of the Constitution it has incorporated a number of different principles and guarantees that may not always conform with each other. The interpretation of the constitutional provisions should establish consistency and unity between the conflicting provisions.[55] This also means that an individual constitutional provision cannot be viewed in isolation and interpreted exclusively in the manner the initiators understood.[56] The implementation of the new provisions poses a particular challenge, according to the Court, as viewed on their own they appear to be in conflict with fundamental values recognized by Switzerland under international law. The Court highlighted that it is currently up to the political authorities to create the necessary balance between the constitutional values at the legislative level.

---

[50]   Keller, Lanter, Fischer (Ch 1, n 12) 123; Biaggini (Ch 1, n 12) 340; Auer, Aubert, Somer (Ch 1, n 91) 672; Tarek Naguib, 'Halbdirekte Demokratie und Rechtsstaat im Konflikt: Quo vadis? Einblicke in die eidgenössische Kontroverse zum Umgang mit menschenrechtswidrigen Volksinitiativen und verfassungswidrigen Bundesgesetzen' in Michael Wrase, Christian Boulanger, Anna Schulze (eds), *Die Politik des Verfassungsrechts: Interdisziplinäre und vergleichende Perspektiven auf die Rolle und Funktion von Verfassungsgerichten* (Nomos 2013) 283, 297–299.

[51]   Moeckli, 'Switzerland' (Ch 2, n 14) 41–42.

[52]   Kiener, Krüsi (Ch 1, n 15) 239.

[53]   Art. 72(3), Art. 121(3)–(6), and Art. 123a of the Federal Constitution. See Keller, Lanter, Fischer (Ch 1, n 12) 121–154; Kiener, Krüsi (Ch 1, n 15) 239; Biaggini (Ch 1, n 12) 329–330.

[54]   *X v Migration Office of the Canton of Thurgau*, BGE 139 I 16, Decision of the Federal Court of 12 October 2012.

[55]   Ibid para 4.2.1.

[56]   Ibid.

However, then the Court stated that even if the new constitutional provisions had been directly applicable in the case, this could not have changed the outcome: 'in the event of a conflict of norms between international law and later legislation, the case law generally assumes the primacy of international law'.[57] The analysis of the Federal Supreme Court about popular initiatives that violate international law is *obiter dictum* in this judgment. Nonetheless, it indicates the approach the Court might take once a case arrives where the conflict between new constitutional provisions adopted through popular vote and international law must be resolved. However, this possible post-vote remedy does not prevent potentially unconstitutional norms from becoming part of the legal system and cannot substitute for the control and correctional functions of a remedy within the authorization procedure.

Lastly, remedies are not available against the decisions of the Italian Constitutional Court. Although the referendum authorization is decided by a judicial body that evidently possesses the necessary expertise in constitutional adjudication, the lack of remedies means that there is no control over potential errors in the decision-making. The injuries of the initiators and voters cannot be rectified and the exercise of discretionary powers by the Court is left unchecked.

4.2   Remedies by Regular Courts

As a general trend, the referendum authorization decisions of election commissions and governmental bodies can be challenged before regular courts.[58] In states where referendum authorization is left to election commissions (or governmental bodies), the procedure is regarded as akin to administrative decision-making, where judicial oversight of administrative actions is the norm in most European states.[59] The first instance referendum authorization decision can be appealed before regular courts with administrative law jurisdiction in Latvia and Hungary.[60] The approximation of referendum authori-

---

[57]   Ibid para 5 (DeepL Translator).
[58]   See Chapter 2, section 4.2.
[59]   Giulio Napolitano, 'The Rule of Law' in Peter Cane, Herwig C.H. Hofmann, Eric C. Ip, Peter L. Lindseth (eds), *The Oxford Handbook of Comparative Administrative Law* (Oxford University Press 2020) 434; Li-Ann Thio, 'Courts and Judicial Review' in Peter Cane, Herwig C.H. Hofmann, Eric C. Ip, Peter L. Lindseth (eds), The *Oxford Handbook of Comparative Administrative Law* (Oxford University Press 2020) 721.
[60]   Beyond these two selected states, the same applies for Russia, Lithuania, Moldova, and Georgia. See LIDD data dashboard > Explore data > By Instrument/Item > Theme: Substantive/Formal procedure on http://lidd-project.org/data/, accessed 15 March 2022.

zation procedures to administrative procedures also highlights their concrete review element and that they center around the permissibility of a voting event.

In Latvia, the refusal decision of the Central Election Commission can be appealed by the initiators before the Senate of the Supreme Court Department of Administrative Law.[61] The Latvian referendum Act does not contain extensive procedural rules on the appeal. It ensures that the appeal procedure is prompt, as the Supreme Court has to decide within one month about the petition.[62] The referendum Act also states that the applicants – thus the initiators – have to provide justifications for the appeal and that the burden of proof shall lie with the participants in the administrative proceeding.[63] Since the referendum authorization procedure lacks any fact-finding and is solely about the interpretation of legal limits, it follows that the initiators and the Central Election Commission have to provide reasons for their interpretation of the legal limits. The Court adjudicates the case within these claims.[64] For the judicial procedure, the rules of the Administrative Procedure Law provide detailed procedural rules, but they do not contain specific provisions for referendums. The Supreme Court examines the case as a court of first instance,[65] thus the provisions of the first instance procedure are applicable for referendum cases.[66] The applicant may appeal the first instance decision within 30 days, arguing that the administrative act is invalid or that there has been a serious procedural law violation that caused a significant infringement of rights or legal interests.[67] The appeal has to identify the applicant and their contact details. It also has to contain the claim and the grounds for the application. It can contain a request for oral procedure or legal aid.[68] In cases where the appeal does not conform with these conditions, the judge does not reject the application but leaves it 'not proceeded with' until the defects of the application are corrected.[69] By establishing admissibility conditions for referendum appeals but at the same time offering opportunities for correcting the appeals, the law does not impose undue burdens on the initiators that would limit their access to the remedy.

---

[61] Art. 23(1 prim)(1) Law On National Referendum, Legislative Initiative and European Citizens' Initiative.

[62] Art. 23(1 prim)(3) Law On National Referendum, Legislative Initiative and European Citizens' Initiative.

[63] Art. 23(1 prim) Law On National Referendum, Legislative Initiative and European Citizens' Initiative.

[64] See also section 5.1. of this chapter, on claim limitations.

[65] Art. 23(1 prim) Law On National Referendum, Legislative Initiative and European Citizens' Initiative.

[66] Chapter 10–31 Administrative Procedure Law.

[67] Art. 184 Administrative Procedure Law.

[68] Art. 186 Administrative Procedure Law.

[69] Art. 192 Administrative Procedure Law.

Even though the remedy seems accessible, only four of the 13 rejected citizen-initiated referendums have been challenged since 2012: the citizenship initiative,[70] the initiative against the euro,[71] and two initiatives related to education.[72]

In Hungary, both the approval and the rejection decision of the National Election Commission can be challenged at the Curia.[73] The Curia has 90 days to either amend or uphold the decision of the National Election Commission.[74] The legal provisions contain a number of admissibility conditions for the petition. The applicant has to submit the appeal within 15 days from the publication of the resolution of the National Election Commission.[75] The appeal can only be submitted personally, or via post, or via certified electronic document.[76] The appeal has to contain the grounds for challenging the first instance decision, which may either be a legal violation or an unlawful exercise of discretionary powers.[77] The appeal must also contain the name, address, and personal identification number of the applicant.[78] Legal representation is mandatory in the procedures of the Curia.[79] If the applicant does not attach the proof of legal representation, then the court provides a deadline to correct the defect. If the applicant fails to submit an appeal that is in line with the other conditions, the Curia rejects the appeal without considering its merits.[80] The Curia rejects between 11 and 17 per cent of the appeals based on defects in the submissions,[81] thus these conditions create a hurdle to the accessibility of remedies. Some of these – for instance, the substantive requirement to justify the appeal – are rea-

---

[70]   Judgment No. SA-1/2014 of 12 February 2014 of the Supreme Court; Judgment No. SA-1/2013 of 11 February 2013 of the Supreme Court.

[71]   Judgment No. SA-3/2014 of 28 March 2014 of the Supreme Court.

[72]   Judgment No. SA-1/2020 of 2 March 2020 of the Supreme Court; Judgment No. SA-2/2018 of 11 May 2018 of the Supreme Court.

[73]   Art. 29 Act CCXXXVIII of 2013 on Initiating Referendums, the European Citizens' Initiative and Referendum Procedure and Art. 222 Act XXXVI of 2013 on Electoral Procedure.

[74]   Art. 30 (1) Act CCXXXVIII of 2013 on Initiating Referendums, the European Citizens' Initiative and Referendum Procedure.

[75]   Art. 29 Act CCXXXVIII of 2013 on Initiating Referendums, the European Citizens' Initiative and Referendum Procedure.

[76]   Art. 223(1) Act XXXVI of 2013 on Electoral Procedure.

[77]   Art. 223(3) Act XXXVI of 2013 on Electoral Procedure.

[78]   Art. 224(3) Act XXXVI of 2013 on Electoral Procedure.

[79]   Art. 224(5) Act XXXVI of 2013 on Electoral Procedure.

[80]   Art. 231 of Act XXXVI of 2013 on Electoral Procedure.

[81]   See <https://www.valasztas.hu/documents/20182/305738/Statisztik%C3%A1k+az+elb%C3%ADr%C3%A1lt+n%C3%A9pszavaz%C3%A1si+kezdem%C3%A9nyez%C3%A9sekr%C5%91l.pdf/a0655454-ecd7–412f-ab08–8a23dc419f5e>, accessed 15 March 2022.

sonable requirements. However, in the last five years, eight appeals have been rejected solely based on the omission of the personal identification number of the applicant,[82] even though the identification of the applicant would have been possible through the other personal data they provided or through their legal representation. This strict interpretation of the admissibility conditions also contributes to the high rejection rates in Hungarian referendum authorization procedures.

4.3   Remedies by Constitutional Courts

In the member states of the Council of Europe, parliaments are just as popular institutional choices for referendum authorization as election commissions. However, remedies are available in only half of these cases.[83] If remedies are provided against parliamentary decisions, then it is almost exclusively to constitutional courts.[84] The choice of the parliament for authorizing referendums highlights the link between direct and representative democracy. From a procedural perspective, this choice – especially coupled with a constitutional court review – highlights the abstract review element of referendum authorization and the fact that the procedure is about a legislative proposal.

The rejection of the referendum request can be appealed by the initiators in Liechtenstein and Slovenia.[85] In Liechtenstein, the People's Rights Act states only that the initiators have the right to appeal the declaration of invalidity by Parliament.[86] The Act on the State Court specifies that the appeal has to be submitted within four weeks of the publication of the resolution, and the appeal has to contain justifications describing the alleged rights violation.[87] Legal representation is not necessary in the procedure.[88] The Court rejects the application only if it is not submitted within the statutory deadlines or due to obvious lack of jurisdiction.[89] Consequently, the appeal procedure of the State Court seems to be accessible for the initiators. Even though Liechtenstein has

---

[82]   Decisions Knk.II.40.646/2021/9; Knk.IV.37.874/2019/2; Knk.VII.37.282/ 2019/2; Knk.VII.37.124/2019/2; Knk.IV.37.123/2019/2; Knk.VII.38.104/2017/2; Knk. VII.37.842/2017/2; and Knk.IV.37.841/2017/2 of the Curia.

[83]   See Chapter 2, section 4.2.

[84]   The one exception is Serbia, where the Supreme Court can review the parliamentary decision. See Art. 41 Law on Referendum and People's Initiative.

[85]   Liechtenstein: Art. 70 and Art. 70b People's Rights Act; Slovenia: 47/13 Constitutional Act on Amending Articles 90, 97, and 99 of the Constitution of the Republic of Slovenia.

[86]   Art. 70(1)(b) People's Rights Act.

[87]   Arts 15–16 Act on the State Court.

[88]   Art. 41 Act on the State Court.

[89]   Art. 43 Act on the State Court.

a continually active referendum practice, the State Court has been involved in the referendum authorization only four times: twice regarding the initiative of the Prince where the Court did not assess the merits of the appeals due to the lack of standing,[90] and twice reviewing the rejection decisions of the Parliament.[91] The lack of extensive judicial practice can be due to the low rejection rates in the parliamentary authorization: the Parliament has only rejected two citizen-initiated referendums since 1990 and both have been challenged before the Court.[92]

In Slovenia, the referendum Act determines the deadlines for the appeal and for the adjudication of the appeal. The initiators of the referendum have 15 days from the rejection decision of the National Assembly to challenge the decision at the Constitutional Court. The Constitutional Court decides within 30 days.[93] The legal provisions governing the procedure of the Constitutional Court do not contain specific rules for referendum authorization procedures. The Act on the Constitutional Court prescribes the rules of reviewing the constitutionality and legality of regulations and general Acts to be applied for any 'other' procedure in the jurisdiction of the Court.[94] According to these rules, the request to the Court must identify the challenged Act, contain a statement of reasons about the inconsistencies between the Act and the Constitution, and provide information able to ascertain the applicants' standing.[95] The Court rejects the request if these conditions are not fulfilled.[96] Out of the 14 cases about referendum authorization that have been adjudicated by the Constitutional Court,[97] such a rejection has only occurred in one case: a local referendum aiming to prohibit the building of mosques.[98]

---

[90] Decision 2002/67 of 9 December 2002 of the State Court, and Decision 2002/73 of 3 February 2003 of the State Court. Both cases concerned the constitutional reform initiated by the Prince.

[91] Decision 2004/70 of 9 May 2005 of the State Court on a climate change initiative, and Decision 2013/183 of 28 February 2014 of the of the State Court on a pension reform.

[92] Auer, Aubert, and Somer (Ch 1, n 91) 671–672; Wilfried Marxer, *Direkte Demokratie in Liechtenstein: Entwicklung, Regelungen, Praxis* (Ch 4, n 38) 155.

[93] Art. 21 Referendum and Popular Initiative Act.

[94] Art. 49 Constitutional Court Act.

[95] Art. 24b Constitutional Court Act.

[96] Art. 25 Constitutional Court Act.

[97] See <https://www.us-rs.si/decisions/?q=referendum&caseId=&df=&dt=&af=&at=&pri=1&vd=&vo=&vv=&vs=&ui=&va=&page=1&sort=&order=&lang=en#show-decision-results>, accessed 15 March 2022.

[98] Decision U-I-111/04 of 28 April 2004 of the Constitutional Court, Official Gazette of the Republic of Slovenia, No. 51/2004.

5.   THE SCOPE OF REMEDIES

Beyond the availability and accessibility of the right to remedy, the scope of these remedies warrants a closer look. Referendum cases are special in the sense that the authorization procedure is purely about deciding a legal question. The *a priori* nature of the referendum authorization means that there is not a factual dispute behind the case,[99] it is 'only' about the legality and constitutionality of the referendum proposal. It follows that the authorizing state institution does not have to establish the facts of the case or conduct an evidentiary procedure, and the factual basis cannot be the subject of the remedy. Consequently, in referendum authorization procedures some traditional questions about public law remedies are not relevant. For instance, the question whether both legal and factual questions can be reviewed (*de novo* review) is not meaningful. It is, however, still important to assess the limits of the remedy and the decisional competence of the judicial body – that is, the competence of the courts to go beyond the claim and to change or annul the first instance decision.

5.1   Claim Limitations

One question that arises about the scope of the remedy is whether the court is bound by the claim of the applicants or whether it can review the referendum authorization decision for the violation of legal limits not mentioned in the application. Claim limitations highlight that the remedy procedure is primarily about remedying the applicant's injury and the protection of individual rights.[100] Meanwhile, providing an option for the court to step beyond the claims emphasizes the protection of legality and the rule of law.[101] This question is relevant for the remedy procedures of regular courts, while constitutional courts as guardians of the constitutional order usually do not face claim limitations. The Liechtenstein State Court, for instance, exercises its jurisdiction *ex officio* in every stage of the proceedings.[102] The Slovene Constitutional Court is also not bound by the petition when reviewing the legality or constitutionality of legislation and other general acts.[103]

The question of claim limitations has appeared multiple times in the case law of the Hungarian Curia. Most recently, the court analyzed the question in relation to citizen appeals against the government-initiated referendum on the

---

[99]   Nobles, Schiff (n 2) 676–701.

[100]   Thio (n 59) 726.

[101]   Raymond T. Koopmans, 'Natural Justice Rediviva? The Right to a Fair Hearing in European Law' (1992) 39(1) *Netherlands International Law Review* 175–186, 180.

[102]   Art. 39 Act on the State Court.

[103]   Art. 30 Constitutional Court Act.

prohibition of gender reassignment surgeries for minors.[104] In all the cases, the Curia has stated that the protection of the constitutional order has priority over claim limitations in referendum authorization procedures. In other administrative law cases, the court is bound by the claim, but in referendum authorization procedures it must evaluate all the potential legal grounds for refusing the authorization.[105] In some of the cases this means that the Curia bases its decision on a completely new legal ground. When citizens submitted an initiative that aimed to restrict the special healthcare privileges of government ministers, the National Election Commission rejected it based on two arguments. First, the Commission claimed that the question does not belong to the competence of the National Assembly as it is regulated by government decrees. Second, the Commission reasoned that the question cannot be regarded so important as to warrant the exceptional use of direct democracy.[106] The first ground for rejection is an explicit substantive limit on referendums, while the second limit was derived from the preamble of the referendum Act.[107] The Curia upheld the rejection decision but based the reasoning on the substantive limit on person- and organization-related matters falling within the competence of the National Assembly.[108] The court also highlighted that the Commission erred in basing its decision on the preamble of the referendum Act instead of relying on explicit limits.[109] It has been a long-standing practice of the Curia to *ex officio* review all possible grounds for rejection.[110] This practice clearly emphasizes the correctional function of remedies and prioritizes the protection of the rule of law. However, with the abundance of limits in the Hungarian referendum rules, it also makes it even harder to initiate a successful referendum.

In contrast, the Latvian Administrative Procedure Law states that the court has to render a judgment on the subject-matter of the application, as set out by the applicant, not exceeding the limitations of the claim.[111] In the practice of the Latvian Supreme Court this question has not yet appeared. This might be due to the small number of cases in Latvia. Also, most referendum authorization cases center exclusively around the question of whether the legislative

---

[104] Decision Knk.II.40.646/2021/9 of the Curia.

[105] Decisions Knk.VII.38.177/2018/2; Knk.II.40.646/2021/9; Knk.VII.38.257/2018/2; Knk.IV.37.300/2012/4; Knk.IV.37.361/2015/3; and Knk.IV.37.340/2015/3 of the Curia.

[106] Decision 1041/2018 of the National Election Commission.

[107] Act CCXXXVIII of 2013 on Initiating Referendums, the European Citizens' Initiative and Referendum Procedure.

[108] Decision Knk.VII.38.257/2018/2 of the Curia para 23.

[109] Ibid para 28.

[110] See Decisions Knk.IV.37.340/2015/3 and Knk.IV.37.361/2015/3 of the Curia.

[111] Art. 249 Administrative Procedure Law.

initiative has been fully elaborated.[112] The adherence to claim limitations high-lights that the appeal is in the hands of the appellants, and that the court offers remedy for the violation of their rights. At the same time, the appellants carry the burden of establishing the legality or illegality of the referendum proposal. The Latvian referendum law explicitly states that the burden of proof shall lie with the participants of the administrative proceedings.[113] This solution empha-sizes the control function of remedy rights.

5.2   Decisional Competence

The decisional competence of the judicial bodies can either allow the annul-ment or the revision of the challenged decision. This means that if the court finds that the first instance decision-maker has erred in the interpretation of legal limits, it can either repeal the decision and refer the case back for a new procedure or remedy the illegality through the revision of the challenged deci-sion. The choice between the revision and the annulment competence reflects various policy considerations.[114] The annulment of the challenged decision allows the first instance decision-maker to correct both the substantive and procedural defects of its decision. The annulment respects the decisional competence of the first instance body and protects the separation of powers.[115] However, it prolongs the procedure and can lead to a back-and-forth between the different instances.[116] The revision competence contributes to procedural economy and ensures the timely ending of the procedure but it encroaches on the competence of the first instance decision-maker.[117] It can provide a remedy against the substantive defaults of the decision, but not against the procedural violations committed in the first instance procedure. This last element has little practical relevance because none of the selected states offers extensive and mandatory participation rights in the first instance referendum authorization

---

[112] See Judgment No. SA-3/2014 of 28 March 2014 of the Supreme Court on the rejection of the euro, Judgment No. SA-1/2014 of 12 February 2014 of the Supreme Court on the citizenship referendum, or Judgment No. SA-1/2020 of 2 March 2020 of the Supreme Court on education reform.

[113] Art. 23 (1 prim) (4) Law On National Referendum, Legislative Initiative and European Citizens' Initiative.

[114] Katharina Pabel, 'Verwaltungsprozessrecht' (2007) 15 *Journal für Rechtspolitik* 287–297, 289.

[115] Klaus Rennert, 'Administration, Administrative Jurisdiction and Separation of Powers' [2018] 1 *ELTE Law Journal* 147–155, 152–153.

[116] Pabel (n 114) 289.

[117] Rennert (n 115) 152–153.

procedure.[118] Still, it is worth mentioning that the revision competence could be ineffective for remedying procedural law violations.

The Hungarian Curia serves as an example. The court decides the merits of the case by the adoption of a resolution, either upholding or altering the resolution of the National Election Commission.[119] In other administrative law cases, if the Curia notices that the administrative body or the lower-level court conducted a procedure in serious violation of procedural rules, it annuls the lower-level decision and instructs the administrative body or court to conduct a new procedure that adheres to the procedural guarantees. In referendum cases, the Curia does not have an annulment competence, and the appeal procedure itself cannot remedy the violations of procedural rules. This means that if the National Election Commission commits a procedural law violation (for instance by not deciding by majority vote) or if there are other procedural shortcomings (for example regarding the standing of parties), the Curia has no means to correct the violation.[120] It can state in its resolution that procedural rights have been violated, but it cannot offer any effective remedy. This question came up in a referendum authorization case in 2018.[121] The popular initiative aimed to introduce a mandatory referendum for all legislative Acts that require a qualified majority in parliament. The initiative was rejected by the National Election Commission and the rejection decision was challenged at the Curia. The initiator claimed that their right to a fair procedure was violated because they had not been afforded an opportunity to present their arguments in the open session of the election commission. In rejecting the appeal, the Curia did not reference the election procedure law, which clearly states that the election commission can freely decide whether or not to allow for an oral presentation of arguments.[122] Instead, the court reasoned that it has no competence to remedy procedural law violations and did not evaluate the merits of the claim.[123]

Apart from Hungary, all other states offering remedies have opted for providing an annulment competence to the judicial bodies. In Liechtenstein, the State Court can repeal the decision of the Parliament and refer the case back for a new decision that takes account of the legal opinion of the Court.[124] Similarly,

---

118 See Chapter 8, section 4.

119 Art. 30 Act CCXXXVIII of 2013 on Initiating Referendums, the European Citizens' Initiative and Referendum Procedure.

120 Decision Knk.IV.37.222/2016/9 of the Curia.

121 Decision Knk.VII.37.868/2018/2 of the Curia.

122 Art. 43 Act XXXVI of 2013 on Electoral Procedure. See also Chapter 8, section 4.

123 Decision Knk.VII.37.868/2018/2 of the Curia, para 22.

124 Art. 17 Act on the State Court. See also Decision 2013/183 of the State Court.

the Constitutional Court of Slovenia can abrogate the order of the National Assembly.[125] This solution respects the decisional authority of the parliaments. It is also in line with the traditional decisional competences of constitutional courts: they can annul or set aside legislative Acts but cannot actively take the place of the legislature.[126]

6.   CONCLUSIONS FROM THE STATE PRACTICE

The right to an effective remedy ensures that the first instance decision-maker is held accountable, and a further state authority can correct the potential errors of the legal interpretation of the limits. The availability of the remedy can enhance the quality of the first instance referendum procedure by incentivizing the state institution to carry out a thorough and unbiased procedure. In addition, it provides an opportunity for the parties to express their arguments and participate in the procedure. The right to an effective remedy ensures that the parties to the authorization procedure can appeal to a court, and that the legal interpretation of the limits is in the hands of a judicial organ with experience in legal adjudication.

The provision of remedy rights is especially important in cases where the first instance authorization procedure is conducted by a state institution which might lack the necessary independence, impartiality, or professional competence to carry out the review of the legal limits. Yet the analysis of the state practice shows that remedies are available against the decisions of election commissions but not necessarily against the decisions of parliaments (or presidents). As the examples of Slovenia and Liechtenstein show, it is possible to integrate constitutional court remedies into the parliamentary referendum authorization procedure, thus ensuring that both the correctional and control functions of remedies are fulfilled. Slovakia and Croatia also enable the constitutional courts to review the referendum proposal, although their solutions cannot be deemed a remedy procedure and do not offer the parties any control over the decision-making.

When remedies are provided in a referendum authorization procedure, then most states make them available only for initiators against rejection decisions. The initiators of the referendum are directly affected by the rejection as they are prevented from promoting the referendum and exercising their right to vote. Only in Hungary can voters appeal the first instance referendum author-

---

[125]   Art. 21 Referendum and Popular Initiative Act. See also Decision No. U-II-1/15 of 28 September 2015 of the Constitutional Court, Official Gazette Republic of Slovenia No. 80/15, para 38.

[126]   Sadurski (Ch 1, n 104) 57.

ization decision. The involvement of voters can introduce a further guarantee against referendum proposals violating formal or substantive limits reaching the polls. The voters can be provided remedy rights based on multiple justifications. They can claim that their right to vote is affected or that they are individually affected by the content of the referendum proposal. However, the most convincing reason for involving voters already at the stage of the referendum authorization is that everyone has a legal interest in upholding constitutionality and the rule of law, and everyone would be affected by an unlawful referendum. The provision of remedy rights to voters can ensure that the citizens have full control over the legality of the referendum authorization procedures: the initiators can appeal against the unlawful rejection of the referendum proposal, while the voters can oversee that the legal limits are applied against unlawful proposals.

The examples of the selected states show that if remedies are provided, then they are generally accessible. None of the states impose such hurdles that would significantly limit access to the remedies. Similarly, the effectiveness of the remedies does not seem to be affected by the decision competence of the authorizing state institutions. Claim limitations rarely apply, which makes the correctional potential of the remedy procedure even stronger. Meanwhile, the annulment powers, which are the norm in the selected states, ensure that the decisional competence of the first instance state institution is respected but still enable the courts to determine how the legal limits should be interpreted.

10. Conclusions on referendum authorization procedures in Europe

In recent years, a number of referendums have been organized in European countries that fell short of the ideal of direct democracy. The rise of populism in some European countries has also contributed to the criticism of referendums. In some of the votes, such as the Brexit referendum, the Russian constitutional referendum, or the Hungarian migrant quota referendum, the empowerment and the genuine will-formation of the voters seemed secondary to the political gains of the governments and the political parties. In other instances, such as the defense of marriage referendums in Central Europe or the referendums on the rights of foreigners and asylum seekers in Switzerland, the popular votes directly targeted the rights of minorities and vulnerable groups.

I make the argument that more emphasis should be laid on the legal construction of direct-democratic instruments and specifically on the legal construction of citizen-initiated and state institution-initiated referendums. Citizen-initiated referendums can be genuine tools of democratic empowerment because they allow the voters to react to governmental actions between elections. The voters can formulate their own policy or legislative ideas in a proactive referendum proposal or react to governmental decisions by confirming, rejecting, or abrogating legal acts. The legal design of these instruments can largely determine how the referendum practice can strike a balance between empowering citizens and protecting the core values of liberal democracy and the rule of law. The genuine empowerment through referendums presupposes that voters can express their preferences clearly and the freedom of vote is ensured. It is also crucial that the referendums do not annihilate core democratic values, fundamental rights, or the rule of law, because unfettered popular sovereignty can be detrimental to minorities as well as to democracy itself. In contrast, referendums initiated by state institutions tend to offer the least democratic empowerment and are often tools of populist politics, as the Hungarian government-initiated referendums show. It cannot be assumed that state institutions will not propose unconstitutional or unlawful referendums, thus these direct-democratic instruments should also be constructed in a way that the checks and balances of the constitutional order apply. The relevant international norms, most importantly the Code of Good Practice on Referendums by the Venice Commission, underline this point. The

Code explicitly emphasizes that the referendum design should protect the free vote as well as the constitutional order and the rule of law.

The questions of referendum design are not new in the legal or political science literature on direct democracy. However, the book lays emphasis on the procedural side of the referendum design. It focuses on procedures that enforce the legal rules on referendums and specifically on the procedures for authorizing the referendum issue. When deciding which referendum proposals can go forward to a popular vote and how the legal provisions regulating referendums should be interpreted, state institutions exercise effective control over the referendum process. Parliaments, presidents, election commissions, or courts have a final say in whether the citizens can exercise their right to vote. If there is a lack of certain procedural guarantees, the decision can arbitrarily restrict the right of citizens to exercise popular sovereignty. Alternatively, the decision-making process might not be able to effectively protect the right to vote along with other fundamental rights, democratic values, or the rule of law. Thus, I argue that the legal rules governing referendums should not be seen as static, but equally emphasis should be paid to constructing the procedures enforcing them.

The book provides an overview of referendum authorization procedures in the member states of the Council of Europe. The focus is primarily on citizen-initiated referendums. The data collection shows that citizen-initiated referendums are also popular instruments of direct democracy throughout Europe. While some states, such as Switzerland or Italy, have a long-standing practice of citizens initiating referendums, a large number of states from the former Eastern Bloc have introduced these instruments since the fall of the Soviet Union. Even though the voters can theoretically initiate referendums in 25 member states of the Council of Europe, only 15 have held at least one referendum since 1989–90. The number of states that frequently use these direct-democratic instruments is even lower. This already suggests that both the legal rules governing citizen-initiated referendums and their enforcement should be investigated when trying to understand the practice (or the lack of it). Although, referendums initiated by state actors are prevalent choices among the direct-democratic instruments, very few legal and procedural constraints are imposed on these instruments. Consequently, the legal and procedural analysis of these instruments pose challenges.

A clear distinction between citizen-initiated and institution-initiated referendums is that most European states impose a number of substantive and formal legal limits for citizens initiating referendums. In contrast, state institutions are usually relatively free of constraints to propose referendums. There is a clear correlation between the number of formal and substantive legal limits imposed on referendums and the number of referendum events held. Even though there are some states that have held referendum events regardless of the extensive legal limits imposed on citizen-initiated referendums (Hungary, Malta), the most frequent users of these instruments impose few limits on these instruments (Italy, Liechtenstein, Switzerland). The most common formal limit imposed on citizen-initiated referendums is the requirement of clarity. Among the substantive limits, the majority of states prohibit referendums on state finances, including budgetary issues, taxes, or other financial obligations. Questions about pardon and amnesty or emergency powers are also common exceptions from citizen-initiated referendums. Referendums on fundamental rights and freedoms are also often prohibited.

The member states of the Council of Europe mostly entrust the enforcement of formal and substantive limits on citizen-initiated referendums to parliaments, election commissions, or constitutional courts. In rare cases, presidents or governments can authorize referendums. Regular courts usually provide remedies in referendum authorization procedures. Meanwhile, referendum authorization procedures are less frequently devised for referendums initiated by state institutions.

A common trend is that while the technical registration and the formal review of the citizens' referendum proposal is entrusted to election commissions and governmental bodies, the substantive authorization is left to parliaments or constitutional courts. While legal remedies are always provided against the decisions of election commissions and governmental bodies, the decisions of parliaments and constitutional courts are often final. When comparing the number of referendum events to the institutional choices, no clear correlation could be found. Parliaments, election commissions, or constitutional courts are common choices in states with extensive referendum practice and in states without practice. This suggests that the institutional choice alone does not determine the referendum practice and that any of these institutions can be an appropriate choice for referendum authorization.

Nonetheless, by looking into the nature of referendum authorization procedures, I establish that certain state institutions are more suited to decide about referendums than others. The first inquiry in this regard is about the legal or political nature of referendum authorization. The right to vote in a referendum is a political right and the referendum allows the citizens to participate in politics. Still, the referendum authorization procedure cannot be deemed political once legal limits are imposed and a corresponding authorization procedure is available. This applies both for citizen-initiated and state institution-initiated referendums. In the referendum authorization procedure, the state institutions decide whether the referendum proposal violates any legal limits. Consequently, the legal limits serve as legal standards for the procedure. I use the analogy of the political question doctrine to show that referendum authorization involves legally resolvable issues and necessitates competence in deciding legal disputes.

The state institution authorizing referendums needs competence in legal adjudication also because it conducts an abstract and a concrete review of the referendum proposal. The assessment of the referendum proposal against the substantive limits is akin to the abstract review of legislation in constitutional adjudication. The initiators submit a draft legal act or a generally worded question for authorization. The state institution reviews the submission against the constitution, international law, or other substantive limits. The state institution has to decide how the referendum proposal would fit into the legal system if adopted in the popular vote. This analysis is *a priori* and detached from any individualized legal dispute.

However, the referendum authorization is primarily about the concrete controversy of whether the proposal can reach the ballots. The initiators ask for a 'permit' to continue the referendum process. The ultimate aim of the procedure is to decide whether the referendum can take place, which brings concreteness into the review. The referendum authorization differs from the concrete review in constitutional adjudication in one significant aspect. In the case of concrete review, the applicants traditionally aim to decide an individual legal dispute and challenge the legal act regulating the dispute. Thus, the court reviews the legal act and decides about its applicability in the individual case. In referendum authorization, the individual dispute is about whether the voters can exercise their right to vote, while the challenged 'legal act' is the referendum proposal. In most cases there is no topical connection between the referendum proposal and the right to vote. The authorization procedure itself makes a connection when the state institution assesses the clarity of the referendum proposal and its adherence to other formal limits, and thus protects the right to vote.

The legal nature of referendum authorization accompanied with the abstract and concrete dimensions of the review necessitates that the state institution authorizing referendums has experience in legal adjudication or even in constitutional adjudication. As the data collection shows, a variety of state institutions can be involved in the review of the formal and substantive limits. All the potential state institutions – presidents, parliaments, governments, election commissions, regular and constitutional courts – carry out referendum authorization as an ancillary task to their other constitutional functions. Even in states with extensive use of referendums, such as Switzerland or Liechtenstein, the annual number of referendum authorization cases would not warrant the establishment of a specialized state institution that only adjudicates referendum cases. In other European states, the referendum authorization procedure is even more exceptional. Thus, the competence to authorize referendums is an additional task for state institutions primarily conducting other constitutional functions. Since the competence to authorize referendums confers the task of legal/constitutional adjudication, the state institutions that already have such functions are better equipped to decide about referendums. This means that solely based on the nature of referendum authorization, election commissions and regular and constitutional courts are more suitable to authorize referendums than governments, parliaments, or presidents.

It also follows from the nature of referendum authorization procedures that procedural guarantees should be available for the initiators and the voters. Both the initiators and the voters have a legal interest in the outcome of the referendum authorization. The decision is about their right to vote and directly participate in public matters. Thus, their involvement in the procedure should be guaranteed to some extent. The need for procedural guarantees is also affirmed if we look into the legal limits the state institutions have to enforce. The authorizing state institutions have to apply broadly worded substantive and formal limits in most European states. When evaluating the most common substantive and formal limits, I have found that almost all limits confer considerable discretion on the state institution to define the permissible scope of referendum issues. This increases the chance of arbitrary decision-making and the development of inconsistent practice. The procedural guarantees in the referendum authorization can play a crucial role in keeping the state institution checked and accountable.

The traditional fair trial guarantees are not fully applicable to referendum authorization because it is not a traditional civil or criminal dispute. It is a future-oriented, *a priori* legal dispute about the permissibility of the referendum issue and the exercise of constitutional rights. By comparing the Code of the Venice Commission to the fair trial catalogues of the ICCPR and the ECHR, as well as to the rule of law literature, four procedural guarantees – the independence and impartiality of the decision-maker, the right to a reasoned decision, the right to be heard, and the right to an effective remedy – are compatible with referendum authorization procedures. These guarantees are also minimum requirements to ensure that the rights of the initiators and voters are represented in the procedure and to reduce the risk of arbitrary decision-making.

In the book I analyze how these four procedural guarantees appear in the referendum practice of eight European states with diverse institutional solutions and various practices with referendums. Croatia, Liechtenstein, Slovenia, and Switzerland entrust parliaments to authorize referendums, but in Liechtenstein and Slovenia judicial remedies are also available. Hungary and Latvia leave referendum authorization to election commissions with an appeal to regular courts. In Slovakia, the President authorizes referendums, while Italy involves only regular and constitutional courts in the procedure. Only Hungary and Slovakia have devised the same authorization procedure for both citizen- and institution-initiated referendums, while the other states either do not have rules or apply more lenient rules to referendums initiated by state actors.

The state practice related to the four procedural guarantees shows that election commissions and courts can better incorporate referendum authorization into their other constitutional functions and are better at providing procedural guarantees for the parties than parliaments, governments, or presidents. Parliamentary and presidential decision-making fares especially poorly in providing procedural guarantees to the participants.

Even though the independence and impartiality of the authorizing state institutions have not been questioned often in the state practice, parliaments and governments face an inherent strategic and ideological conflict when deciding about referendums. The members of the parliament and the government are dependent on periodical elections by voters, which creates a strategic conflict when they try to balance their task to uphold the legal limits on direct democracy and keep their electoral support. In addition, a potential ideological conflict also arises, when voters want to take away decision-making powers over important economic, social, and political questions that would otherwise be decided by parliaments or governments. It is difficult to assess to what extent these potential conflicts influence the referendum practice; however, none of the other state institutions authorizing referendums face similar challenges.

The parliaments and presidents entrusted with referendum authorization only exceptionally provide reasons for their decisions. Even in cases where legal reasoning would be necessary to formulate an appeal, no justification is provided by the parliaments. Similarly, the right to be heard or other forms of participation rights are not guaranteed in these procedures and the right to an effective remedy is rare. Due to the lack of reasoning and of participation rights, the parliamentary and presidential referendum practices are not transparent and concerns about the arbitrary interpretation of legal limits are difficult to dispel.

Nonetheless, some best practices can be identified that can alleviate the shortcomings of the parliamentary and presidential procedures. From the states that rely on parliaments to authorize referendums, the examples of Slovenia and Liechtenstein can be highlighted. Both states allow the initiators to challenge the rejection decisions at the constitutional courts, thus providing correctional and control mechanisms over their review of the legal limits. Liechtenstein also involves experts in the decision-making process, while Slovenia is the only state where the parliament provides a detailed reasoning for its decisions. Although the parliamentary procedures do not accommodate participation rights, the parties are able to submit written arguments in the appeal procedures and react to the developments in the case.

The procedures of election commissions and judicial bodies are better equipped with procedural guarantees, although the participation rights of the parties might not be the same as in other public law disputes. The two states with referendum authorization by election commissions, Hungary and Latvia, have similar strengths and weaknesses. The composition of both election commissions might raise concerns about the political independence of the bodies, but it is difficult to ascertain the bias in current practice. The election commissions provide detailed reasoning for their decisions and allow remedies against their decisions. However, participation rights are limited in their procedures. In Hungary, the active involvement of the parties is at the discretion of the National Election Commission, while in Latvia the Central Election Commission does not even allow the initiators to comment on the developments in the case. However, the availability of a judicial remedy can alleviate some of these deficiencies, as for instance in Latvia where the trial provides an adversarial procedure for the parties.

Regular and constitutional courts are involved in the referendum authorization procedure as expert bodies (Croatia, Slovakia), first instance decision-makers (Italy) or appeal forums (Hungary, Latvia, Liechtenstein, Slovenia). The independence of these courts in deciding referendum cases has not raised concerns in most states. The only exception is Hungary, where the case law of the Curia shows some inconsistencies in deciding citizen-initiated referendums, especially if contrasted with the decisions about government-initiated referendums. All the courts provide extensive reasoning for their decisions. A right to be heard is not prevalent even in the judicial procedures, but the initiators of the referendum are usually able to submit written arguments. From a procedural perspective, the practice of the Italian Constitutional Court is exemplary in the provision of extensive participation rights to the initiators and to the civil society.

Even though the referendum authorization procedures of election commissions and courts offer some procedural guarantees, none of the selected states adheres fully to the Code of the Venice Commission. Most states do not provide the necessary safeguards that could ensure that referendums initiated by state institutions adhere to 'superior laws and international law as well as the principles of democracy, human rights, and the rule of law'.[1] These instruments are often deemed as purely political, without legal limits and corresponding authorization procedures. Meanwhile, in the case of citizen-initiated referendums, most of the deficiencies can be found regarding the provision of procedural rights, especially hearing and appeal rights. The lack of participation opportunities can be traced back to multiple reasons.

One potential reason is that referendum authorization is an ancillary task of the state institutions, and the procedure is not regulated as extensively as the other constitutional functions of the state institution. None of the states provides extensive procedural rules for referendum authorization. Meanwhile, the

---

[1]   Revised Code III.1.

rules of the other procedures of the state institution might not be fit for referendum procedures. This can be clearly seen in parliamentary decision-making where the rules of procedure for adopting legislative acts are not appropriate for adjudicating referendum disputes. In the case of election commissions and courts, the rules of civil or administrative procedures can provide sufficient procedural guarantees for referendum authorization. However, in many states – due to the special, abstract dimension of the review – special procedural rules apply for referendum cases that do not offer enough guarantees for the parties. Thus, another reason is that most states lay emphasis on the abstract dimension of referendum authorization and focus only on reviewing the referendum proposal. This approach disregards the fact that referendum authorization is decisive for the referendum event taking place and for the exercise of the right to vote.

The lack of proper procedural guarantees increases the chance of the arbitrary limitation of popular sovereignty. However, the lack of procedural guarantees can also contribute to the inconsistent protection of the rule of law and core democratic values. If the independence and impartiality of the decision-maker is not ensured, then the referendum authorization can be influenced by political or other non-legal considerations. If the decision is not reasoned, then it cannot be ascertained that the decision-maker has exercised its discretion in a non-arbitrary manner. If no participation or remedy rights are available for the initiators of the referendum or the voters, then they are not able to voice their arguments that could contribute to a more well-rounded decision. They are also not able to keep the decision-maker accountable or build trust in the decision-making process.

The state practice shows that none of the states can effectively balance the empowerment of citizens and the protection of the core values of liberal democracy and the rule of law. In Hungary, it is almost impossible for citizens to formulate a referendum proposal that is not rejected. Meanwhile, in Switzerland, it is almost impossible to block a citizen-initiated referendum from reaching the polls. Most selected states have held citizen-initiated referendums that raise questions about the protection of minorities, or fundamental rights and freedoms. Croatia, Slovakia, and Slovenia have held referendums that aimed to prohibit the marriage of same-sex couples. Citizens have wanted to introduce a ban on abortion in Liechtenstein. Italy has held a vote on reproduction rights, and Latvia on the rights of the Russian minority. The Swiss voters have decided about the life-long custody of non-treatable, extremely dangerous sexual and violent offenders.

The institutional and procedural configurations of referendum authorization are just one element of a well-designed direct-democratic instrument. These configurations may not be enough to affect the overall referendum practice and to prevent such controversial referendums. What makes a direct-democratic instrument able to empower citizens to effectively participate in the decision-making and at the same time protect the rule of law depends on multiple elements of the referendum design. The conditions for initiating referendums, such as the required number of signatures, the legal limits imposed on the referendum, or the rules governing the campaign and the voting and quorum rules, all influence the referendum practice. The institutional and procedural settings for authorizing referendums are one element of this system. Focusing on this element puts an emphasis on avoiding arbitrary decision-making instead of on the number of referendums. The non-arbitrary referendum authorization is instrumental for both the exercise of popular sovereignty and the protection of the rule of law. Thus, ensuring the independence and impartiality of the decision-maker, the transparency of the procedure, and the empowerment of the parties through participation and remedy rights are all crucial elements of the overall referendum design.

Bibliography

Abts, Koen, Stefan Rummens, 'Populism versus Democracy' (2007) 55 *Political Studies* 405.

Alber, Elisabeth, 'Ethnic Governance and Direct Democracy: Perils and Potential' in Wilfried Marxer (ed), *Direct Democracy and Minorities* (Springer VS 2012).

Alexy, Robert, *A Theory of Legal Argumentation: The Theory of Rational Discourse as Theory of Legal Justification* (Oxford University Press 2010).

Alivizatos, Nicos C., 'Revision of the Code of Good Practice on Referendums' in Daniel Moeckli, Anna Forgács, Henri Ibi (eds), *The Legal Limits of Direct Democracy* (Edward Elgar Publishing 2021).

Allan, T.R.S., 'Requiring Reasons for Reasons of Fairness and Reasonableness' (1994) 53(2) *The Cambridge Law Journal* 207.

Altman, David, *Direct Democracy Worldwide* (Cambridge University Press 2010).

Anderson, Helen A., 'Frenemies of the Court: The Many Faces of Amicus Curiae' (2015) 49 *U. Ric. L. Rev.* 361.

Arditi, Benjamin, *Politics on the Edges of Liberalism: Difference, Populism, Revolution, Agitation* (Edinburgh University Press 2007).

Atikcan, Ece Özlem, 'The Expression of Popular Will: Do Campaigns Matter and How Do Voters Decide?' in Laurence Morel, Matt Qvortrup (eds), *The Routledge Handbook to Referendums and Direct Democracy* (Routledge 2018).

Auer, Andreas and Michael Bützer (eds), *Direct Democracy: The Eastern and Central European Experience* (Ashgate 2001).

Auer, Andreas, Nicolas von Arx, 'Direkte Demokratie ohne Grenzen? Ein Diskussionsbeitrag zur Frage der Verfassungsmässigkeit von Einbürgerungs- beschlüssen durch das Volk' [2000] *Aktuelle Juristische Praxis* 923.

Auer, Andreas, Nicolas Aubert, Evren Somer, 'So besser nicht: Kritische Anmerkungen zum materiellen Vorprüfungsverfahren für Volksinitiativen im Bund' [2013] *Aktuelle Juristische Praxis* 659.

Baranger, Denis, Christina Murray, 'Systems of Government' in Mark Tushnet et al. (eds), *Routledge Handbook of Constitutional Law* (Routledge 2013).

Baraník, Kamil, 'Slovakia' in Daniel Moeckli, Anna Forgács, Henri Ibi (eds), *The Legal Limits of Direct Democracy* (Edward Elgar Publishing 2021).

Baumann, Robert, 'Völkerrechtliche Schranken der Verfassungsrevision' (2007) 108 *Schweizerisches Zentralblatt für Staats- und Verwaltungsrecht* 181.

Bayles, M.E., *Procedural Justice: Allocating to Individuals* (Dordrecht: Springer Netherlands 1990).

Bell, John, *Judiciaries Within Europe: A Comparative Review* (Cambridge University Press, 2006).

Bell, John and Marie-Luce Paris (eds), *Rights-based Constitutional Review: Constitutional Courts in a Changing Landscape* (Edward Elgar Publishing 2016).

Belov, Martin (ed), *The Role of Courts in Contemporary Legal Orders* (Eleven International Publishing 2019).

Berg-Schlosser, Dirk, Gisèle De Meur, Benoît Rihoux, Charles C Ragin, 'Qualitative comparative analysis (QCA) as an approach' [2009] 1 *Configurational Comparative Methods: Qualitative Comparative Analysis (QCA) and Related Techniques* 1.

Beriger, Julian Ivan, 'Russia' in Daniel Moeckli, Anna Forgács, Henri Ibi (eds), *The Legal Limits of Direct Democracy* (Edward Elgar Publishing 2021).

Besselink, Leonard F.M., 'The Proliferation of Constitutional Law and Constitutional Adjudication, or How American Judicial Review Came to Europe After All' (2013) 9(2) *Utrecht Law Review* 19–35.

Biaggini, Giovanni, 'Die schweizerische direkte Demokratie und das Völkerrecht – Gedanken aus Anlass der Volksabstimmung über die Volksinitiative Gegen den Bau von Minaretten' (2010) 65 *Springer-Verlag Zeitschrift für öffentliches Recht* 325.

Biaggini, Giovanni, 'Constitutional Adjudication in Switzerland' in Armin von Bogdandy, Peter Huber, Christoph Grabenwarter (eds) *Constitutional Judicial Review: Institutions* (Oxford University Press 2020).

Bingham, Tom, *The Rule of Law* (Penguin Books 2011).

Birgelis, Martins, 'Latvia' in Daniel Moeckli, Anna Forgács, Henri Ibi (eds), *The Legal Limits of Direct Democracy* (Edward Elgar Publishing 2021).

Blackstone, William, *Commentaries on the Laws of England in Four Books.* Notes selected from the editions of Archibold, Christian, Coleridge, Chitty, Stewart, Kerr, and others, Barron Field's Analysis, and Additional Notes, and a Life of the Author by George Sharswood. In Two Volumes. (Philadelphia: J.B. Lippincott Co., 1893).

Boggio, Andrea, 'Italy Enacts New Law on Medically Assisted Reproduction' (2005) 20(5) *Human Reproduction* 1153.

Bowler, Shaun, 'When is it OK to Limit Direct Democracy?' (2013) 97(5) *Minnesota Law Review* 1780.

Bowler, Shaun, Todd Donovan (eds), *Demanding Choices: Opinion, Voting, and Direct Democracy* (Ann Arbor, MI: The University of Michigan Press 1998).

Boyron, Sophie, Wendy Lacey, 'Procedural Fairness Generally' in Mark Tushnet, Thomas Fleiner, Cheryl Saunders (eds), *Routledge Handbook of Constitutional Law* (Routledge 2013).

Bradley, Kieran, 'Tribunals and Adjudication' in Peter Cane, Herwig C.H. Hofmann, Eric C. Ip, and Peter L. Lindseth (eds), *The Oxford Handbook of Comparative Administrative Law* (Oxford University Press 2020).

Brunner, Georg, 'Direct vs. Representative Democracy' in Andreas Auer and Michael Bützer (eds), *Direct Democracy: The Eastern and Central European Experience* (Ashgate 2001).

Bugaric, Bojan, Alenka Kuhelj, 'Varieties of Populism in Europe: Is the Rule of Law in Danger?' (2018) 10 *Hague J Rule Law* 21.

Butković, Hrvoje, 'The Rise of Direct Democracy in Croatia: Balancing or Challenging Parliamentary Representation?' (2017) 23(77) *Croatian International Relations Review* 39.

Butler, David, Austin Ranney (eds), *Referendums: A Comparative Study of Practice and Theory* (American Enterprise Institute 1978).

Bützer, Michael, 'Introduction' in Andreas Auer, Michael Bützer (eds), *Direct Democracy: The Eastern and Central European Experience* (Ashgate 2001).

Cappelletti, Mauro, '"Who Watches the Watchmen?" A Comparative Study on Judicial Responsibility' (1983) 31(1) *The American Journal of Comparative Law* 1.

Čepo, Dario, Dario Nikić Čakar, 'Direct Democracy and the Rise of Political Entrepreneurs: An Analysis of Citizens' Initiatives in Post-2010 Croatia' (2019) 16(1) *Anali* 27.

Cheneval, Francis, Mónica Ferrín, 'Direct Democracy in the European Union: An Option for Democratic Empowerment?' in David Levi-Faur, Frans van Waarden (eds), *Democratic Empowerment in the European Union* (Cheltenham: Edward Elgar 2018).

Cheneval, Francis, Alice El-Wakil, 'The Institutional Design of Referendums: Bottom-Up and Binding' (2018) 24(3) *Swiss Political Science Review* 294.

Choper, Jesse H., 'The Political Question Doctrine: Suggested Criteria' (2005) 54 *Duke Law Journal* 1457.

Christmann, Anna, *Die Grenzen direkter Demokratie: Volkentscheide im Spannungsverhältnis von Demokratie und Rechtsstaat* (Nomos Verlag 2012).

Christmann, Anna, 'Direct Democracy and the Rule of Law – Assessing a Tense Relationship' in Wilfried Marxer (ed), *Direct Democracy and Minorities* (Springer 2012).

Christmann, Anna, Deniz Danaci, 'Direct Democracy and Minority Rights: Direct and Indirect Effects on Religious Minorities in Switzerland' (2012) 5(1) *Politics and Religion* 133.

Clark, Tom S., *The Limits of Judicial Independence* (Oxford University Press 2012).

Clayton, Richard, Hugh Tomlinson, *Fair Trial Rights* (Oxford University Press 2010).

Cohn, Margit, 'Form, Formula and Constitutional Ethos: The Political Question/ Justiciability Doctrine in Three Common Law Systems' (2011) 59(3) *The American Journal of Comparative Law* 675.

Colombo, Céline, Hanspeter Kriesi, 'Referendums and Direct Democracy' in Robert Rohrschneider, Jacques Thomassen, *The Oxford Handbook of Political Representation in Liberal Democracies* (Oxford University Press 2020).

Comella, Víktor Ferreres, *Constitutional Courts and Democratic Values: A European Perspective* (Yale University Press 2009).

Cooter, Robert D., and Michael D. Gilbert, 'A Theory of Direct Democracy and the Single Subject Rule' (2010) 110(3) *Columbia Law Review* 687.

Craig, Paul, 'Standing, Rights, and the Structure of Legal Argument' (2003) 9(4) *European Public Law* 493–508.

Craig, Paul, *Administrative Law* (8th edn., London: Sweet & Maxwell Thomson Reuters 2016).

Dalton, Harlon Leigh, 'Taking the Right to Appeal (More or Less) Seriously' (1985) 95(1) *The Yale Law Journal* 62.

Danaci, Deniz, 'The Minaret Ban in Switzerland: An Exception to the Rule?' in Wilfried Marxer (ed), *Direct Democracy and Minorities* (Springer 2012).

Darpö, Jan, 'Pulling the Trigger: ENGO Standing Rights and the Enforcement of Environmental Obligations in EU Law' in Sanja Bogojević, Rosemary Rayfuse (eds), *Environmental Rights in Europe and Beyond* (Hart Publishing 2018).

della, Cananea, Giacinto, *Due Process of Law Beyond the State: Requirements of Administrative Procedure* (Oxford University Press 2016).

Delledonne, Giacomo, 'Appointing and Electing Constitutional Judges: An Evolving Comparative Landscape' in Martin Belov (ed), *The Role of Courts in Contemporary Legal Orders* (Eleven International Publishing 2019).

Dicey, Albert Venn, *Introduction to the Study of the Law of the Constitution* (originally published 8th edn London: Macmillan 1915, Liberty Classics Reprint 1982).

Dixon, Rosalind, Felix Uhlmann, 'The Swiss Constitution and a weak-form unconstitutional amendment doctrine' (2018) 16 (1) *I•CON* 54.

Donovan, Todd, Shaun Bowler, 'Are Voters Competent Enough to Vote on Complex Issues' in M. Dane Waters (ed) *The Initiative and Referendum Almanac:*

A Comprehensive Guide to the Initiative and Referendum Process in the United States (Durham NC: Carolina Academic Press 2003).

Donovan, Todd, Shaun Bowler, 'Direct Democracy and Minority Rights: An Extension' (1998) 42 *American Journal of Political Science* 1020.

Drugda, Šimon, 'The People v Their Representatives: The Slovak Constitutional Court Blocks Referendum on Early Election' (*Verfassungsblog*, 14 September 2021) <https://verfassungsblog.de/the-people-v-their-representatives/>, DOI: 10.17 176/20210914-173356-0.

Druviete, Ina and Uldis Ozolins, 'The Latvian Referendum on Russian as a Second State Language' (2016) 40(2) *Language Problems & Language Planning* 121.

Dudás, Endre, 'Croatian Constitutional Court: The Referendum on the Cyrillic Script' (2015) 9(1) *Vienna Journal on International Constitutional Law* 126.

Dworkin, Ronald, *A Matter of Principle* (Oxford: Clarendon Press 1986).

Dworkin, Ronald, *Law's Empire* (Harvard University Press 1986).

Eisler, Jacob, 'Dissonant Referendum Design and Turmoil in Representation' (2019) *Public Law* (Sweet & Maxwell), <http://dx.doi.org/10.2139/ssrn.3378642>.

Eliantonio, M., Ch.W. Backes, C.H. van Rhee, T. Spronken, A. Berlee, *Standing up for Your Right(s) in Europe: A Comparative Study on Legal Standing (Locus Standi) before the EU and Member States' Courts* (Cambridge: Intersentia 2013).

Elliott, Mark, 'Has the Common Law Duty to Give Reasons Come of Age Yet?' [2011] *Public Law* 56.

Erdős, Csaba, 'A Kúria két határozata a miniszterelnöki ciklusok számának maximalizálására irányuló népszavazási kezdeményezésekről' (2017) 4 JEMA 41.

De Falco, Vincenzo, *Administrative Action and Procedures in Comparative Law* (Eleven International Publishing 2018).

Fatin-Rouge, Marthe Stefanini, 'Referendums, Minorities and Individual Freedoms' in Laurence Morel, Matt Qvortrup (eds), *The Routledge Handbook to Referendums and Direct Democracy* (Routledge 2018).

Fazekas, János, 'Local Governments and Political Question Doctrine in Hungary' (2019) 17(3) *Lex Localis: Journal of Local Self-Government* 809–819.

Featherstone, Kevin, 'What Those Calling for Brexit Could Learn from the Greek Bailout Referendum' (LSE Comments, 6 June 2016) <https://blogs.lse.ac.uk/europpblog/2016/06/06/brexit-and-greek-bailout-referendum/>.

Ferejohn, John A., Larry D. Kramer, 'Independent Judges, Dependent Judiciary: Institutionalizing Judicial Restraint' (2002) 77 *N.Y.U. Law Review* 962.

Fix-Fierro, Héctor, Pedro Salazar-Ugarte, 'Presidentialism' in Michel Rosenfeld and András Sajó (eds), *Oxford Handbook of Comparative Constitutional Law* (Oxford University Press, 2012).

Fordham, Michael, 'Reasons: The Third Dimension' (1998) 3(3) *Judicial Review* 158 <https://doi.org/10.1080/10854681.1998.11427014>.

Forgács, Anna, 'Hungary' in Daniel Moeckli, Anna Forgács, Henri Ibi (eds), *The Legal Limits of Direct Democracy* (Edward Elgar Publishing 2021).

Frey, Bruno S., Alois Stutzer, Susanne Neckermann, 'Direct Democracy and the Constitution' in A. Marciano (ed), *Constitutional Mythologies: New Perspectives on Controlling the State* (New York: Springer 2011) <https://doi.org/10.1007/978-1-4419-6784-8_8>.

Frey, Bruno S., Alois Stutzer, 'Direct Democracy: Designing a Living Constitution' in Stefan Voigt (ed), *Design of Constitutions* (Edward Elgar 2013).

Fuller, Lon L., *The Morality of Law* (Yale University Press 1964).

Fuller, Lon L., 'Forms and Limits of Adjudication' (1978) 92 *Harvard Law Review* 353.

Gamble, Barbara S., 'Putting Civil Rights to a Popular Vote' (1997) 41(1) *American Journal of Political Science* 245.

Gardašević, Đorđe 'Constitutional Interpretations of Direct Democracy in Croatia' 7 (2015) 12 *Iustinianus Primus Law Review* 1.

Gárdos-Orosz, Fruzsina, 'The Hungarian Constitutional Court in Transition – From Actio Popularis to Constitutional Complaint' (2012) 53(4) *Acta Juridica Hungarica* 302.

Garrone, Pierre, 'The Code of Good Practice on Referendums' in Daniel Moeckli, Anna Forgács, Henri Ibi (eds), *The Legal Limits of Direct Democracy* (Edward Elgar Publishing 2021).

Gildersleeve, John, 'Editing Direct Democracy: Does Limiting the Subject Matter of Ballot Initiatives Offend the First Amendment?' (2007) 107(6) *Columbia Law Review* 1437.

Ginsburg, Tom, 'Constitutional Court in East Asia: Understanding Variation' in Andrew Harding, Peter Leyland (eds), *Constitutional Courts: A Comparative Study* (Wildy, Simmonds and Hill Publishing 2009).

Ginsburg, Tom, Mila Versteeg, 'Why Do Countries Adopt Constitutional Review?' (2014) 30(3) *Journal of Law, Economics, & Organization* 587–622.

Glaser, Andreas, 'Das Verwaltungsreferendum' (2012) 113 *Schweizerisches Zentralblatt für Staats- und Verwaltungsrecht* 511.

Glatthard, Jonas, 'Schweiz sagt "Ja, ich will" zur Ehe für alle' (Swissinfo 26 September 2021) <https://www.swissinfo.ch/ger/ehe-fuer-alle-wird-voraussichtlich-realitaet/46979242>.

Glaurdić, Josip, Vuk Vuković, 'Proxy Politics, Economic Protest, or Traditionalist Backlash: Croatia's Referendum on the Constitutional Definition of Marriage' (2016) 68(5) *Europe-Asia Studies* 803.

Gordon III, James D., David B. Magleby, 'Pre-Election Judicial Review of Initiatives and Referendums' (1989) 64 *Notre Dame Law Review* 298.

Guarnieri, Carlo, Daniela Piana, 'Judicial Independence and The Rule of Law: Exploring the European Experience' in Shimon Shetreet, Christopher Forsyth (eds) *The Culture of Judicial Independence: Conceptual Foundations and Practical Challenges* (Leiden: Martinus Nijhoff Publishers 2012).

Habermas, Jürgen, 'Constitutional Democracy: A Paradoxical Union of Contradictory Principles?' (2001) 29(6) *Political Theory* 766–781.

Haider-Markel, Donald P., Alana Querze, Kara Lindaman, 'Lose, Win, or Draw? A Reexamination of Direct Democracy and Minority Rights' (2007) 60 *Political Research Quarterly* 304.

Haller, Walter, 'Das schweizerische System der halbdirekten Demokratie' [1994] *Zeitschrift für Verwaltung* 613.

Halmai, Gábor, 'The Invalid Anti-Migrant Referendum in Hungary' (*Verfassungsblog*, 4 October 2016) , accessed 15 March 2022.

Ham, C.T. van, Holly Ann Garnett, 'Building Impartial Electoral Management? Institutional Design, Independence and Electoral Integrity' (2019) 40(3) *International Political Science Review* 313.

Harding, Andrew, *Constitutional Courts: A Comparative Study* (Wildy, Simmonds & Hill 2009).

Hart, H.L.A., *The Concept of Law* (Oxford: Clarendon Press 1994).

Helmke, Gretchen, Frances Rosenbluth, 'Regimes and the Rule of Law: Judicial Independence in Comparative Perspective' (2009) 12 *Annual Review of Political Science* 345.

Hill, Ronald J., Stephen White, 'Russia, the Former Soviet Union and Eastern Europe' in Matt Qvortrup (ed), *Referendums Around the World* (Palgrave Macmillan 2018).

Hoffmann, Roland, *Verfahrensgerechtigkeit: Studien zu einer Theorie prozeduraler Gerechtigkeit* (Ferdinand Schöningh 1992).

Hug, Simon, George Tsebelis, 'Veto Players and Referendums Around the World' 2002 14(4) *Journal of Theoretical Politics* 466.

Hug, Simon, 'Occurrence and Policy Consequences of Referendums' (2004) 16 *Journal of Theoretical Politics* 321.

Hurst, Robert, 'Der Grundsatz der Einheit der Materie' (DPhil thesis, University of Zurich 2002), <https://doi.org/10.5167/uzh-70565>.

Ibi, Henri, 'Italy' in Daniel Moeckli, Anna Forgács, Henri Ibi (eds), *The Legal Limits of Direct Democracy* (Edward Elgar Publishing 2021).

Ijabs, Ivars, 'After the Referendum: Militant Democracy and Nation-Building in Latvia' (2016) 30(2) *East European Politics and Societies and Cultures* 288.

Inglehart, Ronald, Pippa Norris, 'Trump, Brexit, and the Rise of Populism: Economic Have-Nots and Cultural Backlash' (Harvard Kennedy School Faculty Research Working Paper Series No. RWP16-026, August 2016) <https://www.hks.harvard.edu/publications/trump-brexit-and-rise-populism-economic-have-nots-and-cultural-backlash>.

Issacharoff, Samuel, 'Democracy's Deficits' (2018) 85(2) *The University of Chicago Law Review* 485.

Jackson, Vicki, 'Comparative Constitutional Law: Methodologies' in Michel Rosenfeld and András Sajó (eds), *Oxford Handbook of Comparative Constitutional Law* (Oxford University Press 2012).

Jarinovska, Kristīne, 'Popular Initiatives as Means of Altering the Core of the Republic of Latvia' (2013) 20 *Juridica International* 152.

Kazai, Viktor Z., Ágnes Kovács, 'The Last Days of the Independent Supreme Court of Hungary?' (Verfassungsblog, 13 October 2020) <https://verfassungsblog.de/the-last-days-of-the-independent-supreme-court-of-hungary/>, DOI: 10.17176/2020 1013-233456-0.

Kelemen, Katalin, 'Dissenting Opinions in Constitutional Courts' (2013) 14(8) *German Law Journal* 1345.

Keller, Helen, Markus Lanter, Andreas Fischer, 'Volksinitiativen und Völkerrecht: die Zeit ist reif für eine Verfassungsänderung' (2008) 109(3) *Schweizerisches Zentralblatt für Staats- und Verwaltungsrecht* 121.

Keller, Helen, Severin Meier, 'Independence and Impartiality in *The Judicial Trilemma*' (2017) 111 *American Society of International Law* 344.

Kiener, Regina, *Richterliche Unabhängigkeit* (Stämpfli Verlag AG 2001).

Kiener, Regina, 'Einführung/Europäische Mindeststandards zum Parlamentswahlrecht im Soft Law der Venedig-Kommission' in Andreas Glaser, Lorenz Langer (eds), *Das Parlamentswahlrecht als rechtsstaatliche Grundlage der Demokratie* (Dike Verlag, 2020).

Kiener, Regina, Melanie Krüsi, 'Bedeutungswandel des Rechtsstaats und Folgen für die (direkte) Demokratie am Beispiel völkerrechtswidriger Volksinitiativen' (2009) 110 *Schweizerisches Zentralblatt für Staats- und Verwaltungsrecht* 237.

Kirchgässner, Gebhard, 'Direkte Demokratie und Menschenrechte' in Lars P. Feld, Peter M. Huber, Otmar Jung, Christian Welzel, Fabian Wittreck (eds), *Jahrbuch für direkte Demokratie 2009* (Nomos 2010).

Klaming, Laura, Ivo Giesen, 'Access to Justice: The Quality of the Procedure' (TISCO Working Paper Series on Civil Law and Conflict Resolution Systems No. 002/2008).

Kley, Andreas, 'Die Einheit der Materie bei Bundesgesetzen und der Stein der Weisen' (2019) 120 *Schweizerisches Zentralblatt für Staats- und Verwaltungsrecht* 3.

Kochevar, Steven, 'Amici Curiae in Civil Law Jurisdictions' (2013) 122 *Yale Law Journal* 1653.

Komáromi, László, 'Milestones in the History of Direct Democracy in Hungary' (2013) 9(4) Iustum Aequum Salutare 49.

Komáromi, László, 'Popular Rights in Hungary: A Brief Overview of Ideas, Institutions and Practice from the Late 18th Century until Our Days' (C2D Working Paper Series. 35/2010).

Komáromi, László, 'A népszavazásra vonatkozó szabályozás változásai az Alaptörvényben és az új népszavazási törvényben' (2014) 35 *MTA Law Working Papers* 6.

Komáromi, László, 'Az Alkotmánybíróság határozata a nőkre vonatkozó kedvezményes nyugdíjba vonulási feltételek férfiakra történő kiterjesztésére irányuló népszavazási kezdeményezésről' [2016] 7(1) JEMA 5.

Koopmans, Raymond T., 'Natural Justice Rediviva? The Right to a Fair Hearing in European Law' (1992) 39(1) *Netherlands International Law Review* 175.

Kröger, Sandra, 'Assessing the Democratic Legitimacy of the 2016 Brexit Referendum' (DCU Brexit Institute – Working Paper No.12 2018) <http://dx.doi.org/10.2139/ssrn.3312457>.

Krošlák, Daniel, 'The Referendum on the So-Called Traditional Family in the Slovak Republic' [2015] 1 *Central and Eastern European Legal Studies* 149.

Kriesi, Hanspeter, *Direct Democratic Choice: The Swiss Experience* (Lexington Books 2005).

Krygier, Martin, 'What's the Point of the Rule of Law?' (2019) 67 *Buffalo Law Review* 743.

Krygier, Martin, 'The Challenge of Institutionalisation: Post-Communist "Transitions", Populism, and the Rule of Law' (2019) 15 *European Constitutional Law Review* 544.

Kużelewska, Elżbieta, 'Same-Sex Marriage – A Happy End Story? The Effectiveness of Referendum on Same-Sex Marriage in Europe' (2019) 1(24) *Białostockie Studia Prawnicze* 13.

Lanz, Simon, Alessandro Nai, 'How Elections Shape Campaigning Effects in Direct Democracy' in Laurence Morel, Matt Qvortrup (eds), *The Routledge Handbook to Referendums and Direct Democracy* (Routledge 2018).

Le Sueur, Andrew P., 'Legal Duties to Give Reasons' (1999) 52 *Current Legal Problems* 150.

Lind, E. Allen, Tom Tyler, *The Social Psychology of Procedural Justice* (New York: Plenum Press 1988).

Linder, Wolf, *Schweizerische Demokratie: Institutionen, Prozesse, Perspektiven* (Bern: Verlag Paul Haupt 2012).

Lublin, David, 'The 2012 Latvia Language Referendum' (2013) 32 *Electoral Studies* 385.

Luksic, Igor, Andrej Kurnik, 'Slovenia' in Andreas Auer and Micheal Bützer (eds), *Direct Democracy: The Eastern and Central European Experience* (Ashgate 2001).

Lupia, Arthur, John G. Matsusaka, 'Direct Democracy: New Approaches to Old Questions' (2004) 7 *Annual Review of Political Science* 463.

Lupia, Arthur, 'Shortcuts Versus Encyclopedias: Information and Voting Behavior in California Insurance Reform Elections' (1994) 88(1) *American Political Science Review* 69.

MacCormick, Neil, *Legal Reasoning and Legal Theory* (Oxford University Press 1994).

Macdonald, Roderick A., Hoi Kong, 'Judicial Independence as a Constitutional Virtue' in Michel Rosenfeld, András Sajó (eds), *Oxford Handbook of Comparative Constitutional Law* (Oxford University Press 2012).

MacDowall, Andrew, 'Voters back Viktor Orbán's rejection of EU migrant quotas' (Politico 2 October 2016).

Mangione, Gabriella, 'Presentation at the Conference: Brief Remarks on Referendums in Italy' (2018) 4(1) *International Comparative Jurisprudence* 7.

Marczewska-Rytko, Maria (ed), *Handbook of Direct Democracy in Central and Eastern Europe after 1989* (Opladen: Barbara Budrich Publishers 2018).

Marshall, P.D., 'A Comparative Analysis of the Right to Appeal' (2011) 22(1) *Duke Journal of Comparative & International Law* 1.

Marxer, Wilfried (ed), *Direct Democracy and Minorities* (Springer 2012).

Marxer, Wilfried, 'Foreword' in Wilfried Marxer (ed), *Direct Democracy and Minorities* (Springer 2012).

Marxer, Wilfried, 'Minorities and Direct Democracy in Liechtenstein' in Wilfried Marxer (ed), *Direct Democracy and Minorities* (Springer 2012).

Marxer, Wilfried, 'Initiatives in Liechtenstein: Safety Valve in a Complex System of Government' in Maija Setälä and Theo Schiller (eds), *Citizens' Initiatives in Europe: Procedures and Consequences of Agenda-Setting by Citizens* (Palgrave Macmillan 2012).

Marxer, Wilfried, *Direkte Demokratie in Liechtenstein: Entwicklung, Regelungen, Praxis* (Bendern: Verlag der Liechtensteinischen Akademischen Gesellschaft 2018).

Marxer, Wilfried, 'Liechtenstein' in Daniel Moeckli, Anna Forgács, Henri Ibi (eds), *The Legal Limits of Direct Democracy* (Edward Elgar Publishing 2021).

Mashaw, Jerry L., *Reasoned Administration and Democratic Legitimacy* (Cambridge University Press 2018).

Matsusaka, John G., 'Direct Democracy Works' (2005) 19(2) *Journal of Economic Perspectives* 185.

Matsusaka, John G., *Let the People Rule: How Direct Democracy Can Meet the Populist Challenge* (Princeton: Princeton University Press 2020).

McIntyre, Joe, *The Judicial Function: Fundamental Principles of Contemporary Judging* (Springer Singapore 2019).

Mécs, János, 'Az egyértelműség követelménye az országos népszavazási kérdések hitelesítése során' (Jogi Tanulmányok, ELTE Állam-és Jogtudományi Kar Állam-és Jogtudományi Doktori Iskola, 2018).

Michael, Douglas C. 'Preelection Judicial Review: Taking the Initiative in Voter Protection' (1983) 71 *California Law Review* 1216.

Miles, Joanna 'Standing under the Human Rights Act 1998: Theories of Rights Enforcement & the Nature of Public Law Adjudication' (2000) 59(1) *Cambridge Law Journal* 133.

Miller, Kenneth P., *Direct Democracy and the Courts* (Cambridge University Press 2009).

Moeckli, Daniel, 'Of Minarets and Foreign Criminals: Swiss Direct Democracy and Human Rights' (2011) 11 *Human Rights Law Review* 774.

Moeckli, Daniel, 'Die Teilungültigerklärung und Aufspaltung von Volksinitiativen' (2014) 115 *Schweizerisches Zentralblatt für Staats- und Verwaltungsrecht* 579.

Moeckli, Daniel, 'Referendums: Tyranny of the Majority?' 2018 24(3) *Swiss Political Science Review* 335.

Moeckli, Daniel, 'Völkerrechtliche Vorgaben für den Rechtsschutz in Wahlsachen' in Andreas Glaser, Lorenz Langer (eds), *Das Parlamentswahlrecht als rechtsstaatliche Grundlage der Demokratie* (Dike Verlag, 2020).

Moeckli, Daniel, 'Switzerland' in Daniel Moeckli, Anna Forgács, Henri Ibi (eds), *The Legal Limits of Direct Democracy* (Edward Elgar Publishing 2021).

Möllers, Christoph, *The Three Branches: A Comparative Model of Separation of Powers* (Oxford University Press 2013).

Moore, Michael S., 'The Plain Truth about Legal Truth' (2003) 26 *Harvard Journal of Law and Policy* 23.

Morel, Laurence, 'Referendums' in: Michel Rosenfeld, András Sajó (eds), *Oxford Handbook of Comparative Constitutional Law* (Oxford University Press 2012).

Morel, Laurence, 'Types of Referendums, Provisions and Practice at National Level Worldwide' in Laurence Morel, Matt Qvortrup (eds), *The Routledge Handbook to Referendums and Direct Democracy* (Routledge 2018).

Morel, Laurence, 'The Democratic Criticism of Referendums. The Majority and the True Will of the People' in Laurence Morel, Matt Qvortrup (eds), *The Routledge Handbook to Referendums and Direct Democracy* (Routledge 2018).

Morel, Laurence, Matt Qvortrup (eds), *The Routledge Handbook to Referendums and Direct Democracy* (Routledge 2018).

Mudde, Cas, Cristóbal Rovira Kaltwasser, 'Studying Populism in Comparative Perspective: Reflections on the Contemporary and Future Research Agenda' (2018) 51(13) *Comparative Political Studies* 1667.

Müller, Jan-Werner, *What is Populism?* (University of Pennsylvania Press 2016).

Myers, Jackson A., 'Comment: Transatlantic Perspectives on the Political Question Doctrine' (2020) 106 *Virginia Law Review* 1007.

Naef, Tobias, 'Popular Initiatives Contrary to International Law – A Swiss Dilemma' in Andreas Kellerhals, Tobias Baumgartner, *Rule of Law in Europe – Current Challenges: 8th Network Europe Conference, Moscow, 10th–13th July 2016* (Zürich: Schulthess Verlag 2016).

Naguib, Tarek, 'Halbdirekte Demokratie und Rechtsstaat im Konflikt: Quo vadis? Einblicke in die eidgenössische Kontroverse zum Umgang mit menschenrechtswidrigen Volksinitiativen und verfassungswidrigen Bundesgesetzen' in Michael Wrase, Christian Boulanger, Anna Schulze (eds), *Die Politik des Verfassungsrechts: Interdisziplinäre und vergleichende Perspektiven auf die Rolle und Funktion von Verfassungsgerichten* (Nomos 2013).

Napolitano, Giulio, 'The Rule of Law' in Peter Cane, Herwig C.H. Hofmann, Eric C. Ip, Peter L. Lindseth (eds), *The Oxford Handbook of Comparative Administrative Law* (Oxford University Press 2020).

Nobles, Richard, David Schiff, 'The Right to Appeal and Workable Systems of Justice' (2003) 65(5) *The Modern Law Review* 676.

Norton, Philip, 'Referendums and Parliaments' in J. Smith (ed), *The Palgrave Handbook of European Referendums* (Cham: Palgrave Macmillan 2021) 91–108.

Noyes, Henry S., *The Law of Direct Democracy* (Carolina Academic Press 2014).

Pabel, Katharina, 'Verwaltungsprozessrecht' (2007) 15 *Journal für Rechtspolitik* 287.

Pal, M., 'Electoral Management Bodies as Fourth Branch of Government' (2016) 21(1) *Review of Constitutional Studies* 85.

Pállinger, Zoltán Tibor, Bruno Kaufmann, Wilfried Marxer, Theo Schiller (eds), *Direct Democracy in Europe: Developments and Prospects* (Springer VS 2007).

Pállinger, Zoltán Tibor, 'Potentials of Direct Democracy in an Extremely Majoritarian System: The Case of Hungary' (2016) *Andrássy Working Papers zur Demokratieforschung* 1/2016.

Papayannis, Diego M., 'Independence, Impartiality and Neutrality in Legal Adjudication' (2016) 28 *Revus – Journal for Constitutional Theory and Philosophy of Law* 33.

Phillips, Thomas R., 'The Constitutional Right to a Remedy' (2003) 78 *New York University Law Review* 1309.

Podolak, Małgorzata, 'Rights of Sexual Minorities as the Subject of Referenda in the Republic of Slovenia' (2018) 24 *Białostockie Studia Prawnicze* 45.

Podolnjak, Robert, 'Constitutional Reforms of Citizen-Initiated Referendum. Causes of Different Outcomes in Slovenia and Croatia' (2015) 26 *Revus Journal for Constitutional Theory and Philosophy of Law* 129.

Podolnjak, Robert, 'Croatia' in Daniel Moeckli, Anna Forgács, Henri Ibi (eds), *The Legal Limits of Direct Democracy* (Edward Elgar Publishing 2021).

Qvortrup, Matt, 'Judicial Review of Direct Democracy' in Matt Qvortrup, *Direct Democracy: A Comparative Study of the Theory and Practice of Government by the People* (Manchester University Press 2014).

Qvortrup, Matt (ed), *Referendums Around the World* (Palgrave Macmillan 2018).

Qvortrup, Matt, 'Introduction: Theory, Practice and History' in Matt Qvortrup (ed), *Referendums Around the World* (Palgrave Macmillan 2018).

Qvortrup, Matt, 'Direct Democracy and Referendums' in Erik S. Herron, Robert J. Pekkanen, Matthew S. Shugart (eds), *The Oxford Handbook of Electoral Systems* (Oxford University Press 2018).

Rädler, Peter, 'Independence and Impartiality of Judges' in David Weissbrodt, Rüdiger Wolfrum (eds), *The Right to a Fair Trial* (Springer 1998).

Radosavljevic, Zoran, 'Croatia to Hold Referendum Challenging Same-sex Marriage' (Reuters, 8 November 2013).

Rainey, Bernadette, Elizabeth Wicks, Clare Ovey (eds), *Jacobs, White, and Ovey: The European Convention on Human Rights* (7th edn, Oxford University Press 2017).

Ratto, Fabio Trabucco, 'The Advantages and Disadvantages of Italian Referendum Tools' (2018) 24 *Białostockie Studia Prawnicze* 151.

Rawls, John, *A Theory of Justice* (Oxford University Press 1971).

Raz, Joseph, 'On the Autonomy of Legal Reasoning' (1993) 6 *Ratio Juris* 1.

Raz, Joseph, *The Authority of Law: Essays on Law and Morality* (2nd edn., Oxford University Press 2009).

Reid, Andrew, 'Buses and Breaking Point: Freedom of Expression and the "Brexit" Campaign' (2019) 22 *Ethical Theory and Moral Practice* 623.

Rennert, Klaus, 'Administration, Administrative Jurisdiction and Separation of Powers' [2018] 1 *ELTE Law Journal* 147.

Resnik, Judith, 'Civil Processes' in Mark Tushnet and Peter Cane (eds), *The Oxford Handbook of Legal Studies* (Oxford University Press 2005).

Ribičič, Ciril, Igor Kaučič, *Referendum and the Constitutional Court of Slovenia* (Entwicklung im Europäischen Recht, Vol. 11. Universitätsverlag Regensburg 2016).

Ribičič, Ciril, Igor Kaučič, 'Constitutional Limits of Legislative Referendum: The Case of Slovenia' (2014) 12(4) *Lexlocalis – Journal of Local Self-Government* 899.

Riezzo, Irene, Margherita Neri, Stefania Bello, Cristoforo Pomara, and Emanuela Turillazzi, 'Italian Law on Medically Assisted Reproduction: Do Women's Autonomy and Health Matter?' (2016) 16 *BMC Women's Health* 44.

Rocher, François, André Lecours, 'The Correct Expression of Popular Will. Does the Wording of a Referendum Question Matter?' in Laurence Morel, Matt Qvortrup (eds), *The Routledge Handbook to Referendums and Direct Democracy* (Routledge 2018).

Rooduijn, Matthijs, 'State of the Field: How to Study Populism and Adjacent Topics? A Plea for Both More and Less Focus' (2019) 58 *European Journal of Political Research* 362.

Rousseau, Jean-Jacques, *Of the Social Contract* (Yale University Press 2002).

Rozsnyai, Krisztina F., 'Current Tendencies of Judicial Review as Reflected in the New Hungarian Code of Administrative Court Procedure' (2018) 17(1) *Central European Public Administration Review* 7–23.

Ruth, Saskia P., Yanina Welp, Laurence Whitehead, 'Direct Democracy in the Twenty-First Century' in Saskia P. Ruth, Yanina Welp, Laurence Whitehead (eds), *Let the People Rule? Direct Democracy in the Twenty-First Century* (ECPR Press 2017).

Rybar, Marek, Anna Sovcikova, 'The 2015 Referendum in Slovakia' (2016) 44(1–2) *East European Quarterly* 79.

Sadurski, Wojciech, *Rights Before Courts: A Study of Constitutional Courts in Postcommunist States of Central and Eastern Europe* (Springer 2005).

Sadurski, Wojciech, 'Constitutional Democracy in the Time of Elected Authoritarians' (2020) 18 (2) *I•CON* 324.

Sartori, G., *The Theory of Democracy Revisited* (Chatham, UK: Chatham House Publishers 1987)

Scheppele, Kim Lane, 'Autocratic Legalism' (2018) 85(2) *The University of Chicago Law Review* 545.

Scheppele, Kim Lane, 'The Opportunism of Populists and the Defense of Constitutional Liberalism' (2019) 20 *German Law Journal* 314.

Schiller, Theo and Maija Setälä (eds), *Citizens' Initiatives in Europe: Procedures and Consequences of Agenda-Setting by Citizens* (Palgrave Macmillan 2012).

Schiller, Theo, Maija Setälä, 'Introduction' in Theo Schiller and Maija Setälä (eds), *Citizens' Initiatives in Europe: Procedures and Consequences of Agenda-Setting by Citizens* (Palgrave Macmillan 2012).

Sczostak, Günter, 'Zur Problematik der gerichtsfreien Hoheitsakte' [1958] 12 *Juristische Rundschau* 445.

Sekerák, Marián, 'Same-Sex Marriages (or Civil Unions/Registered Partnerships) in Slovak Constitutional Law: Challenges and Possibilities' (2017) 13(1) *Utrecht Law Review* 34.

Setälä, Maija, Theo Schiller, 'Comparative Findings' in Theo Schiller and Maija Setälä (eds), *Citizens' Initiatives in Europe: Procedures and Consequences of Agenda-Setting by Citizens* (Palgrave Macmillan 2012).

Shetreet, Shimon, 'Judicial Independence: New Conceptual Dimensions and Contemporary Challenges' in Shimon Shetreet, Jules Deschenes (eds), *Judicial Independence: The Contemporary Debate* (Martinus Nijhoff Publishers 1985).

Shetreet, Shimon, 'Judicial Independence and Accountability' in H.P. Lee (ed), *Judiciaries in Comparative Perspective* (Cambridge University Press 2011).

Shetreet, Shimon, 'Creating a Culture of Judicial Independence: The Practical Challenge and the Conceptual and Constitutional Infrastructure' in Shimon Shetreet, Christopher Forsyth (eds), *The Culture of Judicial Independence: Conceptual Foundations and Practical Challenges* (Martinus Nijhoff Publishers 2012).

Shetreet, Shimon, Christopher Forsyth (eds), *The Culture of Judicial Independence: Conceptual Foundations and Practical Challenges* (Martinus Nijhoff Publishers 2012).

Sirico Jr., Louis J., 'Constitutionality of the Initiative and Referendum' (1980) 65 *Iowa Law Review* 637.

Smilov, Daniel, 'The Judiciary: The Least Dangerous Branch?' in Michel Rosenfeld and András Sajó (eds), *Oxford Handbook of Comparative Constitutional Law* (Oxford University Press 2012).

Somer, Evren. *Direct Democracy in the Baltic States* (Peter Lang 2015).

Sossin, Lorne, 'An Intimate Approach to Fairness, Impartiality and Reasonableness in Administrative Law' (2002) 27 *Queen's L.J.* 809.

Stadelmann-Steffen, Isabelle, Adrian Vatter, 'Does Satisfaction with Democracy Really Increase Happiness? Direct Democracy and Individual Satisfaction in Switzerland' (2012) 34 *Polit Behav* 535. DOI: 10.1007/s11109-011-9164-y.

Stone Sweet, Alec, 'Constitutional Courts and Parliamentary Democracy' (2002) 25 *West European Politics* 77.

Stone Sweet, Alec, 'Constitutional Courts' in Michel Rosenfeld and András Sajó (eds), *Oxford Handbook of Comparative Constitutional Law* (Oxford University Press 2012).

Strauss. Peter L. (ed), *Gellhorn and Byse's Administrative Law: Cases and Comments* (New York: Foundation Press 2011).

Suksi, Markku, *Bringing in the People: A Comparison of Constitutional Forms and Practices of the Referendum* (Kluwer Academic Publishers 1993).

Suzuki, Kohei, Mehmet Akif Demircioglu, 'Is Impartiality Enough? Government Impartiality and Citizens' Perceptions of Public Service Quality' [2020] *Governance* 1–38.

Svensson, Palle, 'Views on Referendums: Is There a Pattern?' in Laurence Morel, Matt Qvortrup (eds), *The Routledge Handbook to Referendums and Direct Democracy* (Routledge 2018).

Szakacs, Gergely, Anita Komuves, 'Hungarian Election Panel Clears Questions of LGBT Referendum' (Reuters 30 July 2021).

Talpin, Julien 'Do Referendums Make Better Citizens? The Effects of Direct Democracy on Political Interest, Civic Competence and Participation' in Laurence Morel, Matt Qvortrup (eds), *The Routledge Handbook to Referendums and Direct Democracy* (Routledge 2018).

Tamanaha, Brian Z. *On the Rule of Law: History, Politics, Theory* (Cambridge University Press 2004).

Thio, Li-Ann 'Courts and Judicial Review' in Peter Cane, Herwig C.H. Hofmann, Eric C. Ip, Peter L. Lindseth (eds), *The Oxford Handbook of Comparative Administrative Law* (Oxford University Press 2020).

Tierney, Stephen, *Constitutional Referendums: The Theory and Practice of Republican Deliberation* (Oxford: Oxford University Press 2012).

Tierney, Stephen, *Constitutional Law and National Pluralism* (Oxford University Press 2006).

Tierney, Stephen, 'Democratic Credentials and Deficits of Referendums: A Case Study of the Scottish Independence Vote' in Laurence Morel, Matt Qvortrup (eds)

The Routledge Handbook to Referendums and Direct Democracy (Routledge 2018) 193–94.

Tornic, Ana, 'Direct Democracy in the Slovak Republic' (C2D Working Paper Series 41/2012).

Tschannen, Pierre, 'Die Formen der Volksinitiative und die Einheit der Form' (2002) 103 *Schweizerisches Zentralblatt für Staats- und Verwaltungsrecht* 2–29.

Tushnet, Mark, *Advanced Introduction to Comparative Constitutional Law* (Edward Elgar 2018).

Tyler, Tom R., 'Social Justice: Outcome and Procedure' (2000) 35 *International Journal of Psychology* 117.

Uleri, Pier Vincenzo, 'Institutions of Citizens' Political Participation in Italy: Crooked Forms, Hindered Institutionalization' in Theo Schiller and Maija Setälä (eds), *Citizens' Initiatives in Europe: Procedures and Consequences of Agenda-Setting by Citizens* (Palgrave Macmillan 2012).

Uleri, Pier Vincenzo, 'On Referendum Voting in Italy: YES, NO or Non-Vote? How Italian Parties Learned to Control Referendums' (2002) 41 *European Journal of Political Research* 863.

Vatter, Adrian, Deniz Danaci, 'Mehrheitstyrannei durch Volksentscheide? Zum Spannungsverhältnis zwischen direkter Demokratie und Minderheitenschutz' (2010) 51(2) *Politische Vierteljahresschrift* 205–222.

Visser, Maartje de, *Constitutional Review in Europe: A Comparative Analysis* (Hart Publishing 2014).

Wade, Sir William, Christopher Forsyth, *Administrative Law* (11th edn, Oxford: Oxford University Press 2014).

Waldron, Jeremy, 'The Concept and the Rule of Law' (2008) 43 *Georgia Law Review* 1.

Waldron, Jeremy, 'The Rule of Law and the Importance of Procedure' in James E. Fleming (ed), *Getting to the Rule of Law* (New York: New York University Press 2011).

Waldron, Jeremy, 'Rule-of-Law Rights and Populist Impatience' in Gerald L. Neuman (ed), *Human Rights in a Time of Populism: Challenges and Responses* (New York: Cambridge University Press 2020).

Wall, Alan et al., *Electoral Management Design: The International IDEA Handbook: Revised Edition* (Stockholm: International Institute for Democracy and Electoral Assistance IDEA, 2014).

Waters, M. Dane, 'The Strength of Popular Will: Legal Impact, Implementation and Duration' in Laurence Morel, Matt Qvortrup (eds), *The Routledge Handbook to Referendums and Direct Democracy* (Routledge 2018).

Weingast, Barry R. 'The Political Foundations of Democracy and the Rule of Law' (1997) 91(2) *The American Political Science Review* 245–263.

Wiederkehr, René, *Fairness als Verfassungsgrundsatz* (Bern: Stämpfli Verlag AG 2006).

Žuber, Bruna, Igor Kaučič, 'Slovenia' in Daniel Moeckli, Anna Forgács, Henri Ibi (eds), *The Legal Limits of Direct Democracy* (Edward Elgar Publishing 2021).

Žuber, Bruna, Igor Kaučič, 'Referendum Challenges in the Republic of Slovenia' (2018) 24 *Białostockie Studia Prawnicze* 137–150.

Zweigert, Konrad, Hein Kötz, *An Introduction to Comparative Law* (trans Tony Weir, 3rd edn, Oxford University Press 1998).

Zweigert, Konrad, 'Methodological Problems in Comparative Law' (1972) 7 *Israel Law Review* 465–74.

ONLINE RESOURCES

Croatia

Collection of laws <https://www.zakon.hr/>
Constitutional Court of the Republic of Croatia <https://sljeme.usud.hr/usud/prakswen
.nsf/vPremaClancimaUstavaNew.xsp>
Parliament of the Republic of Croatia <https://edoc.sabor.hr/>

Hungary

National Legal Database <https://njt.hu/translations>
Curia of Hungary <https://kuria-birosag.hu/hu/nepszavugy>
National Election Commission of Hungary <https://www.valasztas.hu/hatarozatok>

Italy

Official Gazette of the Republic of Italy <https://www.gazzettaufficiale.it/>
Constitutional Court of the Republic of Italy <https://www.cortecostituzionale.it/
actionPronuncia.do>
Court of Cassation <https://www.cortedicassazione.it/corte-di-cassazione/it/referen
dum.page>

Latvia

Legislation of the Republic of Latvia <https://likumi.lv/>
Constitutional Court of the Republic of Latvia <https://www.satv.tiesa.gov.lv/en/
cases/>
Supreme Court Senate of the Republic of Latvia <https://www.at.gov.lv/en/tiesu
-prakse/judikaturas-nolemumu-arhivs>

Liechtenstein

Official Gazette and Law Collection of the Principality of Liechtenstein <https://www
.gesetze.li/chrono/suche>
State Court of the Principality of Liechtenstein <https://www.gerichtsentscheidungen
.li/default.aspx>
Parliament of the Principality of Liechtenstein <https://www.landtag.li/de>
State Administration of the Principality of Liechtenstein <https://bua.regierung.li/BuA/
default.aspx?modus=nr>
Referendums <https://www.abstimmung.li/resultat/21>

Slovakia

Official Collection of Laws of the Republic of Slovakia
Collection of Laws <https://www.zakonypreludi.sk/>

National Assembly of the Republic of Slovakia <https://www.dz-rs.si/>

Slovenia

Official Gazette of the Republic of Slovenia <https://www.uradni-list.si/glasilo-uradni
-list-rs/vsebina?urlid=201520&stevilka=770>
Legal Information System of the Republic of Slovenia <http://pisrs.si/Pis.web/>
Constitutional Court of the Republic of Slovenia <https://www.us-rs.si/decisions/?lang
=en>

Switzerland

Fedlex – The publication platform for federal law <https://www.fedlex.admin.ch/en/
home>
Federal Court of the Swiss Confederation <https://www.bger.ch/index.htm>
Federal Assembly of the Swiss Confederation
Federal Council of the Swiss Confederation – Popular initiatives <https://www.bk
.admin.ch/bk/de/home/politische-rechte/volksinitiativen.html>
Federal Chancellery of the Swiss Confederation <https://www.bk.admin.ch/bk/de/
home/politische-rechte/volksinitiativen.html>

Index